DATE DUE

TEXTUAL SOURCES FOR THE STUDY OF RELIGION
edited by John R. Hinnells

# Judaism

# TEXTUAL SOURCES FOR THE STUDY OF RELIGION

*Zoroastrianism* ed. Mary Boyce
*Sikhism* ed. W. H. McLeod
*Islam* ed. A. Rippin and J. Knappert
*Hinduism* ed. Wendy Doniger O'Flaherty

*Further titles are in preparation*

TEXTUAL SOURCES FOR THE STUDY OF

# Judaism

edited and translated
by Philip S. Alexander

The University of Chicago Press

The University of Chicago Press, Chicago 60637
Copyright © Philip S. Alexander 1984
All rights reserved.
Originally published by Manchester University Press in 1984.
University of Chicago Press edition 1990.
Printed in the United States of America

99 98 97 96 95 94 93 92 91 90    6 5 4 3 2 1

Library of Congress Cataloging-in-Publication Data

Textual sources for the study of Judaism / edited and translated
   by Philip S. Alexander.
        p.    cm.
     Reprint. Originally published : Totowa, N.J. : Barnes &
   Noble Books, 1984. (Textual sources for the study of
   religion).
     Includes bibliographical references and index.
     ISBN 0-226-01297-2 (pbk.)
     1. Judaism—History—Sources.  2. Jews—History—
   Sources.  I. Alexander, Philip S.  II. Title: Judaism.
   BM157.T49   1990
   296—dc20                                    90-43464
                                                    CIP

# CONTENTS

# GENERAL INTRODUCTION

This series is planned to meet a fundamental need in the study of religions, namely that for new, reliable translations of major texts. The first systematic attempt to provide such translations was the monumental *Sacred Books of the East* in the nineteenth century. These were pioneering volumes but, naturally, are now somewhat out of date. Since linguistic studies have advanced and more materials have come to light it is important to make some of these findings of twentieth-century scholarship available to students. Books in this series are written by specialists in the respective textual traditions, so that students can work on the secure foundation of authoritative translations of major literary sources.

But it is not only that linguistic and textual studies have advanced in the twentieth century. There has also been a broadening of the perspective within which religions are studied. The nineteenth-century focus was largely on scriptural traditions and the 'official' theological writings of the great thinkers within each tradition. Religious studies should, obviously, include such materials; but this series also reflects more recent scholarly trends in that it is concerned with a much wider range of literature, with liturgy and legend, folklore and faith, mysticism and modern thought, political issues, poetry and popular writings. However important scriptural texts are in a number of religions, even the most authoritative writings have been interpreted and elucidated; their thoughts have been developed and adapted. Texts are part of living, changing religions, and the anthologies in this series seek to encapsulate something of the rich variety to be found in each tradition. Thus editors are concerned with the textual sources for studying daily religious life as exemplified in worship or in law as well as with tracing the great movements of thought. The translations are accompanied by generous annotation, glosses and explanations, thus providing valuable aids to understanding the especial character of each religion.

Books in this series are intended primarily for students in higher education in universities and colleges, but it is hoped that they will be of interest also for schools and for members of some, at least, of the religious communities with whose traditions they are concerned.

John R. Hinnells

# FOREWORD AND ACKNOWLEDGEMENTS

The purpose of this collection of documents is severely practical: to provide material for introductory courses on Judaism in schools and universities. There was a time when I would have criticised anthologies such as this as wrong in principle, but after a number of years teaching Jewish studies at university and examining O and A level religious studies I am fully convinced of their use. Study of primary texts, however small the sample, is far more profitable than reading any number of generalised, second-hand descriptions of a religion.

Given the limitations of space, choosing the texts proved a daunting task. I am sure not everyone will agree with my choice. I would have liked to have included a section on contemporary Jewish theology, but it proved impossible to put one together. Some writers (or their publishers) were unhappy about being anthologised.

All translations from Hebrew, Aramaic, Arabic, Latin, French and German are my own, unless it is otherwise indicated.

I wish to thank the Central Conference of American Rabbis for permission to reproduce from the CCAR *Yearbook* the Columbus platform (9.2.2) and the Responsum on the use of anaesthetic during circumcision (9.2.3).

I am grateful to Alan Unterman, Leon Yudkin, Norman Calder and Harry Lesser for reading my manuscript either in whole or in part, and making comments and corrections. David Blamires obliged me with expert advice on some tricky points of German. My final and best thanks must go to John Hinnells, the editor of the series, without whose encouragement and persistence this work would never have seen the light of day.

P.S.A.

# 1. INTRODUCTION

## 1.1 SCRIPTURE AND TRADITION

In Islamic texts Jews and Christians are called 'People of the Book'. The title is apt and suggestive, for it correctly points to the central role of holy books in both Judaism and Christianity. For Judaism 'the Book' is, of course, the Hebrew Bible.[1] As the embodiment of divine revelation, the Bible is the axis round which Judaism revolves. The Bible, or more strictly the first five books of the Bible — 'The Torah of Moses our Teacher', is the ultimate authority and court of appeal on all matters of belief and practice. This is true at least in theory. What happens in practice is rather different and much more complicated.

The trouble is that the Bible is not a self-sufficient guide. It may be divine revelation, but it communicates through the imperfect medium of human speech. Scripture is often ambiguous, at times it appears to contradict itself, and it fails to legislate for all the circumstances and eventualities of everyday life. Though it is the eternally valid word of God, it requires supplementation: it stands in need of interpretation, of *midrash*. Over the centuries Judaism has generated vast quantities of midrash. Much of the material in this anthology could be loosely classified under this head in that its authors believed that, either directly or indirectly, they were drawing out the sense of Scripture. Midrash is the classic literary form in which Judaism has presented its teachings. The study of midrash is, therefore, one of the most important keys to the understanding of Judaism. The various sects and religious movements within Judaism can often best be characterised by their different styles of Bible exegesis. Indeed, it is hardly an exaggeration to say that the history of Judaism could be written in terms of the history of midrash.

In practice midrash is as important as the text of Scripture itself. If we were to take at its face value the assertion that Judaism's ultimate religious authority, its most holy book, is the Torah of Moses, and try to deduce from the Torah alone the teachings of Judaism, we would go seriously astray. What is important is not the Bible in isolation but the Bible as it has been read and understood by Judaism. What matters is not what Scripture originally meant, or what we think it means, but what Judaism took it to mean. Judaism's understanding of Scripture is recorded in the midrash, and so we must consult midrash as well as Scripture if we are to discover the teachings of Judaism. Scripture and the interpretative tradition are two interlocking components, neither complete without the other.

Judaism recognises the vital role played by tradition, and in the cardinal doctrine of the two Torahs it goes so far as to bestow on tradition the same status as the text of Scripture itself. According to this doctrine Moses received the Law on Sinai in two distinct forms – as Written Law (*Torah shebikhtav*) and as Oral Law (*Torah shebe'al peh*). The former is enshrined in Scripture, the latter in the interpretative tradition. The effect of this teaching is to enrich and complicate the concept of Torah by absorbing tradition into it. Torah is not simply coextensive with the Five Books of Moses, or with the Bible as a whole: Torah = Scripture + Tradition. By categorising their traditions as Oral Law and by tracing them back to the same revelatory event that gave birth to the Written Law, the rabbis were asserting in no uncertain terms the divine authority of their reading of Scripture. They were fully aware of the existence of other groups, such as the Christians, who also regarded the Hebrew Bible as God's word but who construed its meaning in a very different way. The doctrine of the Oral Torah was an affirmation that it is the rabbis who are the recipients of the authentic tradition, *they* are the true interpreters of the Law. By the doctrine of the Oral Law the rabbis were not suggesting that the whole of the Oral Law as contained in Mishnah and Talmud has been transmitted without change from Moses. They acknowledged that much of the substance of the Oral Law came into existence long after Moses' time and was the work of recent scholars. What they are implying is that the principles of interpretation and the dominant ideas can be traced back to Moses. To put their point another way: it is impossible to interpret the Law correctly unless one has studied with the right teachers, with the Sages who stand in a tradition of scholarship leading back in unbroken succession to the greatest master of all – Moses our Teacher. The rabbis sought to justify this claim historically by establishing the line of transmission through which they had received the Oral Law from Moses. The most famous of these Chains of Tradition is found at the beginning of Pirqei Avot (2.1.1).

Scripture and tradition are two interdependent entities, but within the partnership Scripture is given priority. As we have seen, this priority cannot be one of time, since both the Oral and the Written Torah are supposed to have originated at Sinai. Nor is it, in the last analysis, one of authority, since both Scripture and tradition have equal status. The priority of the Written Torah is logical or symbolic: formally at least it is tradition that is brought into relationship to Scripture and not vice versa; tradition is presented as commentary on Scripture. The Written Torah is not merely a source of law or doctrine in Judaism: it also functions as a symbolic centre. The Scroll of the Law is the 'still point' at the heart of the Judaic universe. New ideas and developments within Judaism have to be legitimated by being brought into relationship with the Bible: to validate them it must be shown that they are present somewhere in Scripture. At first sight this would appear to impose extreme restraints on the development of Judaism. In practice, however, the only limiting factor has proved to be the ingenuity of the interpreter, and as the history of Jewish Bible exegesis shows ingenuity has not been lacking. The Hebrew Bible has been forced to receive some astonishingly alien notions. In some types of midrash the text of Scripture is treated almost as a set of arbitrary signs to be manipulated by the exegete at will. This is especially true in certain forms of mystical midrash (see 8.3.1–6). So although at the formal, superficial level it is tradition that is being accommodated to Scripture, at a deeper level the process of Bible interpretation has the effect of accommodating Scripture to tradition. The Written Torah is fixed and inviolable: it forms an absolutely bounded and defined canon of Holy Writ. The Oral Torah, on the other hand, is open-ended, undefined, continually evolving. It mediates between the Written Torah and life: it enables the sacred text to be made relevant to changing historical circumstances. It allows the Bible to be brought up to date without having to resort to endlessly rewriting and altering the biblical text itself.

Jewish Bible interpretation may be pictured as a game played to strict but complex rules. Certain assumptions about the nature of Scripture determine the field of play. First, as divine revelation Scripture must be totally coherent and self-consistent. This means that any one part of it can be interpreted in the light of and harmonised with any other part. Contradictions in Scripture must be apparent, not real. Second, Scripture is polyvalent: it contains different levels and layers of meaning. It is an inexhaustible well of truth, and in a very real sense all truth is implicit in it. There is no question of looking for the one, true, original meaning; Scripture can mean several things at once, according to whether it is considered from the standpoint of its simple, allegorical, mystical or homiletic sense. Third, Scripture is inerrant. Since it originated in the mind of God, it is inconceivable that it should contain errors of fact.

The aims of the game of midrash are, broadly speaking, to explain the obscurities, difficulties and apparent errors of the biblical text; to remove seeming contradictions; to draw out the deeper meanings; to apply Scripture to the heart and conscience of the Jew; and – most importantly – to validate the tradition in terms of Scripture. From a descriptive point of view the interpreter's task appears as twofold – as *ex*egetical and *eis*egetical: it involves both drawing out the meaning implicit in Scripture, and reading meaning into Scripture. There is some evidence to suggest that the classic commentators were aware of this distinction between exegesis and eisegesis, but in general they seem to have thought that they were genuinely bringing out what is present in Scripture. And in practice it is often difficult to separate exegesis and eisegesis, since both can be involved in the same act of interpretation. The Jewish commentators are adept at exploiting real problems in the text as a way of reading their own ideas into the Bible.

The rules of midrash allow a wide variety of moves to be made to achieve the desired ends: Scripture may be compared with Scripture; word-play can be exploited, names etymologised, and even the numerical value of words or phrases computed (a device known as *gematria*). Various attempts were made to formalise the rules of the game. One of the most important is the Baraita of Rabbi Ishmael, which gives 'the thirteen principles [*middot*] by which the Torah is expounded' (2.2.1). The Rabbi Ishmael to whom these principles are attributed is presumably the early second-century C.E. Palestinian scholar

Ishmael ben Elisha, but it is difficult to know what credence to give this ascription. The Baraita is found as a preface to the rabbinic commentary on Leviticus known as Sifra, which may be no earlier in date than the end of the fourth century C.E. It cannot be automatically assumed that the date of Sifra is the date of the Baraita, because the Baraita may not originally have been an integral part of that work.

As a statement of the rules of the game, the Baraita of Rabbi Ishmael is rather puzzling. It is far from complete, and it does not bear an exact relation to the game as actually played. Indeed, rules 5–11 (omitted below), which deal with certain aspects of the relationship between general and specific terms, appear to be an exercise in formal logic and are hard to instantiate from the midrashic literature. The fact is that the rules of the game are best learned not by studying the rule books but by watching the game played. So two examples of midrash have been chosen, dealing with two important passages of Scripture, which exemplify the skills and methods of the *darshan* − the traditional Jewish Bible exegete.

The first example is taken from Targum Pseudo-Jonathan's paraphrase of the Aqedah − the story of the 'binding' of Isaac in Genesis 22 (2.3.1). Etymologically 'Targum' in Hebrew simply means 'translation', from one language into another, but the term is also used technically to denote one of the early Aramaic translations of the Bible. A number of these Bible versions are still extant: their relationship to each other and their origins are a matter of intense scholarly debate. From the Talmuds and other early Jewish texts it is clear that in the early synagogue, as the Bible was being read to the congregation in Hebrew, a translator (known as a *meturgeman*) offered a simultaneous oral rendering of it into Aramaic. The extant Targumim probably represent literary forms of this oral tradition of translation. To judge from the surviving Targumim the translation was by no means literal, but incorporated a great deal of interpretation. The Targumim, consequently, give us a valuable insight into the way in which Bible was interpreted in synagogue, the themes and motifs that were stressed in the context of public worship. They probably bring us close to the content of popular preaching in the early synagogue.

Aramaic is a language cognate with Hebrew, and it is often asserted that the institution of the Targum arose in the post-Exilic period when Aramaic began to replace Hebrew as the vernacular of the Jews of Palestine. This is probably true, but it cannot be the whole story. The Hebrew Bible was almost certainly the basis of education in early Judaism, so even for Aramaic-speakers its language cannot have been totally unintelligible. The Aramaic version served another function, besides that of bridging the linguistic gap between the Aramaic-speaker and the Hebrew Bible. It gave an opportunity of imposing a particular reading on the Hebrew text, of 'rewriting' the Bible in accordance with a particular religious viewpoint, while at the same time leaving the sacred original intact.

From literary analysis it is clear that Targum Pseudo-Jonathan is an extremely complex work with a long history. In its present form it cannot have been edited earlier than the seventh century C.E., since at one point in its translation it appears to allude to the wife and daughter of Muhammad (see Gen. 21:21). However, it has been demonstrated that it contains many old traditions, some of them possibly dating back to the pre-Christian era.

The story of the binding of Isaac is one of the most dramatic and disturbing in the Hebrew Bible, and it took powerful hold on the Jewish religious imagination. Commentators have wrestled with it and suggested many diverse interpretations. It is often printed in the prayer books, and there are allusions to it at solemn moments in the liturgy, such as in the Zikhronot prayers for Rosh Ha-Shanah.[2] The Aqedah is an important motif of Jewish religious art: it is represented in two of the earliest synagogues yet discovered – at Dura Europus on the Euphrates (third century C.E.), and at Beit Alfa in Israel (sixth century C.E.). Many echoes of the Aqedah can be detected even in modern secular Hebrew literature. Christianity too has been deeply affected by the story and has traditionally read it as a typological foreshadowing of the sacrifice of Christ. It is hardly an exaggeration to see the Aqedah as one of the primal myths of European culture. Like the myth of Prometheus, and the legends of Oedipus and Faust, it has entered deep into the European consciousness.[3] Instinctively men have seen it as symbolising profound, if not always obvious, truths.

The second example of midrash is taken from the Mekhilta of Rabbi Ishmael (2.3.2) – an early rabbinic commentary on large portions of Exodus (Exod. 12–23; 31:12–17; 35:1–3). As with so many early rabbinic texts the date of the Mekhilta is a matter of great dispute. The work is first clearly referred to under its current title by the eleventh-century C.E. Talmudic scholar Nissim ben Jacob. However, it is not certain whether in so doing he meant to attribute the work to the second-century C.E. Palestinian scholar, Ishmael ben Elisha, or whether he used the title simply because Rabbi Ishmael is mentioned almost at the beginning of the work. Many modern scholars believe the work contains Tannaitic material, and that it does have a connection with Ishmael, not, indeed, with him personally, but rather with his school. They have seen reflected in the Mekhilta a tradition of Bible interpretation typical of the school of Ishmael, and they distinguish this Mekhilta from the fragmentary Mekhilta of Rabbi Simeon ben Yohai, which they believe emanated from the great rival school of Bible interpretation, that of Rabbi Aqiva. If this is the case, then the Mekhilta of Rabbi Ishmael is probably to be dated to the third century C.E. However, it must be said that the whole academic construction of the rival schools of Aqiva and Ishmael, and their respective styles of Bible exegesis, rests on very shaky foundations, and recently it has been suggested that the Mekhilta of Rabbi Ishmael is, in fact, a post-Talmudic pseudepigraphon: its author, who may have lived as late as 800 C.E., has deliberately set out to give the impression that his work is Tannaitic by using freely the names of Tannaim.[4] Wherever the truth lies between these two positions, there can be no doubt that the Mekhilta is an important and representative rabbinic midrash. The passages quoted below have been excerpted from its elaborate treatment of the account of the giving of the Law on Sinai (Exod. 19–20). For Judaism this event was the supreme historical moment of revelation, unparalleled before or since. It was at Sinai that the Israelites came face to face with God; there they became a covenant people and took upon themselves the yoke of the divine Law.

## 1.2 LITURGY

The prayer book (the Siddur) perhaps more than any other document takes us close to popular Judaism. The prayers which he regularly prays, the forms of worship in which he engages, express the aspirations of the ordinary Jew, and state the main themes which form the framework of his religious universe. Judaism has a genius for the creation of liturgy: its classic prayers and liturgical institutions have had a profound influence on the development of worship in Christianity and, to a lesser degree, in Islam.

The Jewish liturgical tradition is very rich and includes many regional variations and rites. Clearly it can have reached its present state only after a long process of evolution. All the prayers have undergone change in the course of the centuries, and signs of their historical development are sometimes very obvious. A case in point is the Amidah or Eighteen Benedictions, which, despite its name, contains in its current form nineteen benedictions! The simplest way to explain this anomaly is to suppose that at some point in the history of the prayer an additional benediction was inserted, though, with typical religious conservatism, the old name of the prayer remained unchanged. It is often said that the additional benediction is No. 12, the so-called 'Blessing of the heretics' (Birkat ha-Minim). This view is based on a passage in the Babylonian Talmud which runs as follows:

> The Eighteen Benedictions are really nineteen. – Rabbi Levi said: The blessing relating to the heretics [*Birkat ha-Minim*][5] was instituted at Yavneh . . . Our Rabbis taught: Simeon Ha-Paquli arranged the Eighteen Benedictions in order before Rabban Gamaliel at Yavneh. Rabban Gamliel said to the Sages: Can anyone among you frame a benediction relating to the heretics? Samuel the Lesser arose and composed it. [Babylonian Talmud, Berakhot 28b–29a]

From this text it is argued that the Amidah was edited around 100 C.E. at the Academy of Yavneh, and that the Birkat ha-Minim was composed then. It is sometimes further asserted that the 'heretics' in view here were the Judeo-Christians and that the purpose of the additional benediction was to identify them and drive them out of the synagogue. The Birkat ha-Minim has certainly been applied to the Christians. This is evident from the form of it attested in early manuscript fragments from the Cairo Genizah.

> For apostates [*meshummadin*] let there be no hope, and the arrogant kingdom speedily uproot in our day. May the Nazarenes [*Nozerim* = Christians] and the heretics [*minim*] perish in an instant. 'May they be blotted out of the book of the

living, and may they not be written with the righteous' (Ps. 69:29). Blessed are you, O Lord, who subdues the arrogant.[6]

However, some hold the view that the additional benediction is, in fact, No. 15, the Birkat David (Blessing of David). In the form of the Amidah given below (3.1.2), this prayer for the restoration of the Davidic monarchy seems redundant in view of the similar sentiments expressed in benediction 14: '. . . and swiftly establish in it [Jerusalem] the throne of David'. Benediction 15 is missing from the Cairo Genizah fragments of the Amidah. Instead benediction 14 runs as follows:

> Have compassion, O Lord our God, in your abundant mercy on Israel your people, and on Jerusalem your city, and on Zion the abode of your glory, and on your Temple and on your Dwelling, and on the royal House of David your righteous Messiah. Blessed are you, O Lord, God of David, rebuilder of Jerusalem.[7]

If the additional benediction is indeed the Birkat David, then the editing of the Amidah which many suppose took place at Yavneh cannot have involved the insertion of the Birkat ha-Minim. It may, however, have involved rewording and modifying an existing berakhah to serve new ends.

The major rites differ considerably from each other, but the differences should not be overstressed. For the most part they apply to the detailed wording of the prayers. We should also give due weight to the striking similarities between the various rites: the basic structure of the liturgy remains impressively constant. This fact itself suggests the great antiquity of the synagogue service. The two basic prayers are the Shema and the Amidah. The core of the Shema (3.1.1) is made up of three biblical passages – Deut. 6:4–9; Deut. 11:13–21; Num. 15:37–41 – the first of which begins, 'Hear [Shema], O Israel.' Hence the name of the prayer. In the central, biblical verses Israel does not address God; rather, God addresses Israel. In repeating God's words the Jew is seen as assenting to them:

> Rabbi Joshua ben Qorha said: Why does the section 'Hear, O Israel' (Deut. 6:4 ff), precede 'It shall come to pass' (Deut. 11: 13 ff).)? – So that a man may first take upon himself the kingdom of heaven, and afterwards take upon himself the yoke of the commandments. [Mishnah, Berakhot 2:2]

The Shema's assertion of the unity of God is often seen as the fundamental affirmation of Judaism. The Jew dies with this affirmation on his lips (cf. 4.7).[8] The liturgical use of the central verses of the Shema can be traced back to the Second Temple period.

The Amidah is also very ancient and some form of it too may have existed in Second Temple times. The form given below (3.1.2), however, implies that the Temple has been destroyed. Traditionally the prayer is divided into three sections – praise (berakhot 1–3), petition (berakhot 4–16), and thanksgiving (berakhot 17–19). This division is explained in the Talmud thus:

> Rav Judah said: A man should never petition for his needs either in the first three benedictions or in the last three, but in the middle ones, for Rabbi Hanina said: In the

first three benedictions he is like a servant who addresses a eulogy to his master; in the middle ones he resembles a servant who requests largess from his master; and in the last ones he resembles a servant who has received largess from his master and takes his leave. [Babylonian Talmud, Berakhot 34a]

Though both the Shema and the Amidah may be prayed privately, they are in origin and essence communal prayers. Note the use of the communal 'we'. Judaism has a tradition of private, individual prayer, but its literary forms appear to have been originally different. Typical of private prayer was the opening formula: 'May it be your will, O Lord my God ... that ...'.[9] Communal prayer, however, came to be dominated by the berakhah formula. This is illustrated in the first benediction of the Shema, which opens: 'Blessed are you, O Lord our God, king of the world, creator of lights,' and ends: 'Blessed are you, O Lord, creator of lights.' The Amidah and the Shema are the two basic building blocks of the fixed, communal liturgy. The Amidah is recited at the morning (Shaharit), afternoon (Minhah) and evening (Arvit/Ma'ariv) services, though it is not strictly obligatory for the latter. The Shema is recited before the Amidah morning and evening. The forms of the Shema and the Amidah given below are for weekday services. Other forms are used on Sabbaths and festivals. In the case of the Shema, the Sabbath and festival forms do not differ dramatically from that used on weekdays. The Sabbath and festival Amidot, however, are very different. Only the first three and the last three blessings are retained, and an additional central benediction – the Qedushat ha-Yom (Sanctification of the Day) – appropriate to the day in question, is inserted. In the Musaf, or additional service, for Rosh Ha-Shanah *three* additional berakhot are inserted, making a total of nine. The literary and historical relationship between the festival and the weekday Amidot is highly problematic.

Judaism marks strongly the passage of time. It segments the year into profane and holy time. In holy time men turn aside from their ordinary, secular employment and concentrate on the worship of God. These holy times may correspond with significant points in the natural year (e.g. Shavu'ot is a harvest festival), or they may commemorate significant events in the history of the people (e.g. Hanukkah recalls the re-dedication of the Temple by Judas Maccabaeus in 164 B.C.E.). The Jewish year consists of a cycle of fasts and festivals, each with its distinctive ideas and rituals, which builds up to a climax in the Days of Awe (Yamim Nora'im), the period stretching from Rosh Ha-Shanah to Yom Kippur (see Appendix B).

The most frequently recurring holy time is Sabbath, which runs from sunset on Friday to sunset on Saturday. Certain rituals signal the transition from secular to sacred time and back again: Qiddush (Sanctification) marks the beginning of Sabbath (3.2.1), Havdalah (Separation) its end and the return to secular pursuits (3.2.2). The great antiquity of the Qiddush and Havdalah rites is evident from the fact that their precise nature is minutely discussed in the Mishnah (see 5.1.1). For the observant Jew, passage into and out of holy time should entail more than crossing an invisible temporal boundary line: it should involve a radical change of attitude. The rituals and prayers of Qiddush and Havdalah help the Jew to make the appropriate mental orientation.

The central locus of prayer and ritual in Judaism is the synagogue. But Judaism has also old and sanctified rituals that belong to the home. The most colourful and elaborate of these home rites is the Passover Seder. The Passover commemorates the escape of the ancient Israelites from slavery in Egypt, under the leadership of Moses. The centre of the Seder ceremonies is the re-enactment of the last meal eaten by the Israelites before they left Egypt, on the night when the 'Angel of Death' destroyed all the firstborn of the land of Egypt but 'passed over' the houses of the Israelites without causing any harm. Preparations for the meal and the meal itself are full of symbolism. During the meal the story of the Exodus is dramatically retold, using a service book known as the *Haggadah shel Pesah* (Narration of the Passover). The text of the Passover Haggadah (3.3.1) has all the marks of a work which has grown up over a long period of time. It draws on diverse sources – the Bible, the Mishnah, the Midrashim. It contains prayers, psalms, children's songs and folk tales. Most of it is in Hebrew, but parts are in Aramaic. The 'seams' between the various sections are very evident: transitions are abrupt, with little concern for stylistic or thematic continuity. The text is more or less stable now, but many divergent early forms are extant. The earliest surviving version is in the Siddur of Sa'adiah Gaon (882-942 C.E.). It was probably not long before Sa'adiah's time that the Haggadah emerged as a separate, independent service book for the Passover meal. The Haggadah is one of Judaism's most popular books. It has gone through hundreds of printed editions and has been one of the fields where traditionally Jewish artists have been allowed to exercise their skills. It is the most commonly illustrated text in Judaism, and some of the medieval illuminated Haggadot are fine enough to be compared with the great illuminated Christian books of hours.

## 1.3 TALES OF THE SAINTS AND SCHOLARS

All religions have their holy men, and Judaism is no exception. But religions differ as to the types of men they set apart and venerate; they disagree about the qualities and activities which constitute sainthood. In Judaism religious authority is invested first and foremost in the rabbi – the teacher. Spiritual leadership has traditionally lain with a body of scholars who spend their time debating and analysing the intricacies of the Torah, and, indeed, are such masters of it that they can refute God himself (cf. 4.5). As Jacob Neusner puts it:

> If in other religious traditions holiness is expressed through ascetic, flesh-suppressing disciplines – through sitting on pillars or dwelling in caves, through eating only wormwood and dressing only in rags, the rabbis' sainthood consists in the analysis of

trivial and commonplace things through practical and penetrating logic and criticism. Their chief rite is *argument*. To be sure, they pray like other people, but to them learning in Torah is peculiarly 'ours', praying is 'theirs' – that of ordinary folk. Their heroes are men of learning, and they turn their biblical heroes, beginning with Moses himself, into men of learning.[10]

The central role of the rabbi – the Torah expert – in Judaism is the direct result of the central role of Torah. The rabbi is, in a sense, the embodiment of Torah and his authority stems from his close association with it. He is not, however, an oracular interpreter; he does not simply announce the meaning of Torah *ex cathedra*. He is a lawyer, and as such must present a properly worked out case to support his opinions; and he can be sure that any views he expresses will be debated and challenged by his peers.

Judaism also knows a pattern of spiritual leadership based not on knowledge painstakingly acquired through study but on charisma. The charismatic leader exercises authority in virtue of some innate personal quality, or some 'gift' he possesses, such as the power to heal the sick or to bring rain in times of drought. Speaking very broadly, the difference between the two types is the difference between the scholar and the wonder-worker, or, to use Talmudic terminology, between the rabbi and the 'man of deed' (*ish ma'aseh*).[11] It is true that the rabbi also may, on occasions, be shown performing wonders. He can do so because his knowledge of Torah gives him access to an awesome spiritual force. But wonder-working has never been seen as the essence of his role or the basis of his authority. Scholarship holds the key to the difference between the two types of leader: while it is possible to be a charismatic leader without being learned (and many charismatic leaders in Judaism have been comparatively uneducated), to be a rabbi and not be expert in Torah would be a contradiction in terms. In principle charisma and scholarship are not incompatible: a spiritual leader may embody both charismatic and intellectual qualities. In everyday life, however, the two types tend to be distinct. When charismatic figures have arisen in Judaism they have often found themselves in conflict with the rabbinic establishment. The Torah scholars have an innate, deep-seated distrust of pure charisma. The clash between charisma and scholarship is a major motif in the stories of Honi the Circle-drawer (4.1) and Haninah ben Dosa (4.2), as well as in the Hasidic tale about the Besht and the student of Rabbi Gershon (see 9.1.1).

Judaism has a long and varied tradition of hagiography. The normal style of the hagiographic tale was, however, largely determined at the beginning of the tradition by the stories of the great scholars recorded in the Talmuds and other early texts. These tales should not, of course, be treated as straightforward history. Their legendary traits are obvious. They were told for edification; they are theology in the guise of story and parable. As the living embodiment of Torah the rabbi is the model whom the ordinary Jew should emulate. The great rabbis are exemplars whose knowledge of Torah and manner of life are held up as the goal towards which every Jew should aspire.

## 1.4 RELIGIOUS LAW

In Judaism the primary mode of religious discourse is law, the primary image of God that of a king who has laid down certain laws for his subjects to obey. The study of the Law has usually been regarded as the highest branch of Jewish learning, the one carrying the greatest prestige. It is the expert in halakhah who has normally held the positions of religious power and authority. Many Jewish thinkers have seen in the halakhah the most distinctive and authentic expression of the Jewish religious genius.

The emphasis on law in Judaism can be seriously misunderstood. The bulk of the authoritative religious texts are legal in character, and the legal tradition appears to consist of endless, highly involved debates about the minutiae of religious practice. The aim seems to be to cover the whole of life with a complex network of rules and regulations. This can be disconcerting, particularly to non-Jews who come from Protestant traditions influenced by the antinomianism of Paul. It has often led to Judaism being accused of 'legalism'.[12] Why is it that law is so central to Judaism?

In the first place it should be observed that Judaism is arguably not a religion in the sense that modern Protestantism is a religion. Judaism might more accurately be defined as the culture of a people, a people for whom the idea of statehood is important, and who in the past have existed as a nation in their land, or have enjoyed a large measure of communal autonomy in foreign lands. There is a considerable body of halakhot which have been inherited from these periods of self-government, aimed at the just regulation of society. So, in addition to strictly religious laws dealing with such matters as the times of prayers and festivals, we find in the halakhah laws of property, of contract, of tort, family, criminal and mercantile law, laws of procedure and evidence. No one can seriously deny that such laws touch on extremely important areas of life which require legislation, but they deal with matters which in Western countries are today regarded as lying solely within the competence of the secular authorities and the civil courts. Judaism, however, traditionally, makes no distinction between the religious and the secular: it does not delimit autonomous spheres for 'Church' and 'State' but pronounces on, and offers detailed guidance for, all aspects of life.

Traditional Judaism regards the Torah as the expression of God's will, given by God to Moses on Sinai. But, as we have seen, the precise import of the Torah is not always clear: it has to be interpreted and applied. The halakhah aims to ensure that God's will is fully expressed in everyday life. The rabbis are not content to remain at the level of such general commands as 'You shall love your neighbour as yourself', but seek to define good-neighbourliness in precise and concrete ways. This is a reasonable, and indeed admirable, point of view, but its inevitable outcome is to cover the whole of life with a grid of rules and regulations.

A standard element in the charge of legalism, whether expressed or implied, is the notion that all the minute rules and regulations of the halakhah have reduced Jews to spiritual bondage: the burden of the Law has crushed all joy and spontaneity out of Jewish religious life. It cannot be denied that there have been Jews who have found the halakhah a burden, and either abandoned it or simplified it, but 'the burden of the Law' is essentially a psychological notion: it depends on an attitude of mind. The observant Jew believes firmly in the concept of the joy of the Law: he regards it as an honour that God has addressed him and given him his commandments, and he fulfils those commandments with joy. That joy can be so intense as to reach the heights of mystical ecstasy.

The manner in which the halakhah is classically formulated can give rise to the impression that the rabbis are interested only in minutiae and hair-splitting. Jewish religious law is formulated casuistically rather than normatively, that is to say, legal norms are expressed not by an abstract statement of principle, but by giving concrete cases in which the norm is or is not observed.[13] Take, for example, the long series of prohibitions in Mishnah, Bava Batra 2:1–5:

> A man may not dig a cistern, nor may he dig a trench, vault, water channel, or washerman's pool, unless it is three hand's-breadths away from his neighbour's wall; and he must plaster it with lime. . . . A man may not open a baker's shop or a dyer's shop under his neighbour's storehouse, nor may he keep a cattle stall near by . . . A man's ladder must not be kept within four cubits of his neighbour's dovecot, lest the marten should jump in. His wall may not be built within four cubits of his neighbour's roof gutter, so that the other can set up his ladder to clean it out.

These prohibitions are all concrete illustrations of the norm that a person, even when he is acting in his own domain, must not cause harm to his neighbour, but that norm is not formally and abstractly expressed. The casuistic method of stating the law is a perfectly reasonable one: it keeps the concrete and specific before the lawyer's mind and it allows a large number of subtle distinctions to be made neatly and graphically. It would be wrong, however, to ignore the fact that behind the mass of concrete instances in the halakhah lie norms. Students of halakhah have always been encouraged to seek those norms. It is further arguable that those norms imply yet more ultimate principles, which fit together to form a total ideology and present a coherent view of the world. If this is so, then halakhah is conceivably being used as a vehicle for the expression of general religious truths. In arguing about the details of the law the rabbis may to some extent have been using legal discourse as a medium for presenting their ideas about God, man and nature, ideas which could also have been expressed in theological or philosophical language.

A final point can be made on the issue of 'legalism'. There is a substantial element in the halakhah which is purely theoretical: it is concerned with matters which can no longer have any practical application. A case in point is the material which describes in minute detail the Temple and its cult. A whole order of the Mishnah – Qodashim – is devoted to the everyday business of Temple ritual. The curious thing is that this material was edited after the Temple had been destroyed, at a time when it could have no immediate, practical use, and the problems of Qodashim have continued to exercise halakhic experts right down to modern times. Why did the rabbis draw with such infinite care the map of a land which no longer existed? Perhaps they felt that in some sense the Temple continued to exist through their words, or that to study the laws of sacrifice was in some way equivalent to offering sacrifice. One thing is certain: the study of the Law was a fundamental command in Judaism, and that study was undertaken for its own sake, and not simply to ascertain one's immediate religious duty, because to immerse oneself in Torah was seen as profoundly formative of general character and outlook.

The laws of the Pentateuch form the bedrock of the Jewish legal tradition, but the most important legal structure raised on that bedrock is the Mishnah (5.1.1). The Mishnah influenced the agenda, language, modes of formulation, and style of argument of all subsequent Jewish law. The Mishnah itself is anonymous, but according to tradition it was compiled around 210 C.E. in Palestine by Rabbi Judah Ha-Nasi. Internal evidence supports this tradition, at least as far as the date is concerned, since the Mishnah does not incorporate any sayings or legal rulings attributed to any authorities later than the time of Judah Ha-Nasi. The work is in the nature of a compilation or digest: it collects, arranges and edits the opinions of the great Palestinian legal experts of the first two centuries of the current era. It appears to have been based on earlier collections of halakhot. The Mishnah itself refers to the Mishnah of Rabbi Aqiva and to the 'First Mishnah': 'Rabbi Yose said: Such was the Mishnah of Rabbi Aqiva, but the First Mishnah included also the suitor's uncle, first cousin, and all that are qualified to be his heirs' (Mishnah, Sanhedrin 3:4). Still more important, form-critical study of the various tractates clearly uncovers different stages of growth. The work is written in Hebrew in a highly condensed, formulaic, almost 'telegraphic' style. A handful of basic formulae are used to express hundreds of legal opinions on a host of diverse topics. One common formula has the structure: 'if $x$ is the case, then authority A says $p$, and authority B says $q$,' where $p$ and $q$ are often fixed opposites such as 'clean/unclean', 'liable/free', 'fit/unfit', 'prohibit/permit'. For example:

> If a man had dedicated his goods to the Temple and he was still liable for the payment of his wife's Ketubbah, Rabbi Eliezer says: When he divorces her he must vow to derive no further benefit from her. Rabbi Joshua says: He need not. [Mishnah, Arakhin 6:1]

On first acquaintance the Mishnah appears to be an orderly work: the material is grouped topically into six major sections, or 'orders' (*sedarim*), and each section is in turn divided into tractates (*massekhtot*). On closer inspection, however, a great deal of confusion begins to emerge: much material appears to be out of place in that it does not relate to the ostensible subject matter of the tractate or context where it is found. One starts seriously to question the rigour of the final editing: the Mishnah begins to look like a very loosely assembled document in which extensive use is made of arbitrary and mechanical literary devices such as catchwords. However, profounder study restores something of the initial impression of order, and the possibility begins to emerge that the Mishnah is carefully organised according to a sophisticated conceptual schema which overarches tractates and orders, and even the work as a whole.

The Mishnah summed up and closed the preceding chapter of Jewish legal history, but at the same time opened a new chapter and inaugurated a process of intense legal dialectic which has continued unbroken down to the present day. The very form of the Mishnah is an open invitation to discussion: it seldom legislates on disputed points of law, but rather states a variety of opinions held by competent halkhic authorities, and argues the 'pros' and 'cons' of the various possible positions. The Mishnah could be described as the edited transcripts of the debates in the great rabbinic academies (Yeshivot) of Palestine.

The debate continued with the Mishnah as the basis of discussion. In the Yeshivot not only of Palestine, but also of Babylonia, the Mishnah was analysed and argued over. Gradually a mass of glosses on it emerged which were finally edited into two great digests known as the Jerusalem and Babylonian Talmuds. The former was probably completed around 400 C.E., before the closing of the Academy of Tiberias and the abolition of the Patriarchate in 425 C.E. by the emperor Theodosius. The latter, according to tradition, was completed about a century later (*c.* 500 C.E.) in the time of the Babylonian Jewish scholars Rav Ashi and Ravina. Each Talmud incorporates the Mishnah, and its commentary, composed largely in Aramaic, is known as the Gemara.

The Babylonian Talmud (5.1.2) has always been esteemed more highly in Judaism than its Palestinian counterpart. This was in part due to the fact that in the Gaonic period the spiritual hegemony of the Jews rested with the Babylonian Yeshivot. But it was also due to the intrinsic merits of the Bavli: it is better edited than the Yerushalmi and its legal analysis is more incisive. The Bavli has the added advantage of being the younger, more recent work. The Babylonian Talmud became the basis of all higher education in Judaism, and it profoundly shaped the thinking of the Jews who studied it. It inculcated belief in the power of argument, of dialectic, to discover truth. It fostered a strong intellectual tradition within Judaism and encouraged Jews to take the view that God has given man certain mental faculties which he must use to discover God's will. According to a famous Talmudic story (see 4.7), argument prevails over even miracle or fresh revelation. The Talmud exemplifies an almost unique method of dialectic – a sort of rabbinic logic (cf. 2.2.1) – echoes of which can be heard in the style even of Jewish non-juristic debate. By stating a variety of legal opinions on most disputed points of law the Talmud built into the halakhah an element of flexibility and left room for subsequent change and development. It defined for all time halakhah not as a static, cut-and-dried code of decided law, but as a dynamic body of legal discussion, full of inner contradictions and dialectical tension.

However, this characteristic, which makes the Talmud such a valuable pedagogic instrument, creates problems: the Talmud is not much use as a guide to Jewish living. For example, if a Jew should turn to the Talmud to find an answer to the simple question of when he should recite the evening Shema, he will not get a straight answer. The Mishnah will present him with three different opinions (Mishnah, Berakhot 1:1), while the corresponding Gemara, far from resolving the matter, will offer him several more, and almost certainly lose him in a legal discussion of labyrinthine complexity (Babylonian Talmud, Berakhot 2a–9b). It is not surprising, therefore, that from time to time halakhic experts have attempted to simplify matters by omitting all the debate and divergent opinion and by presenting only the decided law (*pesaq*). But such an enterprise is fraught with danger, and certain purists condemn it as wrong in principle. They argue that the legal debates provide the proper context of the pesaq and help to define its meaning and reference. Anyone presented with the pesaq, and not the debate that led up to it, is in real danger of misunderstanding its precise sense. Nevertheless, the regularity with which the Jewish legal tradition has thrown up codes in the form simply of pesaqim suggests that such works perform a necessary function. Broadly speaking, Jewish legal tradition may be seen as oscillating between two literary types – the book of halakhot, represented in its purest form by the Talmud, and the book of pesaqim, represented in its purest form by the *Shulhan Arukh* (5.2.1–2). As soon as an authority produces an encyclopaedic compendium of halakhah, recording and discussing the divergent views, a movement begins to extract from it the decided law and to present this in the form of a brief code. But, conversely, no sooner has an influential book of pesaqim appeared than scholars begin to annotate it in order to document its sources and key it back into the broader halakhic debate.[14]

The most important book of pesaqim is unquestionably the *Shulhan Arukh* (*Prepared Table*) of Joseph Caro (1488–1575). Caro was born in Toledo in Spain, but left with his family in the expulsion of 1492. After living for many years in Turkey he finally settled in Safed in Galilee, where his great code was completed. The first printed edition appeared in Venice in 1565. Earlier in his life Caro had produced a classic book of halakhot – the *Beit Yosef*. This took the form of an elaborate commentary on the law code of Jacob ben Asher (*c.* 1270–1340) known as the Arba'ah Turim. Caro's purpose in the *Beit Yosef* was to trace the history of each law from the Talmud down to his own times, recording scrupulously all the conflicting interpretations, and concluding in each case with the pesaq, decided according to the unanimous or majority vote of three major medieval codifiers – Isaac Alfasi (1013–1103), Moses Maimonides (1135–1204) and Asher ben Yehiel (*c.* 1250–1327). The *Beit Yosef* already contains pesaq, and the *Shulhan Arukh* was simply drawing this out and assembling it in handy form. Caro probably intended the two works to be used in conjunction, but the *Shulhan Arukh* completely overshadowed the earlier work in popular esteem and circulated independently of it.

As the fame of the *Shulhan Arukh* increased, so the inevitable glossing began. The most important glosses were produced by the Polish scholar Moses Isserles (1525 or 1530–72). When Caro produced his *Beit Yosef* Isserles had published an extensive set of notes and supplements to it under the title *Darkhei Mosheh*: so when Caro brought out the *Shulhan Arukh* Isserles added brief glosses to it based on the *Darkhei Mosheh*. Isserles' glosses served a number of purposes. They clarified Caro's meaning; they included the opinions of recent Ashkenazi authorities whom Caro had ignored; and they gave much greater place to custom (*minhag*) than Caro had allowed. Isserles also differed from Caro in the procedure he used for determining the pesaq. Whereas Caro had followed the majority opinion, Isserles applied the principle of *hilkheta kevatra'ei*, 'the law is in accordance with the later authorities'. Isserles' glosses, which are known as the Mappah (Tablecloth), were widely regarded as an essential supplement to the *Shulhan Arukh*, and since the 1569–71 Cracow edition of the *Shulhan Arukh* they have been printed along with Caro's text.

By adding the Mappah Isserles destroyed the straightforward simplicity of the *Shulhan Arukh*. Once again the user was faced at many points with a difference of opinion. Attempts were made to fuse together Caro's text and Isserles' glosses, and to create a new, simple book of pesaqim. The most successful of these attempts, the *Qizzur Shulhan Arukh* (*Abbreviation of the Shulhan Arukh*), was compiled by the Hungarian Jewish scholar Solomon Ganzfried (1804–86). It first appeared in 1864 and has been reprinted many times since (5.2.3). Ganzfried wrote for the ordinary, observant Jew, not for the halakhic expert. His style is popular and he spices his text with ethical maxims to sustain the interest. His aim is severely practical, and so he tends not to waste time repeating information which is common knowledge and practice, or which is really of only theoretical interest. The *Qizzur Shulhan Arukh* has circulated widely and has become a standard manual of practice for Ashkenazi Jews.

## 1.5 ETHICAL LITERATURE

Jewish religious law – halakhah – is concerned with conduct: it defines how a Jew must act in all aspects of his daily life. But there is another body of teaching in Judaism, distinct from halakhah and with an extensive literature of its own, which is also, on the face of it, concerned with conduct. This teaching comes under the general heading of *musar* – ethics. At certain points musar and halakhah appear to be trying to occupy the same ground, to be offering guidance for the same situations. Questions naturally arise. Are musar and halakhah, law and morality, in any sense in conflict in Judaism? Are both musar and halakhah really necessary, and if they are, how are they to be demarcated? Judaism has always maintained that musar and halakhah are not, in fact, in competition; they are totally compatible. Nevertheless, it has found it difficult to delimit their respective spheres: at their edges one slips easily into the other. However, some rough differentia are reasonably clear.

In the first place, musar is concerned with broad principles of conduct, halakhah with precise and detailed directions. It can be argued that musar to some extent articulates the norms embodied concretely in the halakhah. This point must, however, be stated with care. It is important to observe that, while it may be true that all the norms expressed in musar are embodied somewhere in halakhah, not all the norms implicit in halakhah fall within the realm of musar, not all halakhot embody moral principles. Many ritual *mizvot* (injunctions) have no obvious moral basis, and it would be artificial to seek one. Moreover, it is rather dangerous to divide the mizvot into 'moral' and 'non-moral'. Such a classification is not obviously present in the biblical text, and it is tendentious if it is meant to imply that the moral mizvot are in some sense superior to the non-moral. This view has been maintained. Christians, for example, argue that, while the moral law is eternally valid, the ritual law no longer applies. Jewish reformers in the nineteenth century also stressed the enduring importance of the moral as against the ritual mizvot (cf. 9.2.1.4). Traditional Judaism, however, emphatically rejects this position: a mizvah is a mizvah, and should be obeyed, whether or not it has a moral basis, whether or not we can see a reason for it (cf. 4.3). However, having given these qualifications their due weight, it remains broadly true that musar is concerned largely with abstract statements of principle, whereas halakhah is concerned with concrete law, and that it is possible to discover in musar many of the norms which apparently lie behind the halakhah.

There is a further, closely related point to be made. Since halakhah deals with concrete law, it is focused on actions; musar, on the other hand, is largely concerned with attitudes of heart and mind. Again we must not press this generalisation too far. Musar does indeed concern itself with concepts such as 'humility' and 'the fear of God', which are primarily attitudes, but it also discusses 'almsgiving' and 'acts of kindness', which are directly linked to conduct, and which can hardly be talked about at all without reference to concrete actions and instances.

Judaism is an intensely ethical religion, with an impressive body of ethical literature. Many of its basic mizvot are clearly ethical, and in principle it allows no distinction to be drawn between obedience to its moral and its non-moral mizvot. Yet in practice it has not accorded to musar the same attention or authority as it has to halakhah. There is no work of musar with a standing and influence in Judaism comparable to that of the great halakhic code, the *Shulhan Arukh*.

The earliest distinctive literary form of musar is the moral maxim – the short, pithy, memorable saying. Such maxims are typical of ancient wisdom literature, and are found in the Bible, especially in the Book of Proverbs. An important rabbinic collection is included in the Mishnah, in the tractate Pirqei Avot (6.1). Within the Mishnah Pirqei Avot is unique: unlike the other tractates it is totally non-legal in character. Why, then, was it included? It seems likely that it was meant to perform some function *vis-à-vis* the rest of the work. That this is so is suggested by its opening Chain of Tradition (2.1.1), which traces the transmission of the Oral Torah from Moses down to the Tannaim. As we have seen, this tradition's purpose was to justify the claims of the Tannaim to be the authentic teachers of the Law, and its presence in the Mishnah serves to validate the Mishnah as a whole as a true expression of the Oral Law. However, a problem arises: if Pirqei Avot has a prefatory function, then why does it not come right at the beginning of the Mishnah, or perhaps even at the end, as a sort of epilogue? Why is it located in the middle, almost at the end of the fourth order, Neziqin? This problem need not unduly trouble us. The present order of the tractates is to some extent arbitrary; other arrangements of the Mishnah are attested. Thus in the Vilna edition of the Babylonian Talmud and in the Naples edition of the Mishnah (1492), Pirqei Avot is the very last tractate of Neziqin, while in Codex Munich 95 of the Babylonian Talmud it stands right at the end of the sixth order, Toharot, just before the Minor Tractates. It is also possible to explain its present position towards the end of Neziqin by appealing to Babylonian Talmud, Ta'anit 24a–b. There we read:

> Rabbah once decreed a fast. He prayed, but no rain fell. Thereupon the people remarked to him: When Rav Judah ordained a fast rain *did* fall. He replied: What can I do? Is it because of our studies? But we are superior to him, because in the time of Rav Judah all studies were concentrated on Neziqin, whereas we study all six orders [of the Mishnah].

This statement appears to indicate that there was a time when only the fourth order of the Mishnah, or, as the text might also mean, only the first four orders, were studied. The last two, dealing primarily with Temple matters and ritual purity, were neglected. If, then, actual study of the Mishnah terminated with Neziqin, it would be reasonable to place Pirqei Avot there as a peroration to the preceding halakhot. So then Pirqei Avot probably serves two purposes within the Mishnaic corpus: first, by its Chain of Tradition it validates the Mishnah as genuine Oral Torah, and, second, by its moral maxims it complements the legal materials. We can only speculate as to the nature of this complementation, but it is not unlikely that the editor of the Mishnah saw expressed in Pirqei Avot some of the moral principles latent in the halakhah.

Pirqei Avot is a collection of maxims arranged according to rather mechanical principles of editing. In the Middle Ages, however, attempts were made to treat musar in a more systematic, philosophic way. One of the earliest, and by far the most important, of these attempts was Bahya ibn Paquda's *Book of Direction to the Duties of the Heart* (*Kitab al-Hidaya ila Fara'id al-Qulub*), written in Arabic at Saragossa in Spain, probably between 1080 and 1090 C.E. (6.2). In the Hebrew version by Judah ibn Tibbon, *Sefer Hovot ha-Levavot*, completed in 1161 C.E., Bahya's work exercised a profound influence on subsequent Jewish musar literature, and established its classic literary form.

For Bahya true religion lies essentially in obedience to God, in fulfilling the duties which God has imposed upon man. Corresponding to man's dual constitution of body and soul, these duties can be divided into two categories – 'the external duties of the body and the limbs' and 'the secret duties of the heart'. Both sets of duties have to be performed, the two categories are complementary.

> We are obliged to serve God both outwardly and inwardly. Outward service is expressed in the duties of the members, such as prayer, fasting, almsgiving, learning and teaching the Torah, fulfilling the commandments concerning the tabernacle, the *lulav*, the fringes [*zizit*], the *mezuzah*, the railing on the roof, and the like, all of which can be wholly performed by man's physical body. Inward service, however, is expressed in the duties of the heart, in the heart's assertion of the unity of God, in belief in him and in his Book, in constant obedience to him and fear of him, in humility before him, love for him and complete reliance upon him, submission to him and abstinence from the things hateful to him. Inward obedience is expressed in the consecration of all our work for his sake, in meditation upon his gracious acts, in all the duties performed by faith and conscience without the use of the external body-members. Thus I have come to know for certain that the duties of the members are of no avail to us unless our hearts choose to do them and our souls desire their performance. [Introduction to *The Duties of the Heart*]

Bahya complains that in the past Jewish thinkers have paid almost exclusive attention to the duties of the limbs, and neglected the duties of the heart. He has in mind here the emphasis in Judaism on the study of the halakhah, and he mentions by name two of the great halakhic compendia which appeared before his time – the *Halakhot Pesuqot* and the *Halakhot Gedolot*. His own aim is to redress the balance, to write a systematic guide which will do for the duties of the heart what the great law codes have done for the duties of the limbs. Bahya's division of duties suggests a way of defining the relationship between musar and halakhah rather similar to the one we proposed earlier: the duties of the limbs are the proper sphere of halakhah, the duties of the heart that of musar.

Bahya classifies the duties of the heart into ten categories and derives them from ten roots – beginning with belief in the unity of God and ending with love for God. These 'roots' appear to mark ten stages on a *via mystica*, a ladder of ascent to spiritual perfection which culminates in true love for God – 'the highest stage and supreme rank for those who obey God'. The ultimate goal is communion with God. Bahya is not concerned with ethics or morality in any strict philosophical sense. He provides a manual for the inner life, a guide to spirituality.

There is only one work which can vie in popular esteem with Pirqei Avot and Bahya's *Duties of the Heart*: it is the *Mesillat Yesharim (Path of the Upright)* by Moses Hayyim Luzzato (1707–46). In broad structure Luzzato's work (6.3) follows the classic pattern laid down in Bahya's *Duties of the Heart*: he traces the path to spiritual perfection. He finds that path mapped out in a famous saying attributed to the late second-century C.E. Palestinian scholar Pinhas ben Ya'ir. The saying is recorded in a number of forms each of which lists the scale of virtues slightly differently. Luzzato uses the version in Babylonian Talmud, Avodah Zarah 20b:

> Rabbi Pinhas ben Ya'ir said: Study leads to watchfulness, watchfulness leads to zeal, zeal leads to cleanliness, cleanliness leads to abstinence, abstinence leads to purity, purity leads to saintliness, saintliness leads to humility, humility leads to the fear of sin, fear of sin leads to holiness, holiness leads to the holy spirit, and the holy spirit leads to the resurrection of the dead; and saintliness is greater than any of these, for Scripture says, 'Then you spoke in a vision to your saintly ones'. [Ps. 89:20]

Luzzato takes the qualities listed here as a ladder of perfection, and in elegant rabbinic Hebrew analyses each of them, from 'watchfulness' through to 'holiness'.

Luzzato was born in Padua in Italy. As a young man he was a brilliant student: he mastered not only traditional Jewish religious literature but secular European literature and the sciences of his age as well. However, through his dabbling in Qabbalah he became the centre of bitter controversy and was suspected of heresy. He was forced to leave Padua (1735). He settled for a number of years in Amsterdam, and it was there he wrote the *Mesillat Yesharim*. The work was published in Amsterdam in 1740. Despite the cloud of suspicion that hung over him, Luzzato's non-Qabbalistic works were widely disseminated and well received. After his tragic death from plague at Acre in Palestine at the age of thirty-six, his reputation grew until he came to be regarded almost as a saint. His standing in eastern Europe was especially high. In the nineteenth and early twentieth centuries, owing to the influence of Rabbi Israel Salanter and the musar movement, the *Mesillat Yesharim* was studied in the great Lithuanian Yeshivot. Along with similar works it was regarded as providing a necessary complement and counterbalance to the study of halakhah.

## 1.6 PHILOSOPHY AND THEOLOGY

Compared with the study of halakhah, the study of philosophy is only a minor tradition within Judaism, pursued in fits and starts and treated from time to time with considerable hostility and reserve. Yet philosophy has left an indelible mark on Judaism: after its encounter with philosophy Judaism could never be the same again. Some of the greatest intellects in its history have been philosophers, and Judaism can boast a number of thinkers, such as Ibn Gabirol and Moses Maimonides, of major historical significance. Within mainstream Judaism philosophy began late – not, in fact till the early Middle Ages. There was, indeed, a flourishing school of Jewish philosophy in Alexandria in Egypt at the turn of the eras. Its most important representative, Philo (*c.* 20 B.C.E.–50 C.E.) attempts to create a synthesis of biblical thought and Platonism. Philo's synthesis was profoundly significant for Christian theology, but its impact on main-line Judaism was negligible. In the period following Philo the torch of Judaism was carried by the great Rabbinical academies of Palestine and Babylonia, and in those institutions the study of halakhah overshadowed all other pursuits. Indeed, the attitude of the rabbis towards Greek wisdom (*hokhmah yevanit*) was distinctly hostile. The influence of Philo was also limited by the fact that he wrote in a highly literary Greek, whereas the languages known and used in the academies were Aramaic and Hebrew. So it was left to the Church fathers, Greek-speaking and gymnasium-educated, to take up and develop the insights of Philo. Judaism had to make a fresh start in the Middle Ages to come to terms with philosophical thought.

Jewish philosophy emerged within mainstream Judaism in the Middle Ages as a side-effect of the ninth-century Islamic cultural renaissance promoted by the Abbasid caliphs of Baghdad. This cultural revival reached its peak under al-Ma'mun (*c.* 813–*c.* 833), son of the famous Harun al-Rashid. Al-Ma'mun, as a great patron of the arts, encouraged scholars like Hunayn ibn Ishaq (*c.* 809–873) to translate the works of ancient Greek science and philosophy into Arabic. Within a short period the writings of Galen, Hippocrates, Dioscorides, Euclid, Ptolemy, Aristotle and Plato were available in Arabic versions. The new fields of knowledge opened up by the translators created an intellectual ferment in Islam, because the teachings of the philosophers at many points appeared to be in conflict with the revealed religion of the Quran. And so a classic confrontation developed between science and religion, reason and revelation. From this confrontation arose Islamic theology, the 'Science of Kalam' (*ilm al-kalam*). The fifteenth-century Islamic scholar Ibn Khaldun defines Kalam as 'a science that involved arguing with logical proofs in defence of the articles of faith and refuting innovators who deviate in their dogmas from the early Muslims and Muslim orthodoxy. . . . In general, to the theologians the subject of theology [*ilm al-kalam*] is to find out how the articles of faith which the religious law has laid down as correct can be proved with the help of logical arguments, so that innovations may be repulsed and doubts and misgivings concerning the articles of faith be removed.'[15] This brings out well the apologetic nature of the Kalam: it is concerned to employ philosophic methods in defence of the faith. What it does not reveal is that the Islam which the *mutakallimun* were defending was not simple, traditional Islam but Islamic teaching reinterpreted and 'purified' in a philosophic fashion. While the theologians attacked the scepticism of the philosophers, they also accepted and built into their theology many philosophical ideas. And they were just as vehement in their attacks on the crudities of Islamic fundamentalists who interpreted the Quran in a very literal way. There were a number of different schools of Kalam. The earliest was the Mu'tazila. Al-Ma'mun gave it his blessing and made it the official form of Islam throughout his domains. Its main centres were at Baghdad and Basra. Towards the end of the ninth century, however, the Mu'tazila began to decline in influence and the Ash'ariyya became the dominant school of Islamic theology.

Jews lived in considerable numbers in Iraq in the early Middle Ages. They spoke Arabic and at least some of them were involved in the great ninth-century renaissance. It was no accident that the first major Jewish philosopher of the Middle Ages was Sa'adiah Gaon (882–942). Though Sa'adiah was born in Egypt, the greater part of his life was spent in Iraq as head of the rabbinical academy of Sura, close to Baghdad. Sa'adiah was a pioneer in many fields: he was an important grammarian, halakhist and liturgist. But his most original contribution was to Jewish philosophy. In his philosophical *magnum opus* – *The Book of Beliefs and Opinions (Kitab al-Amanat wa-al I'tiqadat)* (7.1) – his aims were exactly those of the mutakallimun as defined by Ibn Khaldun: he is concerned to rescue his co-religionists from the doubt and bewilderment they felt when faced with philosophic thought, and to defend the faith against philosophic attack. But like the mutakallimun he redefines the faith and reformulates it in such a way as to make it easier to reconcile faith and reason. For Sa'adiah, of course, the true faith is Judaism, not Islam. He may be accurately described as a Jewish mutakallim, or even, to be yet more precise, as a Jewish Mu'tazilite. His work is the first major product of a distinctly Jewish Kalam.

Sa'adiah was a pillar of orthodox Rabbanite Judaism and his espousal of the methods and ideas of the Kalam did much to establish speculative theology as a legitimate intellectual pursuit in orthodox circles. His influence was greatly extended after Judah ibn Tibbon produced in 1186 a Hebrew version of the *al-Amanat*, under the title *Sefer ha-Emunot veha-De'ot*. Sa'adiah opened the gates to speculative theology and many followed him through. He was not unduly daunted by the task of reconciling reason and revelation, but others thought differently: they were convinced that the concessions which the theologians had made to the philosophers were far too great. In time an anti-philosophic tendency emerged. One of its most important representatives was the Spanish poet and thinker Judah Halevi (before 1075–1141). Judah Halevi expounds his views in the *Kuzari* (7.2), which takes the form of a dialogue between the king of the Khazars and a Jewish scholar [*haver*]. The Khazars were a Turkic people of southern Russia and the Caucasus who converted to Judaism in the eighth century C.E. According to Judah Halevi's account the Khazar king considered and rejected in turn the claims of philosophy, Christianity and Islam before being convinced of the truth of Judaism. The *Kuzari* is a polemic work, as its full title shows – *The Book of Argument and Proof in Defence of the Despised Faith*. Its fictional dramatic setting allows its author to state and then refute the teachings of philosophy, Christianity and Islam.

Judah Halevi was not against reason as such, but against exaggerated claims being made for its authority. He makes a distinction between the sciences concerned with demonstration and proof (logic and mathematics) on the one hand, and the speculative sciences (mainly metaphysics, but to a certain extent also physics) on the other. The former are the proper domain of reason: in logic and mathematics reason has achieved certainty and its findings are not open to dispute. However, in the case of the latter it has manifestly failed to achieve certainty. This is evident from the total lack of consensus both in metaphysics and in physics, and from the fact that the arguments and proofs offered by the philosophers in these subjects are open to serious rational criticism and doubt. On metaphysical questions such as the origin of the world and the nature of God, reason needs the guidance of revelation: on such matters the philosopher must bow to the superiority of the prophet. So long as he does so and acknowledges the limits of reason there need be no conflict between philosophy and revelation.

Certain aspects of Judah Halevi's thought are similar to the teachings of his older contemporary, the great Islamic theologian al-Ghazali (1058–1111). Like Halevi, al-Ghazali stressed the limits of reason and attacked the inconsistencies of the philosophers, particularly in his work *The Incoherence of the Philosophers* (*Tahafut al-Falasifa*). Scholars have long disputed whether or not Judah Halevi knew the writings of al-Ghazali. His statement of the principles of the Kalam (7.2.6–16) is very close to a passage in al-Ghazali's Jerusalem Epistle (*al-Risalah al-Qudsiyah*) which now forms part of his great compendium of Islamic belief and practice *The Revival of the Religious Sciences* (*Ihya ulum al-din*). Halevi's text reads like a direct summary of al-Ghazali's. Indeed, at certain points Halevi is so compressed that his meaning only becomes fully clear by looking at the corresponding passage in al-Ghazali.[16]

Medieval Jewish philosophy reached its peak with Maimonides (1135–1204). Maimonides' great philosophical work *The Guide of the Perplexed* (*Dalalat al-Ha'irin*) was written late in life (*c.* 1190) and he seems to have regarded it as in some sense the culmination of his work. His aims in the *Guide* are broadly the same as those of Sa'adiah in the *Emunot ve-De'ot*, viz. to reconcile the Bible with philosophy and science, and thus to rescue the educated Jew of his generation who had studied philosophy and science from doubt and perplexity over those matters where reason and revelation appeared to be in conflict. For Maimonides philosophy meant above all Aristotelianism. In a letter to Samuel ibn Tibbon, who translated the *Dalalat* into Hebrew under the title of *Moreh ha-Nevukhim*, Maimonides asserted, 'Aristotle arrived at the highest peak of knowledge to which man can attain, save for those who have been vouchsafed an emanation of the divine spirit, so that they reach the stage of prophecy, above which is no higher stage'; and 'the works of Aristotle are the roots and foundations of all works on the sciences'.[17] Maimonides' massive authority made Aristotelianism the dominant school of Jewish philosophy. But, in an important sense, he does not represent 'pure' Aristotle, but Aristotle as seen through the eyes of his later interpreters and systematisers such as the second-to-third-century C.E. Greek commentator Alexander of Aphrodisias. Nor is he above criticising Aristotle when Aristotle holds views (such as the eternity of the world) which are utterly incompatible with Scripture (see *Guide*

B

*of the Perplexed*, II, 13–24).

Few would dispute that Maimonides is one of the greatest intellects ever nurtured by Judaism. However, his standing in Judaism rests not so much on the philosophical *Guide* as on his great halakhic works – the *Mishneh Torah* and (to a lesser degree) the *Commentary on the Mishnah*. Both the *Mishneh Torah* and the *Commentary* contain philosophical passages. These differ from the *Guide* in one very important respect: whereas in the *Guide* Maimonides deliberately adopted an opaque arrangement of his subject matter, and used a difficult style to keep the uneducated at bay, in the earlier halakhic works he was striving for maximum clarity, and so he presents the philosophy in a much more accessible form. The passage quoted in 7.3 is taken from the *Commentary on the Mishnah*. The Arabic *Commentary*, written in Cairo in 1168 C.E., was Maimonides' first major work.[18] The passage quoted sets out to define what are the thirteen fundamental principles of the Jewish faith: it constitutes the single most significant document of Jewish dogmatics. Its context in Maimonides' *Commentary* is important: it forms part of Maimonides' discussion of Mishnah, Sanhedrin 10:1:

> All Israel has a share in the world to come, for it is written, 'Your people shall be all righteous, they shall inherit the land for ever; the branch of my planting, the work of my hands that I may be glorified' (Isa. 60:21). And these are they who have no share in the world to come: he who says that there is no resurrection of the dead prescribed in the Torah, and he who says that the Torah is not from heaven, and an Epicurean. Rabbi Aqiva says: Also he who utters a charm over a wound and says, 'I will put none of the diseases upon you which I have put upon the Egyptians: for I am the Lord who heals you' (Exod. 15:26). Abba Saul says: Also he who pronounces the Name of God [YHWH] with its proper letters.

Faced with expounding this text, Maimonides attempts to define the fundamental beliefs of Judaism – those teachings to which a Jew must assent if he is to have a share in the world to come. It should be noted that the content of Mishnah, Sanhedrin 10:1, has determined in no small measure what Maimonides regards as the dogmas of Judaism.

Maimonides was not the only Jewish thinker to formulate the principles of the Jewish faith, but he was one of the earliest and most eminent to do so, and his formulation has been the most influential. Indeed, the thirteen principles of Maimonides are arguably the nearest Judaism has ever come to a formal creed. However, the principles are best known to Jews not in their full, original form but in two abbreviated versions. The first of these is the hymn *Yigdal*. It is of uncertain authorship, but was probably composed in Italy in the early fourteenth century. Immanuel ben Solomon of Rome (*c.* 1261–post 1328) in his *Cantos* has what appears to be an expanded version of the *Yigdal*. The *Yigdal* has been incorporated direct into the liturgy in most major rites.[19] The second abbreviation is the *Ani ma'amin*, so called because each article opens with the formula 'ani ma'amin be-emunah shelemah', 'I believe with complete faith'. As with the *Yigdal*, the authorship of this work as well as its date are unknown. It is first attested in the fifteenth century. The *Ani ma'amin* did not become part of the traditional liturgy, but it is often printed in prayer books.[20]

Maimonides clearly intended his thirteen principles as a genuine test of orthodoxy: note his words at 7.3.22. However, although his principles were very influential they were never really accepted as a practical criterion of orthodoxy, and subsequent Jewish scholars, such as Hasdai Crescas and Joseph Albo, felt free to disagree with him, and to produce alternative and usually shorter lists of the fundamental beliefs of Judaism.

Maimonides' shadow fell across all subsequent Jewish philosophy in the Middle Ages. Later philosophers and theologians tended to present their views as reactions to and comment on Maimonides. Not everyone by any means danced to his tune. The period after his death was marked by a strong upsurge of anti-rationalism within Judaism, bound up, at least in part, with the spread of the Qabbalah. Maimonides' writings, the *Mishneh Torah* as well as the *Guide*, stirred up a storm of controversy. The anti-rationalists in particular attacked Maimonides and those who followed him for seeking to harmonise the Bible and philosophy. The storm raged across the Jewish world from east to west: bans and counter-bans were issued, letters and pamphlets sent in all directions; emissaries went round rallying support for the various points of view. The seriousness of the situation may be gauged from the fact that in December 1232 at Montpellier the Church authorities burned the *Guide of the Perplexed* as a heretical book. The exact circumstances of this sordid incident can no longer be constructed with any certainty, but the Maimonideans were convinced that informers had been at work and pointed the finger particularly at the anti-Maimonidean scholar Solomon ben Abraham of Montpellier. The anti-philosophical faction got the better of the dispute. Of great importance from their point of view was the ban on the study of philosophy issued at Barcelona in 1305 C.E. by the eminent scholar Solomon ben Abraham Adret (c. 1235–c. 1310). Adret attacked those who were 'infatuated with alien sciences' and paid 'homage to Greek books'. He objected to the philosophers reducing the Bible to 'useless allegories' by arguing such things as 'Abraham and Sarah represent matter and form, and the twelve tribes of Israel are the twelve constellations'. Adret therefore forbade the study of philosophy 'until the student and teacher are twenty-five years old, and until they are sated with the delicacies of the Torah, and so will not remove it from its position of pre-eminence'.[21] Despite the violence of Adret's language his ban was in substance moderate. He claimed to be an admirer of Maimonides, and Maimonides himself would arguably have agreed with him in restricting the study of philosophy to those over twenty-five, since Maimonides regarded philosophy as an esoteric subject to be pursued only by an intellectual elite after rigorous training. But the general effect of the Maimonidean controversy and the ban of Adret was to throw doubt in traditionalist circles on the validity of philosophical study. For centuries afterwards philosophy tended to be frowned upon and regarded as in some sense a dangerous and questionable subject of study. This anti-philosophical attitude has persisted in some orthodox circles right down to the present day.

## 1.7 MYSTICAL LITERATURE

It is notoriously difficult to find a brief definition of mysticism. Many definitions have, of course, been proposed, but none of them really stands up to close examination. Yet, for all its vagueness, 'mysticism' remains an indispensable category to the student of religion: there are certain phenomena which cannot, apparently, be labelled by any other term. Though it is hard to say what mysticism is in the abstract, paradoxically it is not too difficult to recognise mysticism when one actually meets it. This is certainly true in the case of Judaism. The literature and leading ideas of Jewish mysticism are well enough known. Few would deny that Scholem's epoch-making survey *Major Trends in Jewish Mysticism* (1941) correctly maps out the whole field. The real problem lies in trying to distil the essence of this tradition, in discovering what it is that links together the diverse texts and ideas analysed by Scholem, and allows them to be grouped together into a separate category, distinct, say, from philosophy or halakhah.

The mystics were certainly themselves conscious that they were taking a different path to ultimate truth from that followed by the philosopher or the halakhist. This consciousness is particularly strong *vis-à-vis* philosophy, which in many ways tried to occupy the same ground as mysticism. Certain forms of contemplative mysticism owe a debt to philosophy and shade imperceptibly into it, but generally speaking the mystics are not sympathetic towards philosophy, and from time to time they launch attacks on philosophy and ally themselves with the forces of anti-rationalism. The tension between halakhah and mysticism is more subtle and oblique. It surfaces occasionally within Judaism, but it is much less radical than the tension between mysticism and philosophy. And it should always be borne in mind that great halakhists such as Joseph Caro were at the same time mystics and, apparently, found mysticism and the halakhah totally compatible.

Three general characteristics of Jewish mysticism can be isolated. Neither singly nor collectively are these sufficient to define the essence of the tradition, but they will serve to highlight some of its significant features.

First, the mystic's aim is to achieve personal and intimate communion with God, either through ecstatic experience (as in Merkavah mysticism), or through contemplation (as in the Qabbalah). This longing to know God in a direct way is common to mysticism, but the form it takes in Judaism has a distinctly Judaic colouring. Judaism is profoundly conscious of the 'otherness' of God, of the ontological gap which divides man from his Creator. As a result the Jewish mystics shrink from explicitly describing the climax of their mystical experiences as absorption into God, even when, in effect, such absorption and union appear to take place.

Second, the path to communion with God lies for the mystic not through reason or intellect, but through some other faculty of the soul. He seeks for an immediate knowledge of God, not one mediated by ideas. Mystical discourse, consequently, differs profoundly from philosophical. It does not proceed by way of logical argument, by rational proof and demonstration. Rather, it exploits powerful, emotive symbols and imagery which appeal more to the imagination. Particularly in the Qabbalah its language becomes intensely mythic in character.

Third, the mystics are concerned with 'secrets', 'mysteries' and 'hidden things'. This is how they most commonly describe their teachings. Jewish mysticism is concerned with secrets in two senses. (a) It seeks to penetrate below the surface of things, to discover hidden truths. It strives to get behind the world of appearance and diversity to a world of unity and ultimate reality. (b) Its teachings are 'secret' in the sense that they are esoteric, that is, they are meant only for the initiated, not for the vulgar who might misunderstand them. Indeed, 'Jewish esotericism' is one of the few designations which might usefully replace 'Jewish mysticism'. In the Tannaitic era or even earlier, Judaism declared two broad areas of study as esoteric: the first was cosmology (Ma'aseh Bere'shit) − speculation on the origin and nature of the world; the other was theosophy (Ma'aseh Merkavah) − speculation on the nature of God and of his angels. These two subjects have broadly characterised the content of the Jewish mystical tradition ever since. It is in their concern with 'secrets', with an ultimate reality beyond the world of appearance, and with an esoteric doctrine, that mysticism and philosophy in Judaism most obviously overlap. However, they differ profoundly as to the nature of that ultimate reality, and the manner in which it is to be apprehended.

The major early cosmological text is the *Sefer Yezirah* or *Book of Formation* (8.1.1). This unique little work, which Scholem estimates as running to no more than '2,000 words altogether even in its longer version',[22] appears at first reading to be a work of primitive science. In broad outline its teaching is clear: it offers an 'atomic' theory of nature, i.e. it accounts for the diverse phenomena which go to make up the world in terms of varying combinations of a small number of irreducible elements, or 'atoms'. However, its detailed interpretation has proved to be intensely problematic, and a plethora of different readings have been proposed. A major issue of interpretation arises from the fact that the *Sefer Yezirah* appears to present two separate cosmologies, the interrelationship of which it fails to make clear. The first cosmology, expounded in mishnayot 6−15, is based on the first ten numbers of the decimal system, which the text calls the ten Sefirot. It appears to envisage creation as taking place in three phases. Phase one sees the emergence of the first four Sefirot, which correspond to the 'Spirit of the Living God', and the basic elements of Air, Water and Fire. This phase seems to be characterised by a process of 'emanation', though the word itself is not actually used and the text is noticeably reticent about deriving the 'Spirit of the Living God' from God. Phase two takes place within the sphere of the three basic elements and is characterised by the verbs 'engrave' and 'hew out'. In the element of Air, God 'engraves and hews out' the twenty-two fundamental letters of the Hebrew alphabet. In the element of Water, he 'engraves and hews out' the primordial chaos from which the physical world emerged. In the element of Fire, he 'engraves and hews out' the Merkavah – the heavenly world of the Throne of Glory and the angels. Phase three involves the fundamental letters and is characterised by the verb 'to seal'. God takes three of the letters and by arranging them in a variety of combinations establishes in infinite space the boundaries of the universe. The last six Sefirot correspond to the six dimensions of finite space. And so, as the author says with typical brevity, three principles were involved in the creation of the world – limit, letter and number (mishnah 1).

The second cosmology, which runs from mishnah 17 to the end, treats the twenty-two letters of the Hebrew alphabet as the building blocks of the universe. It appears to be based on the notion that speech (that is, language composed of words, which are in turn composed of letters/sounds) 'is not only a means of communication but also an operational agent destined to produce being – it has an ontological value. This value, however, does not extend to every form of language; it belongs to the Hebrew language alone.'[23] Speech does not merely name things; it calls them into being. This idea was probably suggested by the prominence which Genesis 1 gives to God's speech in the process of creation. Following a primitive philological schema, the author analyses the twenty-two letters/speech-sounds of Hebrew into three groups – three 'mothers', seven double letters, and twelve simple. He attempts to establish correlations between each of these groups and three distinct aspects of the cosmos – the 'world' (i.e. the material world), the year (i.e. time), and the human body. At a number of points the author shows empiricist leanings: at least in part he has deduced his system from direct observation of nature – from the recurrence of patterns of threes, sevens and twelves in the perceptible world.

What was it that turned this work of speculative natural philosophy into one of the most important works of Jewish mysticism? First, there was the fact that it dealt with a subject – cosmology – which had been proclaimed as esoteric. Second, there was its concentrated, enigmatic style. There is a highly charged, almost poetic quality about its language, and from time to time, especially at the beginning, it contains strong echoes of Merkavah mysticism. Third, the author's highly inventive use of language provided later mysticism with at least one of its key terms. He appears to have coined the term Sefirah (plural: Sefirot), which was to play such a major role in later Qabbalistic speculation.

The colophon of the *Sefer Yezirah* attributes the work to the patriarch Abraham (mishnah 64). The attribution is, of course, false. The true author is unknown, nor can we be certain as to when the *Sefer Yezirah* was written, or where. The work was certainly well known in the tenth century, for Sa'adiah

Gaon produced an important commentary on it. Scholem's considered opinion is that 'the main part of the *Sefer Yezirah*, though it contains post-talmudic additions, was written between the third and the sixth centuries, apparently in Palestine by a devout Jew with leanings towards mysticism, whose aim was speculative and magical rather than ecstatic'.[24] However, it must be admitted that nearly every assertion here can and has been questioned.

*Heikhalot Rabbati* (*The Greater Treatise on the Heavenly Palaces*) is the central work of early Merkavah mysticism. *Heikhalot Rabbati* forms a part of a considerable body of literature, some of it still available only in manuscript, which emanated from circles of mystics flourishing in Palestine and Babylonia in the Talmudic and post-Talmudic eras. These mystics were intensely interested in the visions of the heavenly world contained in the Bible, especially the awesome description of God's Chariot (*Merkavah*) in Ezekiel. However, they were not content to be simply commentators on the biblical text: they sought to experience for themselves, to see with their own eyes, what Ezekiel saw. There was a strong theurgic element in their mysticism: through fasting and other spiritual exercises, through reciting strange, repetitive hymns full of powerful, emotive words, through invoking the angels by magical names and reciting magical formulae, they practised ascent in trance to God's heavenly throne (8.2.1). The climax of the mystic's ecstacy was to behold the divine glory, and to join with the angels in the celestial Sanctus (the Qedushah). The mystic yearns for communion with God, but before he can reach his desired goal he has to overcome well-nigh insurmountable obstacles. Between him and God's throne lies a region of immense danger across which his soul has to find a way. This idea is classically expressed in the heikhalot literature through the symbolism of the heavenly places (*heikhalot*). God dwells in the innermost of seven concentric palaces, and at the gate of each palace stand fierce guardian angels whose task it is to ward off intruders. To get past the angels the mystic must have *gnosis* – secret knowledge: he needs to know the correct magical names which will 'seal', i.e. neutralise, the powers of the hostile gatekeepers. Each 'seal' acts as a sort of password, enabling him to negotiate the gate. He must memorise correctly the complex procedures for making a successful ascent; if he makes a mistake at any point he can put his soul in dire peril. It is not hard to detect psychic realities behind this imagery.

*Heikhalot Rabbati* contains the deposit of a tradition which evolved over many centuries. Like all such texts it is extremely difficult to date, but it probably reached its present form in the fifth or sixth century C.E. The Merkavah tradition has its roots far back in Palestinian Jewish apocalyptic of the first century C.E. or even earlier, and it continued to flourish through the Talmudic period down to the early Middle Ages. Merkavah texts were known in the early tenth century to Sa'adiah Gaon and to the Qaraites, such as Jacob al-Qirqisani. The Qaraites ridiculed the crudely anthropomorphic ideas of the Merkavah mystics, and it may have been due in part to their criticism, and to the consequent embarrassment felt by Rabbanite scholars such as Sa'adiah, that Merkavah mysticism died out as a living mystical movement. Certain Merkavah texts were, however, transmitted westwards to Europe and North Africa, and aspects of their teaching influenced the medieval German Jewish mystics known as the Hasidei Ashkenaz, and the Qabbalists of Spain. But perhaps the most enduring contribution of Merkavah mysticism to Judaism in general was in the sphere of liturgy. It has long been accepted that the angelology of the Merkavah texts, as well as their solemn, grandiloquent hymns, have influenced the style and contents of certain hymns and prayers used in synagogue. This influence is particularly apparent in the various synagogue Qedushot.[25]

The central text of the medieval Qabbalah is the *Book of Splendour* – the *Zohar* (8.3.1–6). Few other texts have had a comparable influence on the development of Judaism. The *Zohar* has had its critics (some of whom have been virulent in their condemnation), and it was by no means universally acclaimed when it first appeared, but it has been largely due to the *Zohar*'s advocacy that Qabbalistic ideas came to permeate the whole of Jewish life – folklore and custom, liturgy and prayer, ethics and the interpretation of the halakhah. Its influence on Hasidism has been especially profound (see 9.1.1–2). In some circles the *Zohar* has been accorded almost canonic status. It may be ranked alongside the Bible and the Babylonian Talmud as one of the three works which have done most to shape the Judaic world view and fire the Jewish religious imagination.

The bulk of the *Zohar* is in the form of a mystical midrash on the Five Books of Moses, written in a curiously stilted and artificial Aramaic. Strictly speaking it is anonymous, but since it purports to record the discussions of the great second-century C.E. Palestinian scholar, Rabbi Simeon ben Yohai, and his disciples, it was traditionally believed that Simeon was the author. Modern academic study of the *Zohar* rejects this attribution and regards the work as a pseudepigraphon: a later writer has deliberately put his own views into the mouth of a famous early master, in order to conceal his own identity, and also, perhaps, to give his own opinions an aura of antiquity and authority.

But if Simeon ben Yohai did not write the *Zohar*, who did? Since the work as usually printed contains around twenty-four separate treatises of diverse literary form and content, it might seem more realistic to look not for one but for several authors. Some scholars have espoused the view of multiple authorship, or have argued that the *Zohar*, like the Mishnah and early midrashim, contains many different layers of material and has reached its present state only after a long and complex historical evolution. However, from a detailed study of its language, style, imagery and ideas, Scholem has argued that the *Zohar* is, in fact, a unified work by a single author – the medieval Spanish Qabbalist Moses ben Shem Tov de Leon, who died in 1305. He believes that the bulk of the work was composed between 1270 and 1300, and that even the two main parts of the *Zohar*, the Tiqqunei Zohar and the Ra'aya Meheimna (Faithful Shepherd), which he concedes are not by Moses de Leon, were written around the same time, and come from the same Qabbalistic circles to which Moses de Leon belonged; hence their inclusion in his work.[26] Scholem's views on the composition, date and authorship of the *Zohar* are now academic orthodoxy, though we can be sure that the last word has not yet been said on any aspect of this perplexing text.

A major reason why the *Zohar* is so perplexing is that it does not give a systematic exposition of the Qabbalah. Yet study shows that it presupposes right from the start a coherent system of ideas, which the author carried in his head, and which lies behind each separate section of his work. This system was not invented by Moses de Leon: in its essentials he found it already formed and simply applied it. The system itself was the result of the profound speculations on mystical theology among the Qabbalists of Provence and Catalonia in the hundred or so years before the time of Moses de Leon. In fact it is probably true to say that in general Moses was not innovative in the realm of basic mystical ideas, though he produced his own distinctive 'mix', and introduced some important modifications to the system. His real originality lies rather in the skill with which he read Qabbalah into Scripture, and in his enormous facility for finding powerful, arresting imagery and language in which to express Qabbalistic doctrine.

The Qabbalists are theosophists in the strictest sense of the term; that is, they claim to have insight into the inner life of God. They are obsessed with God, but God to the Qabbalists is not the God of the philosophers – pure, unchanging, untroubled being, without body, parts or passions. God is process: his life is full of movement, tension and drama. The main conceptual tool devised by the Qabbalists for analysing and describing the divine life is the Sefirot. God in himself is unknowable: he is beyond all thought, all language. In this aspect of his being he is the Ein Sof, the Unlimited, the Undefined. The Ein Sof, however, has chosen to reveal himself under the form of ten attributes, or modes of self-disclosure, called Sefirot. The Sefirot emanate from the Ein Sof, they are aspects, 'faces', of God. They are not entities lying outside God, but remain within the Godhead. The Sefirot may be all we can know of God, but in knowing them we truly know God. 'The Holy One, blessed be he, has produced ten holy crowns above [the Sefirot], wherewith he crowns and invests himself. He is they and they are he, being linked together like the flame and the coal' (*Zohar*, Aharei Mot, III 70a). In descending order of emanation the Sefirot are: (1) Crown (Keter); (2) Wisdom (Hokhmah); (3) Understanding (Binah); (4) Greatness (Gedullah), or Kindness (Hesed); (5) Power (Gevurah), or Justice (Din); (6) Beauty (Tif'eret), or Mercy (Rahamim); (7) Victory (Nezah); (8) Majesty (Hod); (9) Foundation (Yesod), or Righteous One (Zaddiq); (10) Sovereignty (Malkhut). The intense drama of the divine life is presented by the Qabbalists largely in terms of speculation on the Sefirot, and their various groupings and interrelationships.

How is it possible for the Qabbalists to know what is going on in the inner recesses of God's being? Here a 'doctrine of correspondences' comes into play. It is a fundamental tenet of the Qabbalah that a close correspondence exists between the upper world of the Sefirot and the lower, mundane world of the visible creation. 'The Lord made this world corresponding to the world above, and everything which is above has its counterpart below . . . and yet the whole constitutes a unity' (*Zohar*, Shemot, II 20a). Everything on earth has its 'root' or counterpart in the world of the Sefirot. Since God 'fills all worlds and encompasses all worlds', the Sefirot are reflected in all worlds, and the visible, mundane world pulses to the rhythm of the divine life. What happens in nature and in history, especially in the sacred history of Israel, mirrors and symbolises processes within the being of God. Torah is divine revelation, the utterance of God clothed in human speech and physical letters, and so correspondences between it and the world of the Sefirot are naturally seen as particularly detailed and close. The Torah 'consists entirely of the Name of the Holy One, blessed be he, and every letter of the Torah is bound up with that Holy Name' (*Zohar*, Aharei Mot, III 73a). 'The Torah contains all supernal and recondite mysteries which are beyond man's grasp, all sublime doctrines both disclosed and undisclosed; all essences both of the realm above and the realm below, of this world and of the world to come, are to be found therein' (*Zohar*, Toledot, I 134b). The main business of the Qabbalist is to identify these detailed correspondences between the Torah and the Sefirot, and in the light of them to reread the whole Torah as a symbolic description of the drama of God's inner life. The plain, literal sense of the text is not denied, but a second, esoteric level of meaning is superimposed upon it.

It would be wrong to suppose that the direction of influence is only from the upper world to the lower. The two worlds, in fact, interact. Actions and events in the terrestrial world reverberate in the supernal world: 'The upper world moves in response to the lower world' (*Zohar*, Vayyeze, I 164a). 'Whatever is on earth has its counterpart on high. There is no object, however small, in this world that is not subordinate to its counterpart above, which has charge over it; and so whenever a thing below bestirs itself, there is a simultaneous stimulation of its counterpart that has charge over it above, since the two realms form one interconnected whole' (*Zohar*, Vayyeze, I 156b). So man's sin causes disharmony in the world of the Sefirot, within the life of God himself, and conversely when a man studies Torah, prays and observes the mizvot, he makes *tiqqun* (reparation) and helps to restore harmony to the world of the Sefirot: 'The Holy One, blessed be he, said, as it were, "When Israel is worthy below my power prevails over the universe; but when Israel is not found worthy she weakens, as it were, my power above, and the power of severe Justice [Din] prevails" ' (*Zohar*, Be-shallah, II 65b). When Israel went into exile from her land there was a corresponding alienation within the Godhead: the Shekhinah (= the Sefirah Malkhut, the heavenly counterpart of Keneset Yisra'el) went into exile with them: 'When Israel are in captivity, the Holy One, blessed be he, is, so to speak, in captivity with them, for the Shekhinah never leaves them' (*Zohar*, Aharei Mot, III 66a). And Israel's return to her land will be matched by a reunion of God with the Shekhinah. The redemption of Israel becomes at one and the same time the redemption of God.

This idea that human actions influence the upper world forms the basis of Qabbalistic ethics. It assigns to man an astonishingly exalted position in the scheme of things, giving him a cosmic role which involves him directly in the drama of the divine life. Man stands at the opposite pole of the cosmic process to God: he is God's counterpart on earth, in whom are reflected all the Sefirot. Man's task is to direct back to its source the stream of energy emanating from the Ein Sof. His co-operation is essential to the work of creation. Though not strictly speaking an initiator, he is a completer through whom the potential becomes actual. Consequently his refusal to play his part – his sin and rebellion – is a catastrophe of cosmic proportions.

The Qabbalists were much exercised about the question of man's spiritual constitution. The *Zohar* has a tripartite division of the soul, each part representing a different level of consciousness. The lowest level, closest to the body, is *nefesh*. Implanted in all men at birth, it is the principle of animal vitality. The two other parts of the soul are acquired. *Ruah*, the level above nefesh, emerges when a man rises above a purely animal existence, on to a more spiritual plane. Finally, comes *neshamah*, the highest state of consciousness, which is aroused through the study of Torah, through prayer and the performance of the mizvot. Each of these aspects of the soul has its 'root', its counterpart, in the upper world – nefesh in the Sefirah Malkhut, ruah in the Sefirah Tif'eret and neshamah in the Sefirah Binah. It is only when a man rises to the level of neshamah that he gains insight into the ultimate secrets of the universe. Neshamah is the faculty of the soul through which man achieves true communion with God.

## 1.8 MODERN MOVEMENTS, MODERN THINKERS

Judaism has always been marked by diversity of belief and practice, and both in the past and today takes on many forms. On the whole Judaism is tolerant of religious diversity. For most Jews their Jewishness is an inalienable status conferred by birth: it is not something which arises from assent to certain beliefs, or from adopting certain practices. For much of their history Jews have lived as religious minorities scattered across many lands. The scattered communities have often been separated by geographical, political and cultural barriers, which have made contact difficult, if not impossible. As a result local religious autonomy has been the norm for much of Jewish history; intercommunal authority has been either non-existent or for the most part weak. Since the ending of the Babylonian Gaonate in the Middle Ages Jewry has lacked a central religious authority, and it has certainly never at any time possessed an institution resembling in comprehensive religious power the medieval papacy.

Owing to the isolation of the scattered Jewish communities, different forms of Judaism evolved in different countries. Traditionally Judaism has recognised the legitimacy of local variations in religious practice: local custom (minhag) is fully valid for the members of any given local community. Jewish authorities have usually resisted any attempt to suppress local rites or to supplant one by another. The traditional regional variations within Judaism fall into two broad traditions – the Sefardi and the Ashkenazi. 'Sefarad' was the medieval Hebrew name for Spain, and the Sefardi tradition is (roughly speaking) the tradition which was current among the Jews of Muslim and Christian Spain. This tradition was carried abroad, to the Netherlands, to North Africa and to the eastern Mediterranean, when the Jews were expelled from Spain in 1492. 'Ashkenaz' was the medieval Hebrew name for Germany, and the Ashkenazi tradition has its roots in the practice of the Jewish communities of the Rhineland in the Middle Ages. This tradition spread eastwards into Poland and Russia with the eastward migration of German Jews. The Sefardi and Ashkenazi traditions differ considerably from each other in matters of custom, liturgy and halakhah, but traditionally Sefardis and Ashkenazis have acknowledged the legitimacy of each other's form of Judaism, and in Israel today each community has its own Chief Rabbi.

Despite this broad tolerance and flexibility, Judaism has been torn from time to time by deep division, and has experienced serious schism. The Samaritans, the Christians and the Qaraites are examples of groups which have broken with the main body of Judaism to go their own distinctive ways. The tendency towards fragmentation appears to have become more pronounced since the eighteenth century, and whereas in the past Judaism divided on the whole along regional lines, it now divides more fundamentally along ideological lines, which cut across national and geographical boundaries. At a practical, everyday level the adherents of the various modern varieties of Judaism will recognise each other as Jews, but at certain points religious co-operation and intercommunion, and even social contact, become difficult. This is particularly true of the relationship between modern orthodoxy and non-orthodox groups (especially Reform). Indeed, from a halakhic standpoint orthodoxy would be prepared to question the very Jewishness of certain Reform Jews.

The major modern[27] varieties of Judaism have all arisen within the Ashkenazi tradition. The first to emerge was Hasidism. Hasidism was a powerful religious movement which swept through the Jewish communities of eastern Europe in the eighteenth century. It was strongly 'revivalist' in character: it was marked by extreme fervour and enthusiasm in prayer and worship, and it was led by charismatic figures. In certain interesting ways it was similar to the eighteenth-century revivalist movements in Christendom, such as Methodism under the leadership of John Wesley in England, and the Great Awakening inspired by the preaching of Jonathan Edwards in New England.

The movement was 'marginal' in origin: it seems to have begun among fringe groups in the Jewish community in the remote region of Podolia (then in south-east Poland, now in the Ukrainian SSR). It soon spread westwards and northwards into the more central regions of Volhynia, Lithuania and Galicia. At its height the movement had a very considerable following. Hasidic groups have survived down to the present day: their main centres are in the USA and in Israel.

The effective founder of the movement was Israel ben Eliezer (*c.* 1700–60), who was known from his healing and wonder-working as Ba'al Shem Tov – 'Master of the Good Name' (i.e. the Name of God), hence his common acronym, 'the Besht'. The major source for Israel ben Eliezer's life is a collection of stories known as *The Praises of the Besht (Shivhei ha-Besht)* (9.1.1). Recovering the historical Israel ben Eliezer from these tales is as difficult as recovering the historical Jesus of Nazareth from the Gospels. The tales are full of legendary elements and are not meant as biography in any strict sense of the term. Among the Hasidim story-telling performed an important religious function and it was raised to the level of high religious art. It was a staple of Hasidic preaching, and was widely used for religious instruction and edification. It became a chosen vehicle for the expression of ideas. Some Hasidic tales (such as those told by Rabbi Nahman of Bratzlav) are complex, mystical allegories; the majority, however, purport to relate happenings in the lives of the great Hasidic saints. The original compiler of the *Shivhei ha-Besht* expresses his purpose in collecting the stories quite clearly: 'The reader should realise that I have written all this not simply as stories or as history, but in order that he should perceive in each tale the wonders of the Lord, and infer from it its moral, and so attach his heart to the fear of the Lord, the beliefs of the Sages, and the power of our holy Torah.' The 'folksy', simple character of the tales often conceals great narrative sophistication and skill.

The *Shivhei ha-Besht* was compiled some time after the Besht's death by Dov Baer ben Samuel of Linits, the son-in-law of Alexander Shohat, who had served for many years as the Besht's secretary. Alexander Shohat, not surprisingly, is one of the sources for the tales, but there are many others as well. In the case of the great majority of the tales the compiler scrupulously names the tradent in the opening sentence. Dov Baer's text seems to have passed through many vicissitudes before it reached its present form. His manuscript was first printed in 1814 by Israel Jaffe in Kopys. Jaffe extensively edited the text before printing it. He tells us in his preface:

I was aware that this manuscript was full of mistakes, and certainly if it had been copied over and over the errors would have increased in number until the meaning of the sentences would have been almost unrecognisable, and so I took great pains to free it from error. Therefore, I gathered my strength to set it on my printing-press and to correct it as carefully as I could.

In addition to his editorial work, Jaffe added to the beginning of the text a small collection of stories (Nos. 1–15 in the translation of Ben-Amos and Mintz), which, it seems, he received from the great Zaddiq, Shneur Zalman of Lyady

(1745–1813), of whom he was a follower. The tale quoted below (9.1.1) belongs to this group.

A number of different images of the Besht emerge from the tales, not all of them strictly compatible. In some of the stories the Besht comes across as a wonder-worker of humble origin and little learning who went about writing amulets and performing miracles. In Shneur Zalman's tales, however, he has a much more exalted status: he is known as a great saint who consciously concealed his learning until the right moment arrived for him to reveal himself. Shneur Zalman's tales have probably an underlying apologetic purpose. They are certainly used quite deliberately as a 'corrective' to the other traditions by Israel Jaffe. Towards the end of the preface he writes:

> Since I saw that in the manuscripts from which I copied these tales there were things out of order with regard to the sequence of events and the revelation of the Besht, and since I had heard everything in the name of Admor [Shneur Zalman], whose soul rests in heaven, in the proper order and with the correct interpretation, I will print first what I heard from his holy lips, and after that point in the story, I will set down what is written in the manuscripts.

Hasidism was a deeply divisive force: it split east European Jewry into two warring camps. The main oponents of the Hasidim (known as the Mitnaggedim) lived in Lithuania – the bastion of traditional Rabbanism. The greatest of the Mitnaggedim was the famous Talmudist, Rabbi Elijah, the Vilna Gaon. On a number of occasions the Hasidim were excommunicated by the rabbinic establishment, which even went so far as to call in the secular authorities to suppress them.

Rabbinic opposition to Hasidism was based on many factors. The rabbis were put off by the extravagant fervour of Hasidic worship. They also objected to certain Halakhic practices of the Hasidim, such as their method of ritual slaughter, and to their abandonment of the Ashkenazi rite in favour of the Lurianic prayer book.[28] But at the very heart of the rabbinic opposition lay the fear of the establishment over the growth of Zaddiqism in Hasidic circles. As we have already seen, in traditional rabbinic society religious leadership was based on scholarship: positions of religious authority in the community went to those learned in halakhah. To acquire the requisite knowledge of the halakhah meant studying at one of the great Yeshivot. In the Hasidic movement, on the other hand, authority was based not on learning but on charisma – on the purely personal qualities of the leader. The charismatic leaders of the Hasidic movement are known as Zaddiqim (Righteous Ones). Within Hasidic thought the nature and role of the Zaddiq were defined with some precision (though there were differences of opinion on detailed ideological points). The Zaddiq was a sort of spiritual virtuoso (9.1.2), an extraordinary human being who, by reason of his personal qualities and training, was able to reach the highest levels of 'cleaving' (*devequt*) to God. The role of the Zaddiq was twofold. On the one hand he was expected by intense acts of study and devotion to make tiqqun, to help restore cosmic harmony and thus hasten the final redemption. On the other hand he had a part to play towards his followers: he had to teach, guide and inspire them, and set them an example, and thus bring them closer to God. He was a mediator between man and God. The followers of a Zaddiq regard him with extreme reverence, bordering on worship. They observe all his actions closely; as one Hasid succinctly put it, he came to his Master not to hear him teach but to see how he tied his shoelaces.[29]

Hasidism was essentially an east European phenomenon and reflected the peculiar conditions of east European Jewry. Reform Judaism, by way of contrast, was a western movement and arose as a direct response to the challenge of emancipation. 'Emancipation' is the rather loaded term applied to the political process of removing the disabilities under which the Jews had laboured in Christian lands, and of giving them equal rights and opportunities as full citizens of the States where they lived. Emancipation was broader in scope than mere equality before the law. It opened up the universities to Jewish students, allowed them to enter professions previously barred to them, gave them the vote and permitted them to participate directly in the political process. As a result of emancipation Jews enjoyed greater economic and social freedom. The barriers which had segregated them within society came down, and they found themselves in direct contact with a powerful, non-Jewish culture.

The impact of emancipation on traditional Judaism was profound, and its effects continue down to the present day. Indeed, it is probably not an exaggeration to say that, with the exception of Hasidism, all major modern varieties of Judaism represent varying responses to the challenge of emancipation. The social structures which had discriminated against Jews within society prior to the period of emancipation had not necessarily been bad: they had fostered the cohesiveness of Jews as a group; but they had also effectively insulated the Jewish community from outside ideas and change. Even at the end of the eighteenth century the Jewish communities of Europe were still essentially medieval in their organisation and religious outlook. Within two generations those communities were to be exposed to the untempered blast of Western modernism: they were to feel the full force of historical and scientific rationalism, political liberalism, and the social and economic upheavals of the industrial revolution.

Dissatisfaction with traditional Judaism manifested itself early among emancipated Jews. It was first felt, it seems, at the level of synagogue liturgy. Many Jews became disenchanted with what they saw as the lack of decorum in the traditional synagogue: they objected to the long services and to the exclusive use of Hebrew. They wanted a style of worship less distinctive, more in keeping with that of their Christian neighbours. Dissatisfaction was also felt over certain mizvot, such as the dietary laws, which made socialising with non-Jews difficult. The nationalism and exclusivism of traditional Judaism, particularly the 'Zionism' of the prayer book, was felt to be something of an embarrassment. Exclusivism conflicted with the universalistic notions of the Age of Reason, and now that Jews were being granted equal citizenship it was surely inconsistent for them to continue praying for the restoration of their own Jewish State, for a return to Zion. The Reform movement arose in an attempt to strip Judaism of what were seen as anachronisms, and to reshape it in such a way that it would continue to command the respect and allegiance of modern 'westernized', educated Jews.

In the early days Germany was the centre of Reform. From Germany it was carried, largely by emigrating German Jews, to America. In the New World it struck deep roots: its liberalism, its readiness to innovate and its belief in progress were well suited to the ethos of American society. Reform congregations sprang up independently in a number of places. That these separate endeavours were successfully channelled into an organised movement was largely due to the efforts of Isaac Meyer Wise (1819–1900). To Wise more than to anyone else must be credited the formation of two of the basic institutions of the American Reform movement – the Union of American Hebrew Congregation (1873) and Hebrew Union College (1875). Wise was a moderate reformer. In the 1880s, however, the ideological leadership of the movement increasingly slipped from his grasp and passed into the hands of the radicals led by Kaufmann Kohler, who had only recently come to the United States from Germany.

On 16–18 November 1885 a group of Reform rabbis met in Pittsburgh to formulate the principles of the movement. Though Wise was elected chairman, the conference appears to have been dominated by Kohler. It had been called on his initiative; he drafted the text of the principles and delivered the major speech on them. The final text approved by the conference does not seem to differ significantly from Kohler's draft. The radicalism of the final statement faithfully reflects his views. The 'Pittsburgh platform' (9.2.1) was never officially adopted by the Reform movement in America, but it was widely regarded as the most authoritative statement of Reform principles. Writing in 1907, one of the participants of the Pittsburgh conference, David Philipson, declared that the Pittsburgh platform was 'the most succinct expression of the theology of the reform movement that had ever been published to the world [and it] still stands as the utterance most expressive of the teachings of reformed Judaism'.[30]

Fifty years on from Pittsburgh the feeling was strong within the Reform movement that a new declaration of principles was required. A commission was set up which, after some dissension, finally drafted a new declaration (9.2.2). This was submitted for approval to the Central Conference of American Rabbis (the Reform rabbinical organisation) at its meeting in Columbus, Ohio, in 1937. After debate the statement of the 'Guiding Principles of Reform Judaism' was accepted. Curiously enough, it was David Philipson who moved the motion for acceptance. He did so in the following words:

> I am now the only man living who was at the Pittsburgh Conference. I was not in favour of a new Declaration of Principles but the Conference wanted it and since

there seemed to be so great a desire, especially on the part of the younger men, I was willing to consider it. There are some things in the Declaration that do not entirely please me but I know there are certain things that require compromise. For the sake of continuity, I should like to be the one to move the adoption of this Declaration of Principles.[31]

Comparison of the Columbus and Pittsburgh platforms is instructive. It provides us with a convenient way of monitoring the changes of emphasis and the developments which took place in American Reform thinking between 1885 and 1937.

Reform has introduced changes in religious ritual and practice, and has ignored and modified many aspects of the traditional halakhah. As a result it has been faced with the problem of authenticating itself as a legitimate form of Judaism. It has been forced to establish an ideological position from which it could justify its introduction of change and defend itself against the charge of having arbitrarily altered the Torah for the sake of convenience. Broadly speaking, the line of defence has been to maintain that the halakhah is not an unalterable, divine law, timeless and unchanging, but a human, historically conditioned body of tradition which evolves in response to social needs and historical circumstances. Just as competent authorities have changed the halakhah in the past, so it may be changed today. As the Reform rabbinic expert J. Z. Lauterbach put it:

> In instituting these changes, we are merely doing the same thing which our ancient teachers did. The *Halakhah*, as a complex of laws, forms and customs, is not something fixed or permanent. Its very name, *Halakhah*, suggests movement and progress. There has always been an older and a newer *Halakhah*. From its very beginning, the *Halakhah* was constantly changing and developing. Ours is the youngest *Halakhah*, representing its latest development, but it is still the living stream of *Halakhah*. We also have a complex of laws, forms and customs, whereby we regulate our religious life – our *Halakhah*.[32]

Particularly since the Second World War the attitude of Reform towards the traditional halakhah has changed: it has become much more positive. One of the leading figures in this reappraisal of halakhah has been Solomon B. Freehof. Freehof has devoted a lifetime to delving into one of the classic forms of halakhah – the Responsa literature. He has also written many responsa of his own (9.2.3) on current halakhic problems in which he quotes and discusses the classic halakhic authorities. More than anyone else in Reform he has tried to make good in a concrete way Lauterbach's contention that Reform practice still belongs to 'the living stream of *Halakhah*'. Freehof lays great stress on the importance of minhag, and on the need to allow Reform halakhah to evolve gradually with the organic growth of the movement. He has argued against any attempt to produce a Reform 'Code' – a modern Reform equivalent to the *Shulhan Arukh*.

To Moses Mendelssohn (1729–86) belongs the honour of having inaugurated the modern phase of Jewish religious thought. The traditional

Judaism in which Mendelssohn was reared in his home town of Dessau was still essentially medieval in outlook, but after settling in Berlin in 1743 he mastered the most advanced thought of his day and made the transition to a modern world view. In the end he established himself as a leading German philosopher, a central figure of the German Enlightenment. Mendelssohn moved in two quite separate worlds. In private he adhered to the traditional piety of his upbringing; in public he consorted with the foremost German thinkers, scientists and writers of his day, and was active in the intellectual circles of Berlin. These two worlds might seem, at first sight, incompatible. Certainly some of his contemporaries thought they were. They found it hard to see how a great rationalist thinker could remain an observant Jew. Mendelssohn was invited publicly on a number of occasions 'to do the logical thing' and abandon the religion of his fathers. He himself was aware of a certain tension between his philosophical views and his Judaism, but he was sincerely convinced that they could be honourably reconciled. To the end of his life he remained strongly identified with Judaism.

In this loyalty lay the secret of his influence. Mendelssohn's historical destiny was to be a mediator between two cultures. On the one hand his standing in learned circles in Germany gave him the chance to explain and defend Judaism to the educated non-Jewish world. This he did ably in his German writings. Especially after 1770 he became deeply involved in the debate over Jewish civil rights. He was an articulate and respected ambassador for Judaism, and he could not have played this role so well had it been possible to question his integrity as a Jew. On the other hand, he played an important role within the Jewish world, and there too it was his loyalty to Judaism that gave him leverage. Mendelssohn was looked up to by many German Jews as their spiritual leader: through his Hebrew writings, and above all through his German translation of the Bible, he mediated German culture to his co-religionists. Mendelssohn definitely saw himself as having an important educational and reforming mission within the Jewish community. His achievements as a pure philosopher have proved ephemeral, but his work within the Jewish community bore lasting fruit. He gained many Jewish followers and admirers, men inspired not only by his ideas but perhaps even more by the example of his courage in tackling the non-Jewish, secular thought of his day. Mendelssohn became the father of Haskalah – the Jewish Enlightenment which was to shape decisively the development of nineteenth-century European Jewish culture.

Mendelssohn's most important statement of his views on Judaism is contained in his long essay *Jerusalem, or, On Religious Power and Judaism* (1783) (9.3.1). In 1782, in a preface to Marcus Herz's German version of Manasseh ben Israel's *Vindiciae Judeorum* (1656), he had asserted that neither civil nor ecclesiastical authority had the right to use coercion in religious matters. He was taken to task for this view in an anonymous pamphlet entitled *The Search for Light and Right, in a Letter to Herr Moses Mendelssohn occasioned by his remarkable Preface to Manasseh ben Israel* (published probably in September 1782). The author of the pamphlet[33] argued that Mendelssohn's position seriously undermined traditional Judaism. He wrote:

> Ecclesiastical law armed with coercive power has always been one of the cornerstones of the Jewish religion, and a fundamental article of belief in the religious system of your fathers.

He then made his challenge:

> How can you, my dear Mr Mendelssohn, continue to adhere to the faith of your fathers, yet shake the entire structure by removing its foundations, since you deny the ecclesiastical law, given by Moses, which derives its authority from divine revelation?

The tract came down in the end to yet another invitation to the great Mendelssohn to convert to Christianity. But Mendelssohn took its central point seriously. *Jerusalem* is his attempt to defend his views and to rebut the charges made by the 'Searcher for Light and Right'.

In many ways *Jerusalem* is a classic document of the Enlightenment. It is a powerful but complex work which cannot easily be reduced to a unified system. In the first part Mendelssohn reasserts the central thesis of his preface to Manasseh ben Israel: men should be granted absolute freedom of conscience; neither State nor Church has the power or the right to compel belief or conviction. The task of the State is to promote the welfare of its citizens and, in pursuit of that end, to regulate the relationship between man and man. It is concerned with human behaviour, with overt acts, and it has both the right and the duty in the realm of deeds to coerce men into conformity with its will. But it has no right to interfere with a man's private thoughts and beliefs. The Church is entrusted with the 'cure of souls': it *is* concerned with men's beliefs, with their relationship to God. It has a mission to propagate its teachings, and it is fully entitled to do so, but in fulfilling this mission it should use only persuasion and argument; it has no right to resort to force to compel belief. The basic contention of the first half of *Jerusalem* is crystal-clear: State and Church should be separated; a man's private beliefs are his own business: it is neither right nor feasible to coerce his conscience.

In the second part of *Jerusalem* Mendelssohn turns to his definition of Judaism. As a rationalist he argues that those truths which are necessary for man's happiness – the existence and unity of God, divine providence, the immortality of the soul – are accessible to all men through reason. They are not acquired by supernatural revelation, nor do they need to be validated by miracle. The revelation to Israel at Sinai was not a disclosure of these eternal truths of reason, though it is consonant with and presupposes them. It was not concerned with doctrine at all, but rather with law. Judaism, in Mendelssohn's famous but problematic distinction, is not 'revealed religion' but 'revealed legislation'. The laws given on Sinai were for the Jews alone: they were imposed by God to maintain the separateness of Israel and 'to guide the seeking mind to divine truths – partly eternal, partly historical – on which the religion of the Jewish people is based'.

Mendelssohn was not entirely successful in meeting the central challenge of the 'Searcher for Light and Right' that Judaism does not allow freedom of conscience, but applies coercion to those who transgress the Mosaic laws. He concedes that in ancient Israel religion and State were totally identified: 'Every civil act was invested with sacredness and religious authority, and every act of civic service became *ipso facto* a true act of divine worship. The community was God's community; its concerns were God's; public taxes were an offering to God.' Consequently any violation of the Mosaic law was a civil offence punishable under State law. However, this was the case only until the destruction of the Temple in 70 C.E. Since then State and religion have been separated in Judaism. The Jewish State being now defunct, violations of the Law of Moses are not and cannot be punished as crimes against the State. With the loss of statehood Judaism has renounced all coercive power and become simply a religion.

It is usual to set the thought of Samson Raphael Hirsch (1808–88) against the background of the Reform movement in nineteenth-century Germany, and to see him as representing the rejection of the views of such radical reformers as Abraham Geiger, and as reasserting the intellectual respectability of traditional belief and practice. Hirsch viewed Judaism essentially as a timeless structure of beliefs and practices which was basically unaffected by historical evolution and change. He held a fundamentalist position on the Bible and rejected the findings of the nineteenth-century historical school of biblical scholarship. Yet Hirsch was not opposed to all reform. He advocated the modernisation of certain aspects of Jewish religious life: he was in favour of strict decorum and discipline in synagogue services, and he supported the introduction of sermons in the vernacular, synagogue choirs, and clerical dress for rabbis and readers. Above all he was an innovator in the sphere of Jewish education. In Frankfurt-am-Main, where from 1851 to 1858 he was rabbi to the Orthodox Israelitische Religions-Gesellschaft, he founded a Jewish school system in which not only the Hebrew language and Jewish studies were taught, but such secular subjects as German, mathematics and the natural sciences as well. His position was often summed up in the Hebrew slogan, derived from Mishnah, Pirqei Avot 2:2, 'Torah im derekh erez', 'Torah with secular culture'.[34] Hirsch's views on education, particularly his broadening of the syllabus, were condemned by certain ultra-orthodox rabbinical authorities of his day.

It is perhaps fair to say that Hirsch was not a profound thinker, but he was an excellent propagandist, with a fine command of rhetorical German, a prolific writer, a good organiser and a doughty fighter for his beliefs. He has remained down to the present day one of the mentors of moderate, enlightened traditionalism (a form of Judaism sometimes labelled 'Neo-orthodoxy'), and his writings are still widely disseminated and read in orthodox circles in Europe, America and Israel. The florid style of the extract quoted (9.3.2) perhaps reflects something of Hirsch's sermon style.

Solomon Schechter (1847–1915) is remembered by many today as a scholar who made an important contribution to the historical study of Judaism. His edition of the early commentary on Pirqei Avot, known as the Avot deRabbi Natan, is still standard and many of his essays have acquired the status of classics. His place in Jewish scholarship is for ever assured by the fact that he was closely associated with one of the most important manuscript discoveries in the history of Jewish studies–the Cairo Genizah finds. Schechter was one of the first to recognise the immense importance of a great cache of early manuscripts which turned up in a hidden genizah (store room) in the Ezra Synagogue of Fostat (Old Cairo). He was instrumental in bringing a large quantity of these manuscripts to Cambridge University library, where he began the work of sifting and identifying the texts. But Schechter has another claim to fame. As one of the principal architects of the Conservative movement in the United States he had an important influence on the development of contemporary Judaism. Broadly speaking, Conservative Judaism takes up a position on the spectrum of modern Judaism midway between Orthodoxy and Reform. It combines intellectual liberalism, i.e. liberalism in matters of belief, with strong conservatism in matters of practice.

Schechter was no philosopher: his influence was exerted first and foremost as a teacher. In 1902 he took up a post as president of the Jewish Theological Seminary in New York, and from then until his death he helped to mould the outlook of a talented younger generation of American rabbis. Though he was not strong on theory, his method of historical research had important theoretical implications. Unlike Hirsch, Schechter accepted the principle of historical criticism, even as applied to the Bible. Apparently he agreed with many of the findings of the 'higher critics'. But, like contemporary liberal Christian scholars, he realised that to do so precipitates a crisis of religious authority. If the Bible can no longer be seen in the straightforward, traditional way as a unified, divine revelation, what, then, is the ultimate court of appeal to determine belief and practice in Judaism? In a rare burst of more abstract theologising, in the preface to his collected essays, *Studies in Judaism* (from which 9.3.3 is taken), Schechter tackled this question. His answer is that 'the collective conscience of Catholic Israel as embodied in the Universal Synagogue' is to be decisive on all disputed questions of belief and practice. This concept of 'Catholic Israel' (Kelal Yisra'el) has become one of the ideological cornerstones of the Conservative movement.

Schechter's *curriculum vitae* illustrates a pattern which we find repeated again and again in the lives of other important modern Jewish thinkers. His spiritual Odyssey from the mental world of orthodox Judaism into the world of modern, secular thought was accompanied by a physical migration from the traditional communities of eastern Europe westwards to the great secularised societies of western Europe and the United States. Schechter was born in Rumania, the son of a Habad Hasid, educated at the University of Berlin, held teaching posts in the University of Cambridge and University College, London, and ended his days as head of an academic institution in New York. With variations this pattern was repeated, for example, in the lives of J. D. Soloveitchik (b. 1903) and A. J. Heschel (1907–72). These thinkers were, of course, part of a much greater westward Jewish migration. However, unlike many Jews, in whom the shock of physical and cultural dislocation produced alienation and loss of faith, Schechter, Soloveitchik and Heschel remained loyal to their past and managed to adapt their Judaism to the new conditions. They are interesting examples of the successful modernisation of a traditional faith.

## 1.9 RELIGION AND POLITICS

In Judaism religion and politics are inextricably intertwined. Judaism is not simply a religion in the narrow, modern, Western sense, but the culture of a people – a people who once enjoyed statehood, and who have again achieved statehood in their ancient land. In classic Judaic theology statehood is seen as the crowning of God's promises to the progenitors of the people – the Patriarchs: it marks the highest mode of existence to which the people can attain. Loss of statehood and exile are interpreted as punishment for the sins of the people.

The last time the people enjoyed statehood – prior to the re-establishment of Israel in 1948 – was in 132–5 C.E., when, under the leadership of Bar Kokhba, they briefly asserted their independence of Rome. In the period of exile from 135 to 1948 the longing to return to the homeland and found again the State remained alive. It was enshrined in classic prayers such as the Amidah (see 3.1.2). Exile and redemption (i.e. return to the Land) became a major theological theme of Judaism. However, in traditional Jewish thought that redemption was only to be achieved by divine help, when the Messiah came.

In contrast to this traditional religious Zionism there arose at the end of the nineteenth century a new form of Zionism which proposed that Jews should take their destiny into their own hands, and in an organised fashion set about re-establishing a Jewish State. Its effective founder was Theodor Herzl (1860–1904). In some ways Herzl was a rather unlikely figure to become one of the great shapers of modern Jewish history. He came from a well-to-do Jewish family, but, despite attendance at a Jewish elementary school, his contact with Jewish tradition was rather superficial: his education was very much in the tradition of the German Jewish Enlightenment. Though he studied law at the University of Vienna, his inclinations were towards a literary career. He was making a name for himself in Viennese literary circles as an essayist and playwright when, in 1892, his newspaper – the prestigious *Neue Freie Presse* of Vienna – sent him to Paris as its resident correspondent. It was there he was to experience what looks remarkably like a 'religious' conversion. There is clear evidence that Herzl was already interested in the Jewish question, but such interest as he had hitherto shown hardly prepares us for the spiritual and intellectual upheaval which he underwent there. That upheaval turned him from being a Westernised, assimilated Jew, with a minimal Jewish identity, into a passionately committed Jew, totally dedicated to the cause of Jewish nationalism.

It is not altogether clear what brought this revolution about. Herzl himself said that the Dreyfus affair was a factor. Alfred Dreyfus, a French officer of Jewish extraction, was found guilty by a military court in December 1894 of selling military secrets to the Germans. He was sentenced to life imprisonment on Devil's Island, a notorious penal colony off the coast of French Guiana. Dreyfus's Jewishness was made much of in the antisemitic French press at the time, and his public degredation on 5 January 1895 at the École Militaire was accompanied by anti-Jewish outbursts from the crowd. Dreyfus was later proved totally innocent and, after a struggle which rocked French political life to its foundations, exonerated of all blame. As a reporter Herzl followed the Dreyfus case closely. He was deeply disturbed by the antisemitism which it brought to the surface in one of the most enlightened and cultured States of Europe. It seems to have been this that triggered off his dramatic change of outlook and led him to write his essay *The Jewish State: an Attempt at a Modern Solution of the Jewish Question* (10.1.1). It is interesting, however, to note how early in the Dreyfus affair Herzl's 'conversion' took place. It did not come after Dreyfus had been proved innocent, nor even when the *possibility* of his innocence had emerged. Dreyfus was publicly disgraced in January 1895, but already by May 1895 Herzl had formulated the idea of *The Jewish State*, and the essay was in print by February 1896. By contrast, Bernard Lazare's famous accusation that there had been a miscarriage of justice, *Une erreur judiciaire: la vérité sur l'affaire Dreyfus*, was not published till late October or early November 1896, and Emile Zola's article in the same vein, 'J'accuse!', did not appear in *L'Aurore* till 13 January 1898! Dreyfus himself was not finally cleared till 1906 – two years after Herzl's death. It seems probable, therefore, that at the time of Dreyfus's first trial Herzl was spiritually in a critical state, and that the Dreyfus affair acted, almost incidentally, as the trigger that brought about his conversion. The last eight years of his life were spent in feverish efforts to realise his vision of the rebirth of the Jewish State. He proved to be a natural leader – a strong, self-confident personality endowed with great charisma. And he was a talented organiser. He founded a weekly – *Die Welt* – to promote his new Zionism, and at Basle in 1897 he inaugurated a series of Zionist Congresses which rapidly established the party organisation and the institutions necessary to promote the idea of a Jewish State and to bring it to reality.

Zionism has always been marked by intense ideological debate. Herzl certainly did not have things all his own way. His main ideological opponent was the Russian Jewish thinker Asher Ginsberg (1856–1927), who wrote under the pen name 'Ahad Ha-Am' ('One of the People'). Ahad Ha-Am was the principal exponent of 'cultural Zionism'. His background was very different from Herzl's. He was from eastern Europe and had had an intensely religious upbringing, steeped in the great classics of Judaism. He was later to lose his faith and turn agnostic, but his early training gave him a profound insight into the cultural values of traditional Judaism, and into the crisis which traditionalism faces in the modern world. He appears to have been dismayed by the alienation from traditional Jewish culture of Herzl and his Western followers.

Ahad Ha-Am was by nature cautious, an advocate of gradualism: the Jewish State should emerge naturally as the culmination of long and thorough preparation. Herzl and his followers were moving too fast, and as a result courting disappointing and disaster. Herzl's analysis of the Jewish question was fundamentally wrong. The central issue was not, as he maintained, antisemitism but the disintegration of traditional Judaism. It was not only Jews who were coming out of the ghetto, but Judaism as well, and wherever this was happening it ran the risk of being destroyed by modern secularism. This situation was fraught with danger for the Jewish people, a danger more deadly than antisemitism, for traditional Judaism was the matrix of Jewish identity. Torn from this protective matrix, Jews ran the risk of absorption and assimilation into the powerful host cultures which surrounded them. Priority must be given to cultural renewal, to finding cultural forms appropriate to the post-emancipation situation of the Jewish people, which would enable them to survive as a cultural entity. The immediate purpose of establishing a Jewish community in Palestine should be to form a cultural centre which would lead the way in the cultural revival of the Jewish people throughout the world. Ahad Ha-Am's essay quoted in 10.1.2 was written shortly after the first Zionist Congress at Basle in 1897. It first appeared in the important Hebrew-language periodical *Ha-Shiloah*, which he edited.

Right from the first Zionist Congress it became clear that Zionists were divided into two broad camps – the 'politicals' and the 'practicals'. Both were broadly agreed on the ultimate aim of Zionism – the founding of a Jewish State; they were even in a large measure of agreement as to the means to be used to achieve that aim. Where they differed was on the question of priorities. The political Zionists, of whom Herzl was one, argued that the energies of the movement should be channelled primarily into diplomacy, into winning a charter that would grant the Jews legal sovereignty over some tract of land. When that sovereignty had been granted they could move in *en masse* and establish their State. However, once it was agreed that only Palestine would be acceptable as the location of the Jewish State, the politicals did not rule out practical measures being taken to increase and to support the Jewish presence there. The practicals, on the other hand, while not rejecting political moves entirely, saw the way forward as primarily through piecemeal immigration into Palestine and through establishing the infrastructure of the State first, before proclaiming the State. The practicals became increasingly influential within the Zionist Organisation, and from the tenth congress (Basle, 1911) onwards dominated the movement's policy-making.

On Saturday 15 May 1948 the mandate for Palestine which had been assigned to Great Britain in 1920[35] came to an end. The day before, Friday 14th, at 4.30 p.m. in the museum at Tel Aviv, thirty-seven members of a People's Council (Mo'ezet ha-Am), representing both the Jewish community of Erez Israel and the Zionist movement, declared 'the establishment of a Jewish State in Eretz-Israel, to be known as the State of Israel' (10.2.1).

The Jewish State had at last come into being, but what place were Judaism and Jewish law to occupy in it? This has proved to be socially and politically one of the most divisive issues in Israel. Israeli society embraces a wide range of attitudes and opinions: almost every possible position on the ideological spectrum from Marxism to ultra-orthodoxy can be found. Under present arrangements Judaism and Jewish law are given definite but limited recognition by the State. At first sight a reasonable balance appears to have been struck between the forces of religion and secularism. In practice, however, conflict continues over the role of religion in society. For the religious, limited official recognition of religion is too little. The religious authorities are constantly exerting pressure to maximise and to extend the authority of religious law. For secularists, on the other hand, even limited official recognition of religion is too much. They are irked by the fact that in certain matters they are compelled to submit to the religious courts and to religious law, and argue that this involves unacceptable coercion and curtailment of civil rights. The conflict between secularism and religion flares up from time to time, and can be very bitter, even violent.

The rabbinical courts form a part of the Israeli legal system, and have been granted exclusive jurisdiction, as far as Israeli Jews are concerned, in certain specific matters. One of the basic laws extending official recognition to the these courts was the Rabbinical Courts Jurisdiction (Marriage and Divorce) Law of 1953 (10.2.3). Broadly speaking, all matters touching on personal status are dealt with in accordance with religious law. In recognising the competence of the religious courts (not only the rabbinical, but Muslim and Christian as well) in matters of personal status, the State of Israel has simply perpetuated the system of law in operation under the British mandate and under Turkish rule.

Religious law and the rabbinical courts are granted *limited* jurisdiction within the legal arrangements of the State. The problem is, however, that the religious law (halakhah) covers areas outside those in which the State recognises its competence. The halakhah embraces in principle a complete system of civil and criminal, as well as strictly religious, law. From time to time the State and the secular courts in Israel find themselves at variance with the traditional religious law, and the curious situation arises in which the law of the Jewish State and Jewish law are in conflict. This would appear to have happened in the 'Brother Daniel' case (Oswald Rufeisen v. Minister of the Interior, 1962), when the High Court gave a definition of the fundamental term

'Jew' which was at variance with that of the halakhah. The circumstances of this *cause célèbre* were as follows.

In 1958 Brother Daniel, a member of the Carmelite Order, came to Israel to join his Order's chapter there, and applied for an immigration certificate under section 3(a) of the Law of Return (10.2.2), and for registration as a Jew. Brother Daniel's Jewish origins were beyond dispute. Born Oswald Rufeisen of Jewish parents in Poland in 1922, he had been reared as a Jew and as a young man had trained for two years as a pioneer with a view to emigrating to Israel. The outbreak of the Russo-German war in 1941 prevented him from doing so. During the war he did heroic work in helping local Jewish communities against the Nazis. In 1942, while hiding in a convent from the Nazis, he converted to Christianity, and in 1945 he joined the Carmelite Order. He asked to be sent to the Carmelite chapter in Israel and, after a considerable delay, his religious superiors finally acceded to his request.

The Minister of the Interior, Israel Bar-Yehudah, refused his first application on the basis of a directive he had issued to the offices of the Registry of Citizens, to the effect that 'any person declaring in good faith that he is a Jew and is not of another religion' may be registered as Jewish. After the Fourth Knesset elections of 1959 Bar-Yehudah was replaced by Mosheh Shapira as Minister of the Interior. Brother Daniel again applied for Israeli citizenship under the Law of Return, and was again refused. According to Shapira, a Jew for the purposes of registration is 'a person born of a Jewish mother who does not belong to another religion, or one who has converted in accordance with religious law'. Brother Daniel then took the matter to court and an order nisi was issued against the Minister of the Interior to show cause why he had refused Brother Daniel's application. The case was heard in the High Court in 1962 before a bench of five distinguished judges. The court upheld the Minister's decision (by a majority of four to one) and discharged the order nisi. 10.2.4 gives part of Judge Silberg's judgement in the case. Having thoroughly examined the halakhic sources, Judge Silberg came to the conclusion that according to religious law Brother Daniel, though a convert to Christianity, was still for all essential purposes a Jew. If, therefore, religious criteria were applied to the definition of the term 'Jew' in the Law of Return, then Brother Daniel was entitled to Israeli citizenship under that law. But Judge Silberg proceeded to argue that the Law of Return is *not* a religious but a secular law, and so the religious definition of Jewishness cannot be applied to it. 'Jew' for the purposes of the Law of Return has its ordinary, secular meaning, and in Judge Silberg's opinion 'Jew' in everyday parlance is not used of someone, even of Jewish origin, who is actively professing Christianity.


## 1.10  SOCIETY AND THE JEWS

Judaism has been profoundly influenced by the fact that for much of their history Jews have lived as minorities in the midst of powerful alien, and often hostile, cultures. The aim of this section is to explore the attitudes of the host societies towards the Jew. For the sake of brevity we must confine ourselves to Christian and post-Christian Europe. The first three documents come from the Middle Ages. It is necessary to go back this far in time for two reasons. First, without some knowledge of the position of the Jews in the medieval world it is impossible to understand the modern process of Jewish emancipation. Second, many of the prejudices revealed by these medieval texts have shown a remarkable ability to survive down to the present day.

The charter of Richard I of England (11.1) throws light on the attitude of the secular authorities towards the Jews. On the whole it was protective. As moneylenders Jews played a vital role in the financial arrangements of many medieval States, and the royal exchequer helped itself in a variety of ways to a proportion of their takings. The secular authorities were, consequently, sensitive to anything that might harm the Jews financially. They were also concerned to protect them physically and were inclined to deal firmly with anti-Jewish rioters. No government can lightly regard a breakdown of law and order, for whatever reason. Yet the secular powers could also be cruel. Having by favourable legislation promoted Jewish wealth, the State often proceeded to squeeze the Jews financially dry, and when it could get no more out of them it usually expelled them from its domains in order to liquidate their last remaining assets.

On the face of it Richard's charter is not a grant of rights to *all* the Jews of his realm, only to 'Ysaac, son of Rabbi Joce, and to his children and to their men'. Towards the end, however, *all* Jews do seem to be envisaged. The charter also refers quite explicitly to a similar grant of rights to 'the Jews of England and Normandy' by Richard's father, Henry II (1154–89). An almost identical charter was later granted by Richard's brother, King John, to 'the Jews of England and Normandy' on 10 April 1201, and King John's charter refers to an earlier charter in the time of 'King Henry our father's grandfather' (i.e. Henry I, 1100–35). From all this it is reasonable to conclude that Richard's charter represents a renewal of rights previously granted and that it is in the standard text form used in the Angevin chancellery when bestowing rights and privileges on the Jews.

The date of the charter – 22 March 1190 – is significant. It was signed only six days after the famous York massacre. From the day of Richard's coronation on 3 September 1189 England had been plagued by anti-Jewish riots. The rioting was in part caused by the Crusading fervour aroused by the king's expressed intention of taking the cross. It was also due in part to a general breakdown of law and order throughout the realm while he was in France. The York riots were the culmination of anti-Jewish agitation. Attacked by a mob, the Jews of York barricaded themselves in Clifford's Tower. They held out for a few days, but, realising that their stronghold would soon be taken, they set fire to the tower and, like the Sicarii at Masada in 74 C.E., committed mass suicide.[36] This happened on Friday 6 March 1190. Richard's charter was signed six days later at Rouen in France.

The canons of the Fourth Lateran Council (11.2) illustrate the attitude of the Church towards the Jews. Broadly speaking, it was less favourable than that of the State. Indeed, the secular authorities were forced at times to take action to protect the Jews from the hostility of the ecclesiastical powers. Churchmen tended to see in their stubborn refusal to abandon their ancestral religion a challenge to the authority of the Church. Jews were regarded as a dangerous source of heresy, and every effort was made to convert them, or at least to isolate them and prevent them 'infecting' faithful Christians. Yet within the Church it is possible to detect a variety of attitudes towards Judaism. The Popes and higher clergy tended to be more liberal and tolerant. It was among the lower orders that the bitterest anti-Jewish feelings were to be found. It was the ordinary monks and friars who by their preaching roused the hatred of the masses against the Jews, especially during the period of religious fervour round Eastertide.

The Fourth Lateran Council, convened at the Lateran palace in Rome by Pope Innocent III, is regarded by Church historians as the high-water mark of papal legislation in the Middle Ages. The council appears to have had two major aims: first, to deal with the recrudescence of heresy in Christian lands, and second, to promote a new Crusade. Both these concerns meant trouble for the Jews. The final canons of the council were devoted to defining the position of the Jews in Christian society. Attached to the canons was a decree of the Pope calling for a new Crusade ('Expeditio pro recuperanda Terra Sancta'). A passage in this proclaimed a moratorium on interest to Jewish moneylenders for anyone going on Crusade.

The Ballad of Hugh of Lincoln (11.3) may be used to throw light on the attitude of the uneducated or semi-literate masses. It was among the common people that the most deep-seated prejudice and suspicion were to be found. Latent anti-Jewish hatred flared up with alarming regularity throughout the Middle Ages and led to acts of horrifying brutality. This popular antipathy had many roots. In part it grew out of the traditional Christian negative attitude towards Judaism. The common, ignorant people were most easily moved by the classic anti-Jewish *canard* of the blood-libel, or the charges of deicide and the desecration of the Host. It was also the lower orders of society who suffered most from the activities of the Jewish moneylenders. Most disturbing of all, however, is the fact that the Jew tended to be seen by the masses as some sort of 'bogey-man': he became the focus of irrational fears and superstitions. The Jew was often regarded as being in league with the devil, or even as some sort of devil incarnate.

The version of the Ballad of Hugh of Lincoln quoted in 11.3 was taken down by Jamieson and published by him in 1806. It is, therefore, comparatively modern. The ballad can, however, be traced back much further in time. There is extant an Anglo-Norman version which may be as early as the reign of Henry

III (1216–72). The events the ballad commemorates are supposed to have taken place in 1255. The full story is found in the medieval chronicles such as the *Annals of Waverly* and the *Chronica Majora* of Matthew Paris.[37] According to Matthew Paris's account the Jews of Lincoln kidnapped a young boy called Hugh, and, having cruelly tortured him, they crucified him before a gathering of their people in mockery of the death of Christ.

This story is one of the forms of the 'blood-libel', a standard element in anti-Jewish propaganda in the Middle Ages (and, indeed, in more modern times as well). In its classic early form the blood-libel involved, as in Matthew Paris, the allegation that Jews crucified Christian children at Eastertide in mockery of Christ's passion. Later, however, the motif was added that the ritual slaughter was to obtain the blood of Christians for a variety of nefarious purposes. The allegation has been shown time and again to be utterly groundless: murder for whatever reason is completely contrary to the basic teachings of Judaism. Yet the belief that Jews indulged in ritual murder was widespread among the Christian masses in the Middle Ages. Two medieval English saints, Hugh of Lincoln and William of Norwich,[38] were supposed to have been 'martyred' in this way.

The ballad as reproduced marks a late 'degeneration' of the tradition. It duly records that young Hugh was done to death by the Jews, and that certain miracles attended his death, but it utterly fails to provide a believable motive for the murder. There is no hint that the killing was some black ritual before a conventicle of Jews. Being 'stickit like a swine' is hardly reasonable punishment for having broken someone's window with a football!

The fourth text (11.4) is an excerpt from the transactions of the Assembly of Jewish Notables which met in Paris in 1806 and 1807. Coming from the period when Jewish society was in process of transition from the medieval to the modern world, it provides a paradigm of the attitude of the modern, centralised bureaucratic State towards the Jews. With the rise of the modern State Jews were granted emancipation – that is, they were given full citizenship, with, in theory, equal rights and equal opportunities. But there was a price to pay: they lost their old communal autonomy and were expected to integrate fully – economically, socially, and religiously – into the host State. They had to be loyal Frenchmen, or Germans, or Englishmen first, and Jews second.

The Assembly of Jewish Notables and the Paris Sanhedrin (1807) were a subtle instrument devised by Napoleon for integrating the Jews into the French State, and for reforming what he saw as the abuses of Jewish life. One of his main policy aims was to extend the power of the State into all areas of life, including religion. In 1801 he concluded a concordat with the Pope which gave the State a large measure of control over the Catholic Church in France. Similar measures were later taken to extend State control to other religious denominations as well. In 1806 Napoleon turned to the Jews. But here he was faced with a problem: there was no central organisation with which he could negotiate and through which he could exercise control over the Jews. The

Jewish community in the French empire was simply a collection of autonomous congregations, with no 'chief rabbi' and no overall governing body. Napoleon had to create such a body before he could proceed. This he did by convening the Assembly of Jewish Notables. By an imperial decree of 30 May 1806 delegates were summoned to Paris from all the Jewish communities of the French empire and from the kingdom of Italy. Napoleon exploited the assembly for two main ends. First, he used it as a competent body from which he could elicit information about Judaism and the Jewish way of life. The points on which he wanted information were set out in twelve questions which his representatives put to the assembly. Secondly, he employed the assembly to work out, along lines suggested by himself, certain concrete measures for the reorganisation of French Jewry. Napoleon was broadly satisfied by the answers of the Assembly of Notables, and in February and March 1807 he convened with great pomp and circumstance a Sanhedrin to take those answers and cast them into halakhically acceptable form which would make them religiously binding on Jews.

The final two texts (11.5) are concerned with the Holocaust. The Holocaust – the calculated destruction of around six million Jews in Europe by the Nazis and their followers – marked the climax of centuries of antisemitism. It was Europe's ultimate expression of its hatred and rejection of the Jew. This horrendous event has cast a dark shadow over Jewish life and thought for the last four decades, and has profoundly affected the way Jews look at the world.

The ideology of the Nationalist Socialist German Workers' Party – the Nazi Party – was deeply racist. In particular it was marked by a pathological hatred of the Jews, who were identified as the major cause of Germany's, and indeed of the world's, ills. The Nazis, having come to power when Hitler became Chancellor of Germany in 1933, wasted no time in putting their political programme into effect. Their objective was nothing less than to make Germany, and later German-controlled Europe, 'free of Jews' (*Judenrein*). They persisted in this policy with terrifying dedication to the end of the war. It took priority over immediate military objectives even when defeat was staring Germany in the face. By 1945 the Nazis had managed, by starvation, shooting, gassing and other means, to annihilate a large part of the Jewish community of Europe.

The Nazis were extremely sensitive to the power of propaganda and went to great lengths to dress up their activities in the guise of legality. They tried to keep their true aims and methods secret. They were masters of the use of ambiguous terms and 'code words', and avoided mentioning explicitly in written documents their extermination programme. Their plans to annihilate the Jews were hidden behind such innocuous phrases as 'the complete' or 'final solution of the Jewish question'. They recorded those whom they had murdered in the gas chambers as having been 'specially treated'.

The first of the two Holocaust documents (11.5.1) gives a remarkable insight into the mentality of the men who could perpetrate such atrocities. It was written in November 1946 by an SS officer, Dieter Wisliceny, while he was imprisoned at Bratislava awaiting trial for war crimes. The second (11.5.2) – Herman Göring's letter to Reinhard Heydrich – contained the authorisation from the second most powerful man in the Third Reich to begin the deportation of the Jews from all German-occupied areas of Europe. It inaugurated the final unspeakable chapter in the destruction of European Jewry.

## 1.11 CHRONOLOGY

B.C.E.

| | |
|---|---|
| c. 1290 | Exodus of the Israelites from Egypt. |
| c. 1250–1200 | Conquest of Canaan under leadership of Joshua. |
| 1004–965 | Reign of King David. |
| 965–928 | Reign of King Solomon. First Temple built in Jerusalem. |
| 928 | Division of the Kingdom into the northern Kingdom of Israel and the southern Kingdom of Judah. |
| 722 | Fall of Samaria. End of the northern Kingdom of Israel. |
| 586 | Jerusalem and the Temple destroyed by the Babylonians. Mass deportation of Jews to Babylonia. |
| 586–538 | **Babylonian exile** |
| 538 | Cyrus the Persian captures Babylon and issues an edict permitting the Jews to return to Jerusalem. |
| 538–332 | **Persian period** |
| 520–515 | Second Temple built in Jerusalem. |
| 332 | Alexander the Great conquers Palestine. |
| 332–142 | **Hellenistic period** |
| 167 | Seleucid king Antiochus IV (Epiphanes) proscribes Judaism. Jews rebel under the leadership of Judas Maccabaeus. |
| 164 | Judas recaptures Jerusalem, cleanses and rededicates the Temple. |
| 142 | Simeon, Judas's brother, becomes High Priest and leader of the Jews. Seleucid king Demetrius II formally recognises the independence of Judaea. |
| 142–63 | **The Hasmonaean State** |
| 63 | Judaea loses independence. Pompey incorporates it into the Roman Empire. |
| 63 B.C.E.–330 C.E. | **Roman period** |
| 37 B.C.E.–4 C.E. | Reign of King Herod. 19 B.C.E. Herod begins extensive rebuilding of the Temple. |

C.E.

| | |
|---|---|
| c. 10–c. 220 | **The Tanna'im** |
| 66–74 | First Jewish revolt against Rome. 70: Temple in Jerusalem destroyed. 74: Fall of Masada. |
| 70 | Yohanan ben Zakkai and other leading Pharisees establish the Academy of Yavneh. |
| 132–135 | Second Jewish revolt against Rome, under the leadership of Bar Kokhba. |
| 135–138 | Persecution under the emperor Hadrian. Jerusalem becomes a |

pagan city (Aelia Capitolina). Jews are forbidden to enter Jerusalem.

*c.* 210 Judah Ha-Nasi promulgates the Mishnah.

*c.* 220–*c.* 500 **The Amora'im**

*c.* 220 Rav arrives in Babylonia and founds the Academy of Sura. Academy at Nehardea flourishes under Samuel.

224 Sasanids overthrow Parthian empire.

224–637 **Sasanian empire**

*c.* 235 Sanhedrin at Tiberias.

259 Academy of Nehardea moves to Pumbedita.

306–337 Reign of Emperor Constantine I (the Great). 313: 'Edict of Milan' extends official recognition to Christianity. 330: Constantinople becomes capital of the Roman empire.

330–638 **Byzantine era**

358/9 Patriarch Hillel II promulgates the present Jewish liturgical calendar.

*c.* 390 Traditional date for the completion of the Jerusalem Talmud.

425 Theodosius II abolishes the Patriarchate in Palestine.

*c.* 499 Traditional date for the completion of the Babylonian Talmud.

500–540 **The Savora'im**

589–1040 **The Ge'onim**

622 — **The Islamic period**

622 Flight of Muhammad from Mecca to Medina. 632: Death of Muhammad.

637 Arabs conquer Ctesiphon

638 Arabs conquer Jerusalem

661–750 **Umayyad caliphate**

*c.* 740 Conversion of Khazars to Judaism.

750–1258 **Abbasid caliphate**

762–767 Anan ben David: beginnings of **Qaraism**.

882–942 Sa'adiah Gaon.

1040–1105 Rashi.

*c.* 1075–1141 Judah Helevi.

*c.* 1080 Bahya ibn Paquda writes *Duties of the Heart.*

1096–99 The First Crusade. 1096: Crusaders massacre the Jews of the Rhineland. 1099: Crusaders capture Jerusalem.

1135–1204 Maimonides.

1187 Saladin recaptures Jerusalem from the Crusaders.

1190 Anti-Jewish riots and massacre at York. Richard I renews charter to the Jews of England.

1215 Fourth Lateran Council.

1255 The blood libel at Lincoln.

1264 Charter of Boleslav V (the Pious) of Poland to the Jews (the 'Statute of Kalisz').

*c.* 1286 Moses de Leon composes the *Zohar.*

1290 Expulsion of the Jews from England.

1305 Solomon ben Abraham Adret issues at Barcelona a ban against the study of philosophy.

1480 Inquisition established in Spain. 1483: Torquemada appointed Inquisitor General.

1488–1575 Joseph Caro.

| | |
|---|---|
| 1492 | Conquest of Granada: all Spain united under Ferdinand and Isabella. Expulsion of the Jews from Spain. Columbus discovers America. |
| 1496–97 | Expulsion of the Jews from Portugal. Mass forced conversion. |
| 1525/30–1572 | Moses Isserles. |
| 1626–76 | Shabbetai Zevi. 1665: Shabbetai proclaims himself Messiah at Smyrna. 1666, converts to Islam. |
| 1648–49 | Chmielnicki massacres in Poland. |
| 1654 | Jews arrive in New Amsterdam (New York) and found a congregation. |
| c. 1700–60 | Israel ben Eliezer, Ba'al Shem Tov (the Besht). Beginnings of **Hasidism.** |
| 1707–46 | M. H. Luzzato. |
| 1717–87 | Elimelech of Lyzhansk (Hasidic Zaddiq). |
| 1729–86 | Moses Mendelssohn. Beginnings of **Haskalah.** |
| 1745–1813 | Shneur Zalman of Lyady. |
| 1776 | Declaration of American independence. |
| 1789 | Beginning of the French revolution. |
| 1791 | National Assembly in Paris grants full civil rights to all the Jews of France. Beginnings of **emancipation** in the West. |
| 1804–86 | Solomon Ganzfried. |
| 1806–07 | Napoleon convenes the Assembly of Jewish Notables and the Sanhedrin in Paris. |
| 1808–88 | S. R. Hirsch. |
| 1810 | Reform 'Temple' established at Seesen by Israel Jacobsen. Beginnings of **Reform.** |
| 1814–15 | Congress of Vienna. |
| 1827 | Czar Nicholas I enacts 'Cantonist' legislation. |
| 1835 | Czar Nicholas I enacts legislation delineating the Pale of Settlement. |
| 1844 | Autonomy of the Qahal abolished in Russia. Government-supervised schools established for Jews. |
| 1844–46 | Early Reform synods in Germany. 1844, Brunswick; 1845, Frankfurt; 1846, Breslau. |
| 1847–1915 | Solomon Schechter. |
| 1856–1927 | Asher Ginsberg (Ahad Ha-Am). |
| 1860–1904 | Theodor Herzl. |
| 1873 | Union of American Hebrew Congregations founded. |
| 1875 | Hebrew Union College, Cincinnati, opened. |
| 1881 | Pogroms in Russia. Beginnings of mass emigration of Jews to western Europe and the United States. |
| 1882 | Czar Alexander III passes the 'May laws'. Emergence of Hovevei Ziyyon (Lovers of Zion) in Russia. |
| 1882–1903 | **First Aliyyah.** Around 25,000 Jews from Russia, Romania and Galicia emigrate to Palestine. |
| 1885 | Pittsburgh platform. |
| 1886 | Jewish Theological Seminary, New York, opened. |
| 1892 | Solomon B. Freehof born. |
| 1894–1906 | Dreyfus affair in France. |
| 1897 | First Zionist Congress at Basle. |
| 1903–06 | Widespread pogroms in Russia. |

C

| | |
|---|---|
| 1904–14 | **Second Aliyyah.** Around 40,000 Jews from Russia emigrate to Palestine. Peak period of Jewish emigration to the United States. Around 1,950,000 arrive, mainly from Russia. |
| 1914–18 | First world war. 1917: British capture Jerusalem. |
| 1917 | Russian revolution. 'Balfour Declaration' by the British government. |
| 1919 | Pogroms in Ukraine and Poland. |
| 1919–23 | **Third Aliyyah.** Around 35,000 Jews from Russia, Poland and Romania emigrate to Palestine. |
| 1920 | Mandate for Palestine assigned to Great Britain. The Deutsche Arbeiterpartei (German Workers' Party) changes its name to the Nationalsozialistische Deutsche Arbeiterpartie (National Socialist German Workers' Party = Nazi Party) and adopts the 'Twenty-five Point Programme'. |
| 1924–32 | **Fourth Aliyyah.** Around 88,400 Jews from Poland emigrate to Palestine. |
| 1933 | Hitler becomes Chancellor of Germany. |
| 1933–39 | **Fifth Aliyyah.** Around 215,200 Jews from Poland, Germany and central Europe, fleeing persecution, emigrate to Israel. |
| 1937 | Peel Commission proposes partition of Palestine. Columbus platform. |
| 1939–45 | Second world war. 1939: Poland overrun by Germans. 1940: western Europe overrun by Germans. 1941: Germans invade Russia. **Sixth Aliyyah.** Around 62,500 Jews from Nazi-controlled Europe emigrate to Palestine. |
| 1939 | Peak year for emigration to United States of Jews fleeing Nazi persecution. Around 43,500 arrive. |
| 1941 | Jewish emigration from Germany prohibited. |
| 1942 | The Wannsee conference: the Nazis draw up plans to co-ordinate the 'final solution' of the Jewish problem. **The Holocaust.** By 1945 around six million Jews have been murdered by the Nazis. |
| 1945–48 | **Seventh Aliyyah.** Around 120,000 survivors of the Holocaust emigrate from all over Europe to Palestine. Many enter Palestine illegally. |
| 1947 | United Nations General Assembly votes in favour of partitioning Palestine. |
| 1948 | Declaration of the State of Israel. |
| 1949 | First Knesset convenes in Jerusalem. Chaim Weizmann first President of Israel. David Ben-Gurion Prime Minister. Cease-fire agreements with Egypt, Lebanon, Transjordan and Syria. Israel becomes a member of the United Nations. Mass emigration to Israel: around 240,000 Jews arrive. |
| 1950 | Law of Return enacted. |
| 1953 | Rabbinical Courts Jurisdiction (Marriage and Divorce) Law enacted. |
| 1956 | Suez crisis: the Sinai campaign. |
| 1962 | 'Brother Daniel' case heard before the Supreme Court in Israel. |
| 1967 | Six Day War. West bank of the Jordan overrun by Israel. Jerusalem reunited. |

1973    6 October: Yom Kippur war.
1977    May: Labour Party ousted from power in Israel for the first time since the declaration of the State. Likud form government under Prime Minister Menahem Begin. November: President Sadat of Egypt visits Jerusalem.
1979    26 March: peace treaty signed between Israel and Egypt.


# 2 SCRIPTURE AND TRADITION

*See 1.1. The Bible commentaries in 2.3 form the core of this chapter and should be studied first. They illustrate how traditional Judaism interprets Scripture, and should be read side by side with the biblical text, preferably in a Jewish version, such as* The Holy Scriptures according to the Masoretic Text, *Jewish Publication Society of America, 1917. If this is not available, then any literal translation (e.g. the Revised Version of 1881) will do. 2.2.1 gives some of the rules of Jewish Bible interpretation. 2.1.1 is concerned with the transmission of the Oral Torah and offers a theological legitimation of Jewish tradition. It comes from the beginning of Mishnah, Pirqei Avot, on which see 1.4–5. All the texts in this chapter are pre-medieval in date. Other passages in the anthology relevant to the subject of Torah and the nature of Bible exegesis are: 7.3.7–17; 8.3.2; 9.2.1.3–5; 9.2.2.6; 9.3.1–3.*


## 2.1 THE CHAIN OF TRADITION

### 2.1.1 Mishnah, Pirqei Avot 1:1–18 and 2:8. From Moses to the Tanna'im[1]

1:1. Moses received Torah from Sinai and passed it on to Joshua, and Joshua to the Elders, and the Elders to the Prophets; and the Prophets passed it on to the men of the Great Assembly. They said three things: Be careful in giving judgement, raise up many disciples, and make a fence around the Torah.    [1

2. Simeon the Just was one of the last members of the Great Assembly. He used to say: Upon three things the world stands – on the Torah, on the Temple service, and on acts of kindness.    [2

3. Antigonus of Sokho received Torah from Simeon the Just. He used to say: Do not be like slaves who serve their master only in order to receive their allowance, but be like slaves who serve their master with no thought of receiving an allowance; and let the fear of heaven be upon you.    [3

4. Yose ben Yo'ezer of Zeredah and Yose ben Yohanan of Jerusalem received Torah from them. Yose ben Yo'ezer says: Let your house be a meeting-place for the Sages; sit in the dust at their feet, and drink in their words thirstily.    [4

5. Yose ben Yohanan of Jerusalem says: Let your house be opened wide, and let the poor be members of your household, and avoid talking too much with women. This was meant to apply to a man's own wife, how much more, then, to the wife of his friend! Hence the Sages said: Whenever a man talks much with a woman, he brings evil upon himself, neglects the words of the Torah, and ends by inheriting Gehinnom.                                                                          [5

6. Joshua ben Perahyah and Nittai the Arbelite received Torah from them. Joshua ben Perahyah says: Provide yourself with a teacher, and study along with another student; and when you judge anyone, give him the benefit of the doubt.                                                                          [6

7. Nittai the Arbelite says: Keep your distance from a bad neighbour, avoid the company of a wicked man, and do not lose all hope of retribution.            [7

8. Judah ben Tabbai and Simeon ben Shetah received Torah from them. Judah ben Tabbai says: Do not play the part of advocate, and when the litigants stand before you, regard them as guilty, but when they have left the court regard them as innocent, provided they have acquiesced in the sentence.        [8

9. Simeon ben Shetah says: Examine witnesses thoroughly, and choose your words carefully, lest from them they learn to lie.                                  [9

10. Shemayah and Avtalyon received Torah from them. Shemayah says: Love work, shun office, and see that you do not become known to the authorities.                                                                          [10

11. Avtalyon says: Sages, take care what you say lest you incur the penalty of exile, and go into exile to a place of evil waters, and your students who follow after you drink them and die, and thus the name of Heaven be profaned.      [11

12. Hillel and Shammai received Torah from them. Hillel says: Be one of Aaron's disciples, loving peace and pursuing peace, loving mankind and bringing them near to the Torah.                                              [12

13. He used to say: He who promotes his own name destroys his name; he who does not increase decreases; he who does not learn deserves death; he who exploits the crown to his own advantage perishes.                          [13

14. He used to say: If I am not for myself, who, then, is for me? And when I alone am for myself, what am I? And if not now, when?                          [14

15. Shammai says: Make your study of the Torah a fixed habit; say little and do much, and greet everyone with a cheerful look on your face.              [15

16. Rabban Gamaliel says: Provide yourself with a teacher and remove yourself from doubt, and do not get into the habit of tithing by guesswork.   [16

17. Simeon his son says: All my days I grew up among the Sages and I found nothing better for a man than silence. Expounding [the Torah] is not the chief thing, but fulfilling [it]. Whoever multiplies words occasions sin.          [17

18. Rabban Simeon ben Gamaliel says: On three things the world stands: on justice, on truth and on peace, as it is written: 'Execute the judgement of truth and peace in your gates' (Zech. 8:16).                                      [18

2:8. Rabban Yohanan ben Zakkai received Torah from Hillel and Shammai. He used to say: If you have learned much Torah do not take the credit to yourself, for this was the purpose of your creation. *[19*

## 2.2 THE HERMENEUTICAL RULES

### 2.2.1 The Baraita of Rabbi Ishmael. The thirteen principles by which the Torah is expounded

Rabbi Ishmael says: There are thirteen principles [*middot*] by which the Torah is expounded. *[1*

1. *Mi-qal va-homer.* Inference from a less important case to a more important one. *Example.*[2] On one occasion the fourteenth of Nisan fell on a Sabbath. The Benei Bathyra forgot and did not know whether or not the Passover overrides the Sabbath. They said: 'Is there anyone who knows whether or not the Passover overrides the Sabbath?' They were told: 'There is a certain man who has come up from Babylonia, Hillel the Babylonian by name, who has studied with the two greatest men of the age, and he knows whether or not the Passover overrides the Sabbath.' So they summoned Hillel and said to him: 'Do you know whether or not the Passover overrides the Sabbath?' He said to them: . . . 'It is a case of *qal va-homer.* If the daily offering, neglect of which is not punished by "cutting off" [*karet*], overrides the Sabbath, then is it not logical that the Passover offering, neglect of which *is* punished by "cutting off", will override the Sabbath?' (Babylonian Talmud, Pesahim 66a) *[2*

2. *Umi-gezerah shavah.* Inference from an identical term [i.e. an argument that what holds true in one law will hold true in another, on the ground that a certain significant word or phrase occurs in both laws]. *[3] Example.* Another argument advanced by Hillel to prove that Passover overrides the Sabbath ran as follows: ' "In its appointed time" [*be-mo'ado*] is stated in connection with the Passover (Num. 9:2), and "in its appointed time" [*be-mo'ado*] is stated in connection with the daily sacrifice (Num. 28:2). Just as "its appointed time" which is said in connection with the daily sacrifice overrides the Sabbath, so "its appointed time" which is said in connection with the Passover overrides the Sabbath.' (Babylonian Talmud, Pesahim 66a) *[4*

3. *Mi-binyan av mi-katuv ehad umi-binyan av mi-shenei khetuvim.* Construction of a general principle from one verse and construction of a general principle from two verses. *[5] Example.*[3] 'If he knocks out his slave's tooth' (Exod. 21:27). I might understand this to mean even if it is only a milk tooth that the master knocked out, but Scripture also states: 'If a man strikes his slave's eye . . . and destroys it' (Exod. 21:26). Just as the eye is an organ which cannot grow back again, so also the tooth must be one which cannot grow back again. So far only the tooth and the eye are specifically mentioned. How about other chief organs? Behold, you establish a general principle on the basis of what is common to both of these. The specific character of a tooth is not the same as that of an eye, nor is the specific character of an eye the same as that of a tooth, but what is common to both of them is that loss of them constitutes a

permanent defect: they are chief organs and visible, and if the master intentionally destroys them, the slave gets his freedom in recompense. Perhaps, then, the slave should go free if the master cuts off flesh from his body? Scripture, however, mentions specifically the tooth and the eye. Their loss constitutes a permanent defect: they are chief organs and they are visible, and if the master intentionally destroys them, since they cannot be restored, the slave gets his freedom in recompense. Hence, I can include only such parts of the body the loss of which constitutes a permanent defect, which are chief organs, and which are visible; if the master intentionally destroys them since they cannot be restored, the slaves gets his freedom in recompense. (Mekhilta of Rabbi Ishmael, Nezikin 9) *[6*

4. *Mi-kelal u-ferat.* General and specific [i.e. when a general term or statement is followed by a specific term or statement, the general must be taken to include only what is contained in the specific]. *[7] Example.* Rava raised an objection: 'If it had only stated, "When anyone of you brings an offering to the Lord of beasts [*behemah*]" (Lev. 1:2), then I would agree that wild beasts [*hayyah*] are included in the category beasts [*behemah*], as in the verse: "These are the beasts [*behemah*] which you may eat: the ox, the sheep and the goat, the hart, the gazelle and the roebuck" (Deut. 14:4–5). But the text goes on to state, "Even of the herd and of the flock": sacrifices of the herd and of the flock I have prescribed for you, but not of wild beasts. If this had not been added, we might have supposed that although it was not necessary to bring a wild beast, yet if one did so the sacrifice would be valid. It would be like a student to whom his teacher said, "Bring me wheat," and he brought him wheat and barley. The student would not be regarded as flouting his teacher's words, but rather as adding to them, and it would be valid. Hence Scripture states, "Of the herd and of the flock": sacrifices of the herd and of the flock I have prescribed for you, and not of wild beasts. It would then be like a student to whom his teacher said, "Bring me *only* wheat," and he brought him wheat and barley. He would be regarded not as adding to his teacher's orders, but as flouting them, and it would be invalid.' (Babylonian Talmud, Zevahim 34a–b) *[8*

12.[4] *Davar ha-lamed me-inyano ve-davar ha-lamed mi-sofo.* The meaning of a statement may be determined from its immediate context, and the meaning of a statement may be determined from its end [i.e. from a reference later in the same passage]. *[9] Example.*[5] Our Rabbis taught: In 'You shall not steal' [*lo tignov*] (Exod. 20:15) Scripture refers to theft of persons [i.e. kidnapping]. If you should say: The text could refer to theft of persons, but perhaps it refers only to theft of property, then I would reply: Go and learn from the Thirteen Principles by which the Torah is expounded that the meaning of a verse is to be determined from its context. Of what, then, does the context speak? Of capital offences. Hence the reference here too must be to a capital offence. Another baraita taught: In 'You shall not steal' [*lo tignovu*] (Lev. 19:11) Scripture refers to the theft of property. If you should say: The text could refer to theft of property, but perhaps if refers only to theft of persons, then I would reply: Go and learn from the Thirteen Principles by which the Torah is expounded that the meaning of a verse is to be determined from its context. Of what, then, does the context speak? Of property. Hence the reference here too must be to property. (Babylonian Talmud, Sanhedrin 86a)                                    [10

13. *Ve-khen shenei khetuvim ha-makhhishim zeh et zeh ad she-yavo ha-katuv ha-shelishi ve-yakhria beineihem.* Two passages which contradict each other stand as they are until a third passage can be found to decide between them. *[11] Example.* Rabbi Akiva says: 'One passage says, "You shall sacrifice the Passover-offering to the Lord your God, from the flock and from the herd [*zon u-vaqar*]" (Deut. 16:2), and another passage says, "From the sheep [*kevasim*] or from the goats [*izzim*] you shall take it" (Exod. 12:5). How can both these verses be maintained? You must say: This is a principle in the interpretation of the Torah: two passages opposing each other and contradicting each other stand as they are until a third passage comes and decides between them. Now the passage "Draw out and take for yourselves sheep [*zon*] according to your families, and kill the Passover sacrifice" (Exod. 12:21) decides in this case, since it shows that only from the flock [*zon*] and not from the herd [*baqar*] can the Passover offering come.' (Mekhilta of Rabbi Ishmael, Pisha 4)                                    [12

## 2.3  BIBLE COMMENTARIES

### 2.3.1  Targum Pseudo-Jonathan to Genesis 22:1–19. The sacrifice of Isaac

1. It came to pass after these things – after Isaac and Ishmael had quarrelled. Ishmael said: 'It is right for me to be the heir of my father, since I am his firstborn son;' while Isaac said: 'It is right for me to be the heir of my father, since I am the son of Sarah his wife, but you are the son of Hagar, the handmaid of my mother.' Ishmael answered and said: 'I am more righteous than you, because I was circumcised when I was thirteen years old; and if I had wanted to refuse, I would not have allowed myself to be circumcised. But you were circumcised when eight days old. If you had had knowledge, perhaps you would not have allowed yourself to be circumcised.' Isaac answered and said: 'Behold, I am thirty-seven years old this day. If the Holy One, blessed be He, were to demand *all* my limbs, I would not refuse.' Immediately these words were heard before the Lord of the universe, and immediately the Word of the Lord tested Abraham and said to him, 'Abraham'; and he said, 'Here am I.'                                    [1

2. He said: 'Take now your son, your only son, whom you love, even Isaac, and go into the land of worship; and offer him there for a burnt offering on one of the mountains which I will tell you of.'                                    [2

3. Abraham rose early in the morning, saddled his ass, and took with him his two young men, Eliezer and Ishmael, as well as Isaac his son. He chopped the wood of the olive, the fig and the palm, which are proper for the burnt offering,

and he rose up and went to the place of which the Lord had told him. *[3*

4. On the third day Abraham lifted up his eyes and saw the cloud of glory smoking on the mountain, and he recognised it from afar. *[4*

5. Abraham said to his young men: 'Wait here with the ass, and I and the lad will go yonder to find out if what I was promised – "So shall your seed be" (Gen. 15:5) – will ever be fulfilled. We will worship the Lord of the universe, and come again to you.' *[5*

6. Abraham took the wood of the burnt offering, laid it upon Isaac his son, took in his hand the fire and the knife, and both of them went together. *[6*

7. Isaac spoke to Abraham his father and said, 'Father,' and he said, 'Here am I, my son.' Isaac said, 'Behold the fire and the wood, but where is the lamb for the burnt offering?' *[7*

8. Abraham said: 'The Lord will choose for himself the lamb for a burnt offering, my son.' So they went both of them with a perfect heart together. *[8*

9. They came to the place which God had told him of. Abraham built there the altar which Adam had built, but which had been destroyed in the waters of the flood. Noah had rebuilt it, but it was again destroyed in the generation of the division of tongues (Gen. 11:1–9). Abraham set in order the wood upon it, bound Isaac his son, and laid him on the altar, upon the wood. *[9*

10. Then Abraham stretched out his hand and took the knife to sacrifice his son. Isaac answered and said to his father: 'Bind me well so that I may not struggle in the anguish of my soul, lest a blemish be found in your offering, and I be cast into the pit of destruction.' The eyes of Abraham looked at the eyes of Isaac, but the eyes of Isaac looked at the angels on high: Isaac saw them, but Abraham did not see them. The angels on high answered: 'Come and see these two unique men in the earth. One sacrifices and the other is his victim; the one who sacrifices does not hesitate, the one to be sacrificed stretches out his neck.' *[10*

11. The angel of the Lord called to Abraham out of heaven and said to him, 'Abraham, Abraham,' and he said, 'Here am I.' *[11*

12. He said: 'Do not lay your hand on the lad, nor do him any harm, for it is now revealed before me that you fear the Lord, and that you have not withheld your son, your only son, from me.' *[12*

13. Abraham lifted up his eyes and looked, and behold, a ram – one that had been created on the evening when the work of creation was finished – caught in the branches of a tree by its horns. Abraham went and took the ram, and offered it up for a burnt offering instead of his son. *[13*

14. Abraham gave thanks and prayed there in that place, and said: 'I beseech you by the mercy that is before you, O Lord: it is revealed before you that there was no insincerity in my heart, but I sought to perform your decree with joy; so, when the descendants of Isaac my son shall come to the time of distress, remember them, hear their supplications, and deliver them, and all generations to come will say, "In this mountain Abraham bound Isaac, his son, and there the Shekhinah of the Lord was revealed to him." ' *[14*

15. The angel of the Lord called to Abraham a second time from heaven 16. and said: 'By my Word I have sworn, says the Lord, that, because you have done this thing, and have not withheld your son, your only son, 17. I will surely bless you and I will indeed multiply your sons as the stars of the heaven and as the sand on the sea shore; and your sons shall inherit the cities of their enemies. 18. Because of the merit of your sons all the peoples of the earth shall be blessed, because you have obeyed my voice.' *[15*

19. And the angels from on high took Isaac and brought him to the school of Shem the great, and he was there for three years. And on the same day Abraham returned to his young men, and they arose and went together to Beer-sheba; and Abraham dwelt at Beer-sheba. *[16*

### 2.3.2. Mekhilta of Rabbi Ishmael to Exodus 19–20. The giving of the Torah[6]

19:2. *They encamped in the wilderness.* The Torah was given in public, openly in a place free to all. For if the Torah had been given in the land of Israel, the Israelites could have said to the gentiles, 'You have no share in it.' But it was given in the wilderness, in public, openly in a place free to all, so that anyone wishing to accept it could come and do so. You might suppose that it was given at night, but Scripture says: 'It came to pass on the third day, when it was morning' (Exod. 19:16). You might suppose that it was given in silence, but Scripture says: 'There was thunder and lightning' (Exod. 19:16). You might suppose that they could not hear the voice, but Scripture says: 'The voice of the Lord is powerful, the voice of the Lord is majestic' (Ps. 29:4). *[1*

19:4. *How I bore you on eagle's wings.* How does an eagle differ from all other birds? All other birds carry their young between their feet, because they fear birds flying above them. The eagle, however, is afraid only of men who might shoot at it from below. It prefers that the arrows should lodge in it rather than in its young. A parable: When a man is going along the road with his son walking in front of him, if brigands come from in front to seize the son, the father takes him from in front and puts him behind him. If a wolf comes from the rear to attack the son, the father takes him from behind and puts him in front of him. If brigands come from in front and a wolf from the rear, the father takes the son and puts him on his shoulders. So of God it is written: 'In the wilderness you have seen how the Lord your God bore you, as a man bears his son' (Deut. 1:31). *[2*

19:8. *Moses reported the words of the people to the Lord.* Was there any need for Moses to report? Scripture merely wants you to learn proper manners from Moses. He did not say: 'Since he who sent me knows anyway there is no need for me to report back.' *[3*

19:18. *Because the Lord came down upon it in fire.* This tells us that the Torah is fire, was given from the midst of fire, and may be compared to fire. What is the nature of fire? If a man comes too close to it, he gets burned. If he keeps too far from it, he gets cold. The only thing for him to do is to seek to warm himself before its flames.                                                        [4

19:20. *The Lord came down upon Mount Sinai.* You might suppose that the Divine Glory actually descended from heaven and was transferred to Mount Sinai, but Scripture says: 'I have talked with you from heaven' (Exod. 20:19). Scripture thus teaches that the Holy One, blessed be he, bent down the lower heavens and the upper heaven of heavens on to the top of the mountain, and thus the Divine Glory descended. He spread them upon Mount Sinai as a man spreads his mattress on his bed and speaks from on top of the mattress, as it is written: 'Oh that you would rend the heavens and come down, and make the mountains quake before you, as when fire kindles brushwood, or makes water boil'; and the text goes on: 'When you did terrible things which we did not look for' (Isa. 63:9–64:2). Rabbi Yose says: 'Behold, Scripture says: "The heavens belong to the Lord, but the earth he has given to mankind" (Ps. 115:16). Neither Moses nor Elijah ever went up to heaven, nor did the Divine Glory ever come down to earth. Scripture merely teaches that the Omnipresent One said to Moses: "Behold, I am going to call you from the top of the mountain and you will come up," as it is written: "The Lord summoned Moses to the top of the mountain" (Exod. 19:20).'                                                        [5

20:2. *I am the Lord your God.* Why were the ten commandments not uttered at the beginning of the Torah? They told a parable. To what may this be compared? To a king who entered a city and said to the people: 'May I be your king?' The people said to him: 'You have done nothing good for us, that we should let you rule over us.' What did he do then? He built the city wall for them, he laid on a water supply, and he fought their battles. Then he said to them: 'May I be your king?' They replied, 'Yes indeed!' So, too, the Omnipresent One brought the Israelites out of Egypt, divided the sea for them, brought down for them the manna, brought up for them the well, sent along the quails, and fought for them the battle with Amalek. Then he said to them: 'Am I to be your king?' And they replied, 'Yes indeed!'                                                        [6

*I am the Lord your God.* Why was this said? It was because at the sea God appeared to them as a mighty hero waging war, as it is written: 'The Lord is a man of war' (Exod. 15:3). And at Sinai he appeared to them as an old man full of mercy, as it is written: 'They saw the God of Israel' (Exod. 24:10). And of the time after they had been redeemed what does it say? – 'Like heaven itself in clarity' (Exod. 24:10). Again it says: 'I looked till thrones were placed' (Dan. 7:9); and it also says: 'A fiery stream issued and came forth from before him' (Dan. 7:10). So that the gentiles should not have an excuse for saying that there are two Divine Powers, Scripture declares: 'I am the Lord your God' – I am he who was in Egypt and I am he who was at the sea; I am he who was at Sinai; I am he who was in the past and I am he who will be in the future; I am he who is in this world and I am he who will be in the world to come; as it is written: 'See now that I, even I, am he' (Deut. 32:39).                                                        [7

20:3. *You shall not have.* Why was this said? It was because Scripture states: 'You shall not make for yourself a graven image' (Exod. 20:4). This tells me

only that it is forbidden to *make* one, but how do I know that I should not keep one that has already been made? From the fact that Scripture says: 'You shall not *have* other gods.' *[8*
*Before me.* Why was this said? It was to avoid giving Israel an excuse for saying: 'Only those who came out of Egypt were commanded not to worship idols.' Hence Scripture adds, 'Before me,' as much as to say: 'Just as I am living and enduring to all eternity, so also you and your son and your grandson to the end of all generations shall not worship idols.' *[9*
20:4. *You shall not make for yourself a graven image.* You may not make one that is graven. Perhaps, then, you may make one that is solid? But Scripture goes on to say: 'Nor any kind of likeness.' So you may not make a solid one. Perhaps, then, you may plant a plant as an idol for yourself? But Scripture says: 'You shall not plant for yourself an Asherah' (Deut. 16:21). So you may not plant a plant as an idol for yourself. Perhaps, then, you may make an idol of a tree? But Scripture goes on to say: 'Of any kind of tree' (Deut. 16:21). So you may not make an idol of a tree. Perhaps, then, you may make one of stone? But Scripture says: 'Neither shall you place any figured stone' (Lev. 16:1). So you may not make an idol of stone. Perhaps, then, you may make one of silver or gold? But Scripture says: 'Gods of silver or gods of gold you shall not make for yourselves' (Exod. 20:20). So you may not make an idol of silver or gold. Perhaps, then, you may make one of copper, iron, tin or lead? But Scripture says: 'Nor make for yourselves molten gods' (Lev. 19:4). So you may not make for yourself any of these images. Perhaps, then, you may make an image of a symbol? But Scripture says: 'Lest you deal corruptly, and make for yourselves a graven image, the form of any symbol' (Deut. 4:16). So you may not make an image of any symbol. Perhaps, then, you may make an image of cattle or fowl? But Scripture says: 'The likeness of any beast that is on the earth, the likeness of any winged fowl' (Deut. 4:17). So you may not make an image of any of these. perhaps, then, you may make an image of fish, or locusts or unclean animals, or reptiles? But Scripture says: 'The likeness of anything that crawls on the ground, the likeness of any fish that is in the water' (Deut. 4:18). So you may not make an image of any of these. Perhaps, then, you make an image of the sun, the moon, the stars or the planets? But Scripture says: 'Lest you lift up your eyes to heaven' (Deut. 4:19). You may not make an image of any of these. Perhaps, then, you may make an image of the angels— the Cherubim or the Ofannim? But Scripture says: 'Of anything that is in heaven above' (Exod. 20:4). If it had only stated, 'that is in heaven', then you might have supposed that the reference is only to the sun, moon, stars and planets, but it adds 'above', thus excluding images of the angels, the Cherubim and the Ofannim. So you may not make an image of any of these. Perhaps, then, you may make an image of the deeps and the darkness? But Scripture says: 'that is in the water under the earth' (Exod. 20:4). In the opinion of Rabbi Akiva this rules out even the reflected image. Others say it forbids images of the water demons. To such lengths Scripture goes in pursuit of the evil inclination, to leave it no pretext for

permitting idolatry!                                                                                      *[10*

20:5 *For I the Lord your God am a jealous God.* Jealously do I exact punishment for idolatry, but in other matters I am merciful and gracious. A certain philosopher questioned Rabban Gamaliel: 'It is written in your Torah, "For I the Lord your God am a jealous God". But is there any power in an idol that it should arouse God's jealousy? A hero is jealous of another hero, a wise man of another wise man, a rich man of another rich man, but has an idol the power to provoke jealousy?' Rabban Gamaliel said to him: 'Suppose a man should call his dog by the name of his father, and when taking a vow he should swear, "by the life of this dog." Against whom would the father be incensed? Against the son or against the dog?' The philosopher replied: 'Some idols serve a purpose.' 'What makes you think so?' asked Rabban Gamaliel. The philosopher said: 'There raged a fire in a certain city, but the temple of its idol was saved. Was it not because the idol could take care of itself?' Rabban Gamaliel said to him: 'I will tell you a parable; To what may we compare this? To a king of flesh and blood who goes out to war. Against whom does he wage war – against the living or against the dead?' 'Against the living,' replied the philosopher. Then he said: 'But if they serve no purpose at all, why does God not destroy them?' Said Rabban Gamaliel to him: 'But is it only one object you worship? Behold, you worship the sun, the moon, the stars and the planets, the mountains and the hills, the springs and the glens, and even human beings. Shall God destroy his world because of fools? – "Shall I totally consume all things from off the face of the earth? says the Lord" (Zeph. 1:2).' The philosopher said: 'Since idols cause the wicked to stumble, why does God not remove them from the world?' But Rabban Gamaliel continued, saying: 'Because of fools – for you worship human beings as well – "Shall I cut off man from the face of the earth" (Zeph. 1:3).'                                                                                                       *[11*

*Visiting the iniquity of the fathers on the children.* You might suppose that just as the measure of punishment extends over four generations, so also the measure of reward extends only over four generations. But Scripture says: 'Unto thousands' (Exod. 20:6). I might understand 'Unto thousands' to mean a minimum of thousands, that is, two thousand people, but Scripture also says: 'To a thousand generations' (Deut. 7:9) – generations beyond reckoning and counting.                                                                                                          *[12*

20:8 *Remember the Sabbath day to keep it holy.* 'Remember' and 'Observe' (Deut. 5:12) were both spoken together in one utterance. 'Everyone who profanes it shall surely be put to death' (Exod. 31:14) and 'On the Sabbath day two he-lambs' (Num. 28:9) were both spoken together in one utterance. 'You shall not uncover the nakedness of your brother's wife' (Lev. 18:16) and 'Her brother's husband shall go in unto her' (Deut. 25:5) were both spoken together in one utterance. 'You shall not wear mixed fabrics' (Deut. 22:11) and 'You shall make for yourselves twisted cords' (Deut. 22:12) were both spoken together in one utterance. It is impossible for creatures of flesh and blood to speak like this, but of God it is written: 'God has spoken one utterance and we have heard two' (Ps. 62:12).[7] Scripture also says: 'Is not my word like fire, says the Lord, and like a hammer that breaks the rock in pieces?' (Jer. 23:29). *Remember* and *observe*: Remember it before it comes and observe it after it has gone. On the basis of this passage the Sages said: 'We should always increase what is holy by adding to it some of the non-holy.' [13

*To keep it holy*. To consecrate it with a benediction. On the basis of this passage the Sages said: 'At the beginning of Sabbath we consecrate it by reciting a benediction over wine.' [14

20:11. *And rested on the seventh day*. Is God subject to weariness? Is it not written: 'The Creator of the ends of the earth does not faint or grow weary' (Isa. 40:28)? And it says: 'He gives power to the faint' (Isa. 40:29). And it further says: 'By the word of the Lord the heavens were made' (Ps. 33:6). Why, then, does Scripture say: 'God rested on the seventh day?' It means only that God allowed it to be written about himself that he created his world in six days and rested, so to speak, on the seventh. And you should reason by *qal va-homer*: If he, who suffers no weariness, allowed it to be written that he created his world in six days and rested on the seventh, how much more should man, of whom it is written that he is 'born to toil' (Job 5:7), rest on the seventh day. [15

20:12. *Honour your father and your mother*. Rabbi says: 'The honour of one's father and mother is very dear to him who spoke and the world came into being, for he declared honouring them to be equal to honouring him, fearing them equal to fearing him, and cursing them equal to cursing him. It is written: "Honour your father and your mother"; and correspondingly it is written: "Honour the Lord with your wealth" (Prov. 3:9). So Scripture puts honouring one's parents on a par with honouring the Omnipresent One. It is written: "Every one of you shall fear his mother and his father" (Lev. 19:3); and correspondingly it is written: "You shall fear the Lord your God" (Deut. 6:13). So Scripture puts the fear of one's parents on a par with fear of the Omnipresent One. It is written: "He who curses his father or his mother shall surely be put to death" (Exod. 21:17); and correspondingly it is written: "Whoever curses his God shall bear the responsibility for his sin" (Lev. 24:15). So Scripture puts the cursing of one's parents on a par with cursing the Omnipresent One.' [16

20:18. *Moses drew near to the thick darkness*. What earned him this distinction? His meekness, as it is written: 'The man Moses was very meek' (Num. 12:3). Scripture tells us that whoever is meek causes the Shekhinah to dwell with men on earth, as it is written: 'For thus says the High and Lofty One who inhabits eternity, whose name is Holy: "I dwell in the high and holy place, and also with him who is contrite and humble in spirit" ' (Isa. 57:15). [17

20:19. *You yourselves have seen*. There is a difference between what a man sees for himself and what he hears about from others, for he may have doubts about what others report. Here, however, it says: 'You have seen for yourselves.' [18

20:20. *You shall not make for yourselves gods of silver*. To prevent you saying, 'I shall make them merely for adornment as others do in various countries,' Scripture states: 'You shall not *make* for yourselves.' [19

# 3. LITURGY

*See 1.2. 3.1.1. (the Shema) and 3.1.2 (the Amidah) are the two basic building blocks of the synagogue liturgy. Both these prayers, in some form, go back to the Second Temple period (pre-70 C.E.). 3.2 is concerned with Sabbath liturgy. For some of the laws of Sabbath see below, 5.1.2. 3.2.1 and 3.2.2 illustrate the rituals for demarcating holy and secular time. They should be read alongside 5.1.1, which records a very ancient debate on these rituals between the Houses of Hillel and Shammai. 3.3.1 gives at once a sample of festival liturgy and at the same time illustrates Judaism's most famous and colourful home rite – the Passover Seder. For the synagogue Torah lectionary see Appendix A. For the liturgical year see Appendix B.*

## 3.1 WEEKDAY LITURGY

### 3.1.1 The Shema and its Benedictions
**First morning benediction: Yozer or**
Blessed are you, O Lord, our God, King of the universe, who forms light and creates darkness, who makes peace and creates all things. In mercy you give light to the earth and to those who dwell on it, and in your goodness you renew the work of creation each day continually. How numerous are your works, O Lord! In wisdom you have made them all: the earth is full of your possessions. O King, alone exalted from aforetime, praised, glorified and extolled from days of old, O eternal God, in your abundant mercies have mercy upon us, Lord of our strength, Rock of our refuge, Shield of our salvation, Refuge of ours! [1

The blessed God, whose knowledge is great, prepared and made the sun's rays: he formed a good which brings glory to his name. He set the heavenly luminaries round about his strength. The chiefs of his hosts are holy beings who exalt the Almighty, and continually declare the glory of God and his holiness. Be blessed, O Lord our God, for the excellence of your handiwork, and for the bright luminaries which you have made that they should glorify you. [2

Be blessed, O our Rock, our King and Redeemer, Creator of holy beings; praised be your name for ever, O our King, Creator of ministering spirits, whose ministers stand one and all in the heights of the universe and proclaim aloud with awe in unison the words of the living God and eternal King. They are all beloved, all pure, all mighty, and they all in dread and awe perform the will of their Master; they all open their mouths in holiness and purity, with song and psalm, while they bless, praise, glorify, and ascribe power, holiness and sovereignty to the Name of God, the great, mighty and dreaded King, holy is he; and they take upon themselves the yoke of the kingdom of heaven one from another, and give sanction one to another to sanctify their Creator. In serenity of spirit, with pure speech and holy melody, they all respond in unison and exclaim with awe: 'Holy, holy, holy is the Lord of hosts; the whole earth is full of his glory' (Isa. 6:3). The Ofannim and the Holy Creatures with a great tumult raise themselves up towards the Seraphim; over against them they offer praise and say: 'Blessed be the glory of the Lord from his dwelling place' (Ezek. 3:12).                                                                                         [3

To the blessed God they offer sweet melodies; to the King, the living and ever-enduring God, they utter hymns and declare their praises; for he alone performs mighty acts, and makes new things. He is the Lord of battles; he sows charitable deeds, causes salvation to spring forth, creates healing remedies, and is revered in praises. He is the Lord of wonders, who in his goodness renews the work of creation each day continually, as it is written: 'Give thanks to him who made great lights, for his kindness endures for ever' (Ps. 136:7). Cause a new light to shine upon Zion, and may we all be worthy soon to enjoy its brightness. Blessed are you, O Lord, Creator of the heavenly luminaries.                  [4

**First evening benediction: Ma'ariv aravim**

Blessed are you, O Lord our God, King of the universe, who by his word brings on the evening twilight; who in wisdom opens the gates of heaven, and with foresight makes time pass and the seasons change; who arranges the stars in their watches in the sky in accordance with his will; who creates day and night, rolling back the light before the advancing darkness and the darkness before the light; who makes the day fade, brings on the night, and separates day from night; whose name is Lord of hosts. May the ever-living and eternal God reign over us for ever and ever. Blessed are you, O Lord our God, who brings on the evening twilight.                                                                                [5

**Second morning benediction: Ahavah rabbah**

With a deep love you have loved us, O Lord our God, with great and overflowing pity you have pitied us. Our Father, our King, for the sake of our fathers who trusted in you, and to whom you taught the statues of life, be gracious also to us and teach us. Our Father, merciful and compassionate Father, have mercy on us, and put it into our hearts to understand and to discern, to hear, learn and teach, to heed, to do and to fulfil in love all the words of instruction in your Torah. Give us insight into your Torah, help us to cling wholeheartedly to your commandments, and make us single-hearted to love and fear your name, so that we may never be put to shame. We shall assuredly be glad and rejoice at your saving power, for we have trusted in your holy, great and revered name. Bring us in peace from the four corners of the earth, and make us go in freedom to our land, for you are a God who effects salvation. You have chosen us from all peoples and tongues, and in faithfulness you have drawn us near to your great name, so that in love we might give thanks to you and proclaim your unity. Blessed are you, O Lord, who has chosen his people Israel in love. *[6*

### Second evening benediction: Ahavat olam

With eternal love you have loved the house of Israel, your people; Torah and commandments, statutes and laws you have taught us. Therefore, O Lord Our God, we will meditate on your statutes before we sleep and when we awake; we will rejoice in the words of your Torah and in your commandments for ever, for they bring us life and longevity, and we shall ponder on them day and night. Never take your love from us! Blessed are you, O Lord, who loves his people Israel. *[7*

### The Shema

Hear, O Israel: the Lord our God, the Lord is One.

You shall love the Lord your God will all your heart, with all your soul, and with all your strength. These words that I command you today shall be kept in your heart; you shall teach them to your children, and shall talk about them when you sit at home, and when you walk in the street, when you lie down to sleep, and when you awake. You shall bind them for a sign on your hand, and they shall be for frontlets between your eyes. You shall write them on the doorposts of your home, and on your gates. (Deut. 6:4–9) *[8*

It shall come to pass, if you listen carefully to my commandments which I am giving you today, loving the Lord your God and serving him with all your heart and with all your soul, that I will give your land rain in its proper season, the autumn rain and the spring rain, so that you may harvest your corn, your wine and your oil. I will give grass in your fields for your cattle, and you shall eat and be satisfied. Take good care that your heart is not deceived, and that you do not go astray by serving and worshipping other gods. Should this happen, the anger of the Lord will blaze out against you: he will shut up the heavens, so that there will be no rain; the land will not produce her crops, and you will quickly be obliterated from the good land which the Lord is giving you. So you shall lay up these words of mine in your heart and in your soul, and you shall bind them for a sign on your hand, and they shall be frontlets between your eyes; you shall teach them to your children, talking about them when you sit at home, and when you walk in the street, when you lie down to sleep and when you awake; you shall write them on the doorposts of your home and on your gates: so that you and your children may live long in the land which the Lord promised to give your fathers, for as long as the heavens are above the earth. (Deut. 11:13–21) *[9*

The Lord said to Moses: 'Speak to the children of Israel, and tell them to make a fringe [*zizit*] on the corners of their clothes throughout all their generations, and to put in the fringe at each corner a blue cord. Then when this fringe catches your eye, you will remember all the Lord's commandments and obey them, and not go your own wanton ways, led astray by your own heart and eyes. Thus you will remember and obey all my commandments, and you will be consecrated to your God. I am the Lord your God, who brought you out of the land of Egypt, to be your God: I am the Lord your God.' (Num. 15:37–41) *[10*

**Third morning benediction: Emet ve-yazziv [Ge'ullah]**
True and firm, well founded and enduring, right and trustworthy, beloved and precious, desirable and pleasant, revered and majestic, well ordered and acceptable, good and beautiful is this word to us for ever and ever. It is true that the eternal God is our King, the Rock of Jacob, the Shield of our salvation. Throughout all generations he endures and his name endures; his throne is firmly established, and his kingdom and his faithfulness endure for ever. His words live and endure: trustworthy and desirable for ever and for all eternity, they have been laid upon our fathers and upon us, upon our children, our descendants, and all generations of the seed of Israel, your servants. Upon the former ages and the latter there has been laid a good word that endures for ever and ever; it is true and trustworthy, a statue which shall not pass away. It is true that you are the Lord our God, and the God of our fathers, our King, our fathers' King, our Redeemer, the Redeemer of our fathers, our Maker, the Rock of our salvation, our Deliverer and Rescuer. So were you ever known. There is no God apart from you. *[11*

You have been the help of our fathers from of old, a Shield and Saviour to their children after them in every generation. In the height of the universe is your dwelling, and your judgements and righteousness reach to the farthest ends of the earth. Happy is the man who obeys your commandments, and takes your Torah to his heart. It is true that you are the Lord of your people, and a mighty King to champion their cause. It is true that you are the first and you are the last, and apart from you we have no King, Redeemer or Saviour. From Egypt you redeemed us, O Lord our God, and from slavery you delivered us. All their firstborn you slew, but your own firstborn you redeemed. You divided the Red Sea and drowned the proud, but you caused your loved ones to pass through, while the water overwhelmed their enemies, not one of whom survived. Therefore God's loved ones praised and extolled him, his dear ones offered hymns, songs, praises, blessings and thanksgivings to the King, the God who lives and endures; who is high and exalted, great and revered; who humbles the proud and raises up the lowly; who frees the prisoners, delivers the meek, helps the poor, and answers his people when they cry to him in distress. Praise be to the Most High God, who is blessed and ever to be blessed. Moses and the children of Israel sang to you with great joy, and they all said: 'Who is like you, O Lord, among the mighty ones? Who is like you, majestic in holiness, revered in praises, working wonders?' (Exod. 15:11). With a new song the redeemed praised your name at the seashore. In unison they all gave thanks and acknowledged your kingship, saying: 'The Lord shall reign for ever and ever' (Exod. 15:18). O Rock of Israel, rise up and help Israel; set Judah and Israel free, as you promised, O our Redeemer, whose name is Lord of hosts, Holy One of Israel. Blessed are you, O Lord who has redeemed Israel. *[12*

**Third evening benediction: Emet ve-emunah**
All this is true and trustworthy, and we firmly hold that he is the Lord our

God, besides whom no other god exists, and that we, Israel, are his people. He is the one who delivered us from the hand of kings, our King, who redeemed us from the power of all tyrants. He is the God who avenged us on our foes and paid back all our deadly enemies; who performed great deeds beyond reckoning, and wonders past counting; who placed our souls in life and prevented our feet from slipping; who led us in triumph on the heights of our enemies, and raised our horn over all those who hated us; who performed miracles for us, signs and wonders in the land of Ham, when he took vengeance on Pharaoh; who in his anger smote all the firstborn of Egypt, and brought out his people Israel from among them to enjoy everlasting freedom; who led his children through the divided Red Sea, but drowned their pursuers and enemies in its depths. Then his children saw his power; they praised and thanked his name, and willingly accepted his rule over them. Moses and the children of Israel sang to you with great joy, and they all said: 'Who is like you, O Lord, among the mighty ones? Who is like you, majestic in holiness, revered in praises, working wonders?' (Exod. 15:11). Your children saw your royal power when you split open the Red Sea before Moses. They exclaimed: 'He is my God!' (Exod. 15:2). They said: 'The Lord shall reign for ever and ever' (Exod. 15:18). It is written: 'The Lord has freed Jacob, and rescued him from the hand of a foe too strong for him' (Jer. 31:11). Blessed are you, O Lord, who has redeemed Israel.                                    [13

**Fourth evening benediction: Hashkivenu**

Grant us, O Lord our God, to lie down in peace, and raise us up again, O our King, to enjoy life. Spread over us the canopy of your peace. Guide us with your own good counsel, and save us for the sake of your name. Shield us and keep from us every enemy, disease, violence, famine, and sorrow. Remove the adversary from us before us and behind us, shelter us beneath the shadow of your wings, for you are a God who guards and protects us, a God who is a merciful and compassionate King. Guard us when we go out and when we come in, so that we may enjoy life and peace now and for ever. Blessed are you, O Lord, who guards his people Israel for ever.                                    [14

### 3.1.2 The Amidah (Shemoneh Esreh or Eighteen Benedictions)

1. Blessed are you, O Lord our God and God of our fathers, God of Abraham, God of Isaac, God of Jacob, the great, mighty and revered God, God most high, generous and kind, owner of all things. You remember the pious deeds of the patriarchs, and in love will bring a redeemer to their children's children, for your name's sake, O King, Helper, Saviour and Shield. Blessed are you, O Lord, the Shield of Abraham.                                    [1

2. O Lord, you are for ever mighty. You bring back the dead to life. You have the power to save. Out of loving kindness you sustain the living; with great compassion you revive the dead. You support the falling, heal the sick, free the captives, and keep faith with those who sleep in the dust. Who is like you, Lord of mighty deeds, and who may be compared to you, O King, who brings death and life, and causes salvation to spring forth? You are to be trusted to bring the

dead back to life. Blessed are you, O Lord, who revives the dead. *[2*

3. You are holy, and your name is holy, and holy beings praise you every day. Blessed are you, O Lord, the holy God. *[3*

4. You favour mankind with knowledge, and teach mortals understanding. Favour us with the knowledge, understanding and discernment that come from you. Blessed are you, O Lord, gracious Giver of knowledge. *[4*

5. Turn us back, O our Father, to your Torah; draw us near, O our King, to your service. Bring us back in perfect repentance to your presence. Blessed are you, O Lord, who delights in repentance. *[5*

6. Forgive us, O our Father, for we have sinned; pardon us, O our King, for we have been disobedient; for you pardon and forgive. Blessed are you, O Lord, ever gracious and ready to forgive. *[6*

7. Look on our misery, champion our cause, and redeem us swiftly for your name's sake, for you are a mighty Redeemer. Blessed are you, O lord, the Redeemer of Israel. *[7*

8. Heal us, O Lord, and we shall be healed; save us and we shall be saved; for it is you we praise. Send us complete healing for all our ills, for you, O divine King, are a trustworthy and compassionate Physician. Blessed are you, O Lord, who heals the sick of his people Israel. *[8*

9. O Lord our God, bless this year and all its varied produce for our good. Send a blessing on the earth; satisfy us with your goodness, and make this year as blessed for us as former good years. Blessed are you, O Lord, who blesses the years. *[9*

10. Sound the great horn for our freedom. Raise the banner to rally our exiles, and gather us in from the four corners of the earth. Blessed are you, O Lord, who gathers the dispersed of his people Israel. *[10*

11. Restore our judges as at first, our counsellors as in former times. Remove from us sorrow and sighing. Rule over us, O Lord, you alone, in kindness and compassion, and vindicate us in judgement. Blessed are you, O Lord, the King who loves righteousness and justice. *[11*

12. For slanderers may there be no hope. May all wickedness perish in an instant. May all your enemies be swiftly cut off. Uproot, smash, overthrow and humble swiftly in our days the arrogant kingdom. Blessed are you, O Lord, who breaks the enemies and humbles the arrogant. *[12*

13. Towards the righteous and the pious, towards the elders of your people, the house of Israel, towards the remnant of their scholars, towards the righteous proselytes, and towards us also may your compassion be stirred, O Lord our God. Grant a rich reward to all who sincerely trust in your name; set our portion with them for ever, so that we may not be put to shame; for we have trusted in you. Blessed are you, O Lord, the support and security of the righteous. *[13*

14. To Jerusalem, your city, return in mercy, and dwell in it, as you have promised. Rebuild it soon in our days as an everlasting structure, and swiftly establish in it the throne of David. Blessed are you, O Lord, who rebuilds

Jerusalem. [14

15. Cause the scion of David your servant to spring up swiftly, and let his horn be exalted through your saving power, for we wait for your salvation all day long. Blessed are you, O Lord, who makes the horn of salvation to flourish. [15

16. Hear our supplication, O Lord our God. Spare us and pity us; receive our prayers with compassion and favour; for you are a God who listens to prayers and petitions. O our King, do not turn us out of your presence empty-handed, for you hear with compassion the prayers of your people Israel. Blessed are you, O Lord, who hears prayer. [16

17. O Lord our God, receive with pleasure your people Israel and their prayers. Restore the service to the sanctuary of your House. Accept with love and approval the fire-offerings of Israel and their prayers, and may the service of your people Israel be ever pleasing to you. May our eyes witness your return in mercy to Zion. Blessed are you, O Lord, who brings back his Shekhinah to Zion. [17

18. We give thanks to you, for you are the Lord our God and the God of our fathers for ever and ever; you are the Rock of our life, the Shield of our salvation in every generation. We will give thanks to you and praise you for our lives that are held in your hand, for our souls that are in your care, for your miracles that are with us every day, and for your wonders and your benefits that we experience every moment – morning, noon and night. You are all-good, for your mercy has no end; you are all-compassionate, for your kindness knows no limit: we have always put our hope in you. For all this, O our King, may your name be continually blessed and exalted for evermore. May all that lives give thanks to you and praise your name in sincerity, O God, our salvation and our help. Blessed are you, O Lord, whose name is All-Good, and to whom it is proper to give thanks. [18

19. Grant peace, well-being, blessing, grace, lovingkindness and compassion to us and to all Israel, your people. Bless us, O our Father, all of us together, with the light of your face; for by the light of your face you have given us, O Lord our God, the Torah of life, love and kindness, righteousness, blessing, mercy, life and peace. May it be good in your sight to bless your people Israel at all times and at every hour with your peace. Blessed are you, O Lord, who blesses his people Israel with peace. [19

## 3.2 SABBATH LITURGY

### 3.2.1 Qiddush for Sabbath evening

'(There was evening and there was morning –)[1]

The sixth day. So heaven and earth were finished and all their host. On the seventh day God had finished the work he had been doing, and he ceased on the seventh day from all the work he had been doing. God blessed the seventh day and made it holy, because on it God ceased from all the work of creating which he had been doing' (Gen. 1:31 – 2:3).  [1

*The blessing for the wine.* Blessed are you, O Lord our God, King of the universe, who creates the fruit of the vine.  [2

*The blessing for the day.* Blessed are you, O Lord our God, King of the Universe, who has made us holy through his commandments and has taken pleasure in us. In his love and goodwill he has given us his holy Sabbath as an inheritance, a memorial of creation, for it is the first named of the holy assemblies. (Lev. 23:1–38), a reminder of the going forth from Egypt. For you have chosen us and set us apart as holy from all the nations and in love and goodwill have given us your holy Sabbath as an inheritance. Blessed are you, O Lord, who makes the Sabbath holy.  [3

*The blessing for the washing of the hands (Netilat Yadayim).* Blessed are you, O Lord our God, King of the universe, who has made us holy through his commandments, and has given us the commandment concerning the washing of the hands.  [4

*The blessing for the bread.* Blessed are you, O Lord our God, King of the universe, who brings forth bread from the earth.  [5

### 3.2.2 The Havdalah service for the end of Sabbath

Behold, God is my salvation, I will trust and not be afraid, for Yah, the Lord, is my strength and my song, and he has proved to be my salvation. You shall draw up water with joy from the wells of salvation. Salvation comes from the Lord: may your blessing rest on your people. The Lord of Hosts is with us, the God of Jacob is our refuge. The Jews had light and joy, gladness and honour – so may it be with us as well! I will raise the cup of salvation and call on the name of the Lord.  [1

*The blessing for the wine.* Blessed are you, O Lord our God, King of the universe, who creates the fruit of the vine.  [2

*The blessing for the spices.* Blessed are you, O Lord our God, King of the universe, who creates spices of different kinds.  [3

*The blessing for light.* Blessed are you, O Lord our God, King of the universe, who creates the lights of fire [*bore me'orei ha-esh*].  [4

*Havdalah.* Blessed are you, O Lord our God, King of the universe, who has made a distinction between the holy and the profane, between light and darkness, between Israel and the nations, between the seventh day and the six working days. Blessed are you, O Lord, who has made a distinction between the holy and the profane.  [5

### 3.3 PASSOVER LITURGY

#### 3.3.1 Two extracts from the Passover Haggadah[2]

**I**

This is the bread of poverty which our fathers ate in the land of Egypt. Let all who are hungry come and eat; let all who are in need come to our Passover feast. Now we are here; next year may we be in the land of Israel! Now we are slaves; next year may we be free! [1

Why is this night different from all other nights? On all other nights we may eat either leavened or unleavened bread, but on this night only unleavened bread. On all other nights we may eat other kinds of herbs, but on this night only bitter herbs. On all other nights we do not need to dip our herbs even once, but on this night we must dip them twice. On all other nights we may eat either sitting or reclining, but on this night we all recline. [2

We were Pharaoh's slaves in Egypt, but the Lord our God brought us out from there with a strong hand and an outstretched arm. If the Holy One, blessed be he, had not brought our fathers out from Egypt, then we, our children, and our children's children would still be Pharaoh's slaves in Egypt. So even though all of us were wise, all of us clever, all of us elders, all of us knowledgeable in the Torah, yet we would be duty-bound to tell the story of the coming out from Egypt. The more a man tells the story of the coming out from Egypt, the more he is to be praised. [3

Once Rabbi Eliezer, Rabbi Joshua, Rabbi Eleazar, Rabbi Aqiva, and Rabbi Tarfon, were reclining together at Benei Beraq, and they spent the whole night retelling the story of the coming out from Egypt, until their students came and said: 'Our Masters, it is now time to recite the morning *Shema*!' [4

Rabbi Eleazar ben Azariah said: 'I am now about seventy years old, yet I never understood why the story of the coming out from Egypt should be recited at night, until Ben Zoma gave the explanation. It is because Scripture says: "So that you may remember the day when you came out from the land of Egypt all the days of your life" (Deut. 16:3). "The days of your life" would have implied only the daytime; but "*All* the days of your life" means the nights are included as well.' However, the other Sages explain the words differently: 'The days of your life' would have implied only in this world; but '*All* the days of your life' means in the Messianic age as well. [5

Blessed be the Omnipresent One, blessed be he, who gave the Torah to his people Israel. The Torah speaks of four sons: one wise, one wicked, one simple, and one who does not know how to ask. What does the wise son say? – 'What is the meaning of the precepts, statutes, and laws which the Lord our God has given you?' (Deut. 6:20). You, on your part, must instruct him in the laws of the Passover, and explain to him that we must not round off the Passover meal with after-dinner entertainment. What does the wicked son say? 'Why is this rite observed by you?' (Exod. 12:26). 'By *you*', note well, not by *him*. In that he excludes himself from the community, he denies a fundamental principle; so you in turn must set his teeth on edge, and reply: 'It is because of that which the Lord did for me when I came out from Egypt' (Exod. 13:8). 'For *me*', mark well, not for *him*. If he had been there, he would not have been redeemed. What does the simple son say? 'What is this?' (Exod. 13:14). You shall say to him: 'With a strong hand the Lord brought us out from Egypt, from slavery' (Exod.

13:14). As for the son who does not know how to ask, you must take the initiative yourself, as Scripture says: 'You shall tell your son in that day, "It is because of that which the Lord did for me when I came out from Egypt" ' (Exod. 13:8). [6

'You shall tell your son in that day . . .' You might suppose you should begin the instruction on the first day of the month of Nisan, but Scripture stipulates 'In that day'. From 'In that day' you might suppose that you should begin the instruction while it is still daytime; but Scripture goes on to state: 'Because of *that*'. I can only say, 'Because of *that*,' when the unleavened bread and bitter herbs are actually set out in front of you. [7

In the beginning our fathers were idolators, but now the Omnipresent One has brought us to worship him, as Scripture says: 'Joshua said to all the people: "This is what the Lord, the God of Israel, says: Long ago your forefathers, Terah and his sons Abraham and Nahor, lived beyond the Euphrates, and they worshipped other gods. But I took your father Abraham from beyond the Euphrates, and led him through the length and breadth of the land of Canaan. I gave him many descendants: I gave him Isaac, and to Isaac I gave Jacob and Esau. I granted to Esau Mount Seir as his inheritance, but Jacob and his sons went down to Egypt" ' (Josh. 24:2–4). [8

Blessed be he who keeps his promise to Israel, blessed be he! For the Holy One, blessed be he, had already computed the end of their slavery, so as to fulfil what he had promised to Abraham in the Covenant between the Pieces, as Scripture says: 'The Lord said to Abram: "Know this for certain that your descendants shall be aliens in a land that is not theirs; they shall be enslaved and oppressed there for four hundred years. But I will punish that nation whom they serve, and afterwards they shall come out with great possessions" ' (Gen. 25:13–14). It is this promise which has stood by our fathers and by us. For it is not simply a matter of one man rising up against us to destroy us. Rather, in every generation men have risen up against us to destroy us, but the Holy One, blessed be he, has saved us from their hands. [9

II

Rabban Gamaliel says: 'Whoever does not mention the following three things at Passover has not fulfilled his duty – the Passover sacrifice, unleavened bread, and bitter herbs.' The Passover sacrifice which our fathers used to eat while the Temple still stood – what was the reason for it? It was a reminder that the Holy One, blessed be he, passed over the houses of our fathers in Egypt, as Scripture says: 'You shall say: "It is the sacrifice of the Lord's Passover, for he passed over the houses of the Israelites in Egypt, when he smote the Egyptians, but spared our houses." The people bowed down and prostrated themselves' (Exod. 12:27). This unleavened bread which we eat – what is the reason for it? It is a reminder that the dough of our fathers had not yet become leavened when the King of the kings of kings, the Holy One, blessed be he, revealed himself to them and redeemed them, as Scripture says: 'They baked unleavened bread with the dough which they had brought out of Egypt, for it was not leavened;

because they had been driven out of Egypt without delay, and so they could not get ready for themselves provisions for the journey' (Exod. 12:39). These bitter herbs that we eat – what is the reason for them? They are a reminder that the Egyptians made the lives of our fathers bitter in Egypt, as Scripture says: 'They made their lives bitter with hard labour, work with mortar and with brick, and all kinds of work in the fields; in whatever work they were employed, they were treated harshly' (Exod. 1:14).                                                                  [10

In every generation each of us is duty bound to regard himself as if he in person had come out from Egypt, as Scripture says: 'You shall tell your son, "It is because of that which the Lord did for *me* when *I* came out from Egypt" ' (Exod. 13:8). It was not only our fathers that the Holy One, blessed be he, redeemed, but he redeemed us also, along with them, as Scripture says: 'He brought *us* out from there, to bring us in and give us the land which he had solemnly promised to our fathers' (Deut. 6:23).                                        [11

Therefore, we are duty-bound to thank, praise, laud, glorify, exalt, honour, bless, extol, and adore him who performed all these miracles for our fathers and for us. He has brought us out from slavery to freedom, from sorrow to joy, from mourning to holiday, from darkness to great light, and from bondage to redemption. Let us, then, sing before him a new song. Hallelujah!                    [12

# 4. TALES OF THE SAINTS AND SCHOLARS

*See 1.3. All the tales quoted in this chapter are taken from early sources (second to fifth centuries C.E.) and illustrate the classic style of Rabbinic hagiography. They are typically fast-moving, highly compressed, and often very witty. 4.3 comes from the Pesiqta deRav Kahana, a homiletic midrash on the Torah and Haftarah readings for festivals and special Sabbaths, possibly dating from the fifth century C.E. The Avot deRabbi Natan – the source of 4.4 – is a commentary on Pirqei Avot (on which see 1.5, and 6.1 below), and may be as early as the third century C.E. On the Mishnah, the source for 4.1, and on the Talmud, the source for 4.5–7, see 1.4. 9.1.1 below gives an example of later Hasidic hagiography.*

## 4.1 HONI THE RAINMAKER (MISHNAH, TA'ANIT 3:8)

Once they said to Honi the Circle-drawer: 'Pray for rain to fall.' He replied: 'Go and bring in the Passover ovens, so that they don't get softened.' He prayed, but rain did not fall. So what did he do? He drew a circle on the ground, and, standing in it, he addressed God: 'Lord of the world, your children have turned to me, because I am like a son of the house before you. I swear by your great name that I will not stir from here until you take pity on your children.' Rain began to fall drop by drop. Honi said: 'This is not what I asked for, but for rain to fill the cisterns, pits and caverns.' It began to come down in torrents. He said: 'Nor is this what I asked for, but for rain of goodwill, blessing and graciousness.' Then it rained in moderation, and it continued till the Israelites were forced to go up from Jerusalem to the Temple Mount because of the rain. The people came to Honi and said: 'Just as you prayed for the rain to come, pray now for it to go away!' He replied: 'Go and see if the Strayers' Stone has disappeared!' Simeon ben Shetah sent word to Honi: 'If you had not been Honi, I would have excommunicated you! But what am I to do? You importune God and he does what you want, like a son who importunes his father and gets his way. Scripture says of you: "Let your father and your mother be glad, and let her that bore you rejoice" (Prov. 23:23).'

## 4.2 HANINAH BEN DOSA THE HEALER (BABYLONIAN TALMUD, BERAKHOT 34b)

Our masters have taught: Once when Rabban Gamaliel's son fell ill, he sent two students to Rabbi Haninah ben Dosa to ask him to pray for him. When he saw them, he went to the upper room and interceded for him. When he came down, he said to the students: 'Go, for the fever has left him.' They said to him: 'Are you a prophet?' He replied: 'I am neither a prophet, nor the son of a prophet, but this is how I am favoured. If my prayer is fluent in my mouth, I know that the sick person is favoured; if not, I know that God has rejected him.' The students sat down and made a note of the precise time. When they came to Rabban Gamaliel, he said to them: 'By the worship! You have neither subtracted nor added, but that is exactly how it happened. It was at that time that the fever left him and he asked us for a drink of water.'                    [1

On another occasion, when Rabbi Haninah ben Dosa had gone to Rabban Yohanan ben Zakkai to study Torah, the son of Rabban Yohanan ben Zakkai fell ill. He said to him: 'Haninah, my son, pray that he may recover.' Haninah put his head between his knees and prayed, and he recovered. Rabban Yohanan ben Zakkai said: 'Even if Ben Zakkai had squeezed his head between his knees all day long, no one would have paid any attention to him!' His wife said to him: 'Is, then, Haninah greater than you?' He said to her: 'No, he is like a slave before the King, but I am like a prince before the King.'                    [2

## 4.3 RABBAN YOHANAN BEN ZAKKAI ANSWERS A GENTILE OBJECTOR (PESIQTA DERAV KAHANA 4:7)

A gentile once posed a problem for Rabban Yohanan ben Zakkai. 'Don't the things you Jews do,' he said, 'appear to be a kind of sorcery? You bring a heifer, slaughter it, burn it, pound it to ashes, and gather its ashes up. Then when one of you suffers defilement through contact with a corpse, you sprinkle on him two or three drops of the ash mixed with water, and tell him: "You are cleansed!" ' (cf. Num. 19:1–13). Rabban Yohanan replied: 'Has the spirit of madness ever possessed you?' He answered, 'No.' 'Have you, then, ever seen anyone possessed by the spirit of madness?' 'Yes.' 'And what do you do in this case?' 'You bring roots, fumigate him with their smoke, sprinkle water on him, and the spirit of madness flees.' Rabban Yohanan then said: 'Do your ears not hear what your mouth is saying? The man defiled by contact with a corpse is also possessed by a spirit, the spirit of uncleanness, as Scripture says: "I will cause the false prophets and the spirit of uncleanness to depart from the land" ' (Zech. 13.2). When the gentile had gone, Rabban Yohanan's students said: 'Master, you knocked him over with a straw, but how are you going to answer us?' Rabban Yohanan replied: 'By your lives! the corpse of itself does not have power to defile, nor does the mixture of ash and water of itself have power to cleanse, but it is a decree of the Holy One, blessed be he. The Holy One, blessed be he, has said: "I have laid it down as a statute, I have issued it as a decree, and you are not permitted to transgress my decree. This is the statute of the Torah" (Num. 19:1).'

## 4.4 RABBI ELIEZER GOES TO STUDY WITH YOHANAN BEN ZAKKAI (AVOT DERABBI NATAN A.6)

What were the beginnings of Rabbi Eliezer ben Hyrcanus? He was twenty-two years old and had still not studied Torah. Once he said: 'I am going to study Torah with Rabban Yohanan ben Zakkai.' His father Hyrcanus said to him: 'You shall not taste a bite of food till you have plowed an entire furrow.' He rose early in the morning, plowed an entire furrow and went off. Some say: That day was Sabbath eve and he dined at his father-in-law's. But others say: He tasted nothing from six hours before the Sabbath started till six hours after it ended. As he was walking along the road he saw a stone; he picked it up and put it in his mouth. (Some say: It was cattle dung.) He went and spent the night in a hostel. Then he went and sat before Rabban Yohanan ben Zakkai in Jerusalem – until his bad breath became noticeable. Rabban Yohanan ben Zakkai asked him: 'Eliezer, my son, have you eaten anything today?' Silence. Again he asked him, and again silence. Rabban Yohanan sent for the proprietors of the hostel and asked them: 'Did Eliezer have anything to eat at your place?' They replied: 'We thought he was eating with you, master.' He said to them: 'And I thought he was eating with you! You and I, between us, left Rabbi Eliezer to perish!' Rabban Yohanan ben Zakkai said to Rabbi Eliezer: 'Just as the bad breath came forth from your mouth, so shall your fame in Torah spread abroad.' [1

When Hyrcanus, Rabbi Eliezer's father, heard that he was studying Torah with Yohanan ben Zakkai, he declared: 'I shall go and ban my son from all my possessions.' They say: That day Rabban Yohanan ben Zakkai sat expounding in Jerusalem with all the important men of Israel sitting before him. When he heard that Hyrcanus was coming he set guards and told them: 'If Hyrcanus comes, don't let him sit down.' Hyrcanus arrived and they would not let him sit down, but he pushed his way up to the front until he found himself beside Zizit ben Ha-Keset, Naqdimon ben Gorion, and Ben Kalba Shavu'a. He sat among them trembling. They say: On that day Rabban Yohanan ben Zakkai fixed his gaze on Rabbi Eliezer and said to him: 'Deliver the exposition!' 'I cannot,' Rabbi Eliezer replied. Rabban Yohanan pressed him to do it, and the other students pressed him as well. So he rose and delivered a discourse on things such as the ear had never heard before. As each word came from his mouth Rabban Yohanan ben Zakkai rose to his feet and kissed him on the head and exclaimed: 'Rabbi Eliezer, my master, you have taught me the truth!' Before the session had ended, Hyrcanus, the father, rose to his feet and declared: 'My masters, I came here only in order to ban my son Eliezer from my possessions. Now all my possessions shall be given to Eliezer my son. All his brothers are disinherited and shall have none of them.'                                                    [2

## 4.5 THE HEAVENLY VOICE (*BAT QOL*) IS RULED OUT OF COURT (BABYLONIAN TALMUD, BAVA MEZI'A 59A–B)

We learnt elsewhere: If it was cut up into rings and sand put between each ring, then Rabbi Eliezer declared it clean, but the Sages declared it unclean. This was the oven of Akhnai. Why was it called the oven of Akhnai? Rav Judah said in Samuel's name: 'It was so called because they surrounded it with arguments like a snake [*akhna*] and proved it unclean.' It was taught: On that day Rabbi Eliezer brought forward all the arguments in the world to support his view, but they refused to accept them. He said to them: 'If the halakhah agrees with me, let this carob tree prove it.' The carob tree was uprooted and hurled from its place a hundred cubits (or, according to some, four hundred cubits). 'No proof can be brought from a carob tree,' they said to him. Again he said to them: 'If the halakhah agrees with me, let this stream of water prove it.' The stream flowed backwards. 'No proof can be brought from a stream of water,' said they. Again he said to them: 'If the halakah agrees with me, let the walls of the schoolhouse prove it.' The walls started to lean as if about to fall. Rabbi Joshua rebuked them and said: 'When the pupils of the Sages are disputing about halakhah what business have you to interfere?' The walls did not fall, for the sake of Rabbi Joshua's honour, nor did they resume the upright, for the sake of Rabbi Eliezer's honour. (They are still standing in the inclined position.) Again Rabbi Eliezer said: 'If the halakhah agrees with me, let it be proved from heaven.' A *bat qol* went forth and said: 'Why do you dispute with Rabbi Eliezer, seeing that in every case the halakhah agrees with him!' But Rabbi Joshua stood up and exclaimed: 'It is not in heaven!' (Deut. 30:12). What did he mean by this? Rabbi Jeremiah said: 'He meant: The Torah has already been given on Mount Sinai, so we pay no attention to a *bat qol*, since you long ago wrote in the Torah at Mount Sinai: "You must follow the majority opinion" (Exod. 23:2).' Rabbi Nathan met Elijah and asked him: 'How did the Holy One, blessed be he, react on that occasion?' He replied: 'He laughed and said: My sons have defeated me, my sons have defeated me!'

## 4.6 MOSES VISITS RABBI AQIVA'S ACADEMY (BABYLONIAN TALMUD, MENAHOT 29B)

Rav Judah said in Rav's name: 'When Moses went up to heaven he found the Holy One, blessed be he, sitting and adding crowns to the letters of the Torah. Moses said: "Lord of the universe, why has this become necessary?" He replied: "At the end of many generations there shall arise a man, Aqiva ben Joseph by name, who shall derive from each of these strokes heaps and heaps of halakhot." "Lord of the universe," said Moses, "show him to me." He replied: "Turn round." Moses went and sat down behind the eight rows of Aqiva's students and listened to the discussion. Being unable to follow their arguments, he was ill at ease. However, when they came to a certain topic and the students said, "Master, how do you know this?" and he replied, "It was given as halakah to Moses on Sinai," Moses' mind was set at rest. He returned to the Holy One, blessed be he, and said: "You have such a man and yet you choose to give the Torah through me!" He replied: "Be silent! This is what I have decided." Then Moses said: "Lord of the universe, you have shown me his Torah, show me now his reward." "Turn round," said he. Moses turned round and saw them weighing out Aqiva's flesh in the meat market. "Lord of the universe," cried Moses, "such a reward for such Torah!" He replied: "Be silent! This is what I have decided." '

## 4.7 THE MARTYRDOM OF RABBI AQIVA (BABYLONIAN TALMUD, BERAKHOT 61B)

Our rabbis taught: Once the wicked government issued a decree forbidding the Jews to engage in the study of the Torah. Pappus ben Judah came and found Rabbi Aqiva publicly holding meetings and engaging in the study of Torah. He said to him: 'Aqiva, are you not afraid of the government?' He replied: 'I will tell you a parable. A fox was once walking alongside a river, and he saw fish darting in shoals from one place to another. He said to them: "From what do you flee?" They replied: "From the nets which men cast out for us." He said to them: "Would you like to come up on to dry land so that you and I can live together in the way that my ancestors lived with your ancestors?" They replied: "Are you the one men call the cleverest of animals? You're not clever;

you're stupid. If we are afraid in the element in which we live, how much more should we be afraid in an element in which we would die!'' So it is with us. If we are in our present plight while sitting and studying Torah, of which it is written, "It brings you life and longevity" (Deut. 30:20), how much worse off would we be if we were to go and neglect it.' They say that a few days later Rabbi Aqiva was arrested and thrown into prison, and Pappus ben Judah was also arrested and thrown into prison beside him. He said to him: 'Pappus, who brought you here?' He replied: 'Happy are you, Rabbi Aqiva, for you have been arrested for busying yourself with Torah! But alas for Pappus, who has been arrested for busying himself with trivial things!' When Rabbi Aqiva was taken out for execution, it was the time for reciting the Shema. While they combed his flesh with combs of iron, he was taking upon himself the yoke of the kingdom of heaven. His students said to him: 'Our teacher, are you prepared to go this far!' He said to them: 'All my life I have been troubled by the words "With all your soul" (Deut. 10:12; 26:16, etc.), which I understand to mean "Even if God takes your soul". I said: "When shall I ever have an opportunity of fulfilling this?" Now that I have an opportunity, shall I not fulfil it?' He prolonged the word 'one' [ehad][1] and expired while saying it. A bat qol went forth and said: 'Happy are you, Rabbi Aqiva, because you expired with the word "one" on your lips!'

# 5. RELIGIOUS LAW

*See 1.4. It is perhaps best to begin the study of this section with 5.2.3. This should be read in conjunction with Lev. 3:17; 7:26–27; 17: 10–14; 19:26; Deut. 12:16, 23–25; 15:23, which give the biblical basis for the laws regarding the salting of meat. The biblical basis for the laws of Sabbath (5.1.2) may be found in Exod. 20:8–11; 31:12–17; 35:2–3; Num. 15:32–36; Deut. 5:12–15. 5.1.1 is concerned with the rites of Qiddush and Havdalah, for which see further 3.2.1–2 above. In 5.2.1–2 the Shulhan Arukh is given with the glosses of Isserles. For another type of legal text – a Responsum – see 9.2.3 below. The texts quoted in 10.2.1–4 below throw light on the relationship between Jewish religious law and the law of the Jewish State.*

## 5.1 THE TALMUD

### 5.1.1 Mishnah, Berakhot 8:1–8. Differences between the House of Shammai and the House of Hillel

1. These are the differences between the House of Shammai and the House of Hillel with regard to the meal. [1

The House of Shammai says: 'One recites the blessing over the day first, and then the blessing over the wine.' The House of Hillel says: 'One recites the blessing over the wine first, and then the blessing over the day.'  [2

2. The House of Shammai says: 'They wash the hands first, and then mix the cup.' The House of Hillel says: 'They mix the cup first, and then wash the hands.'  [3

3. The House of Shammai says: 'He wipes his hands on the napkin, and lays it on the table.' The House of Hillel says: 'He lays it on the cushion.'  [4

4. The House of Shammai says: 'They sweep the room first, and then wash the hands.' The House of Hillel says: 'They wash the hands first, and then sweep the room.'  [5

5. The House of Shammai says: 'Light, food, spices, and Havdalah.' The House of Hillel says: 'Light, spices, food and Havdalah.'  [6

The House of Shammai says: '. . . who created the light of fire [she-bara me'or ha-esh].' The House of Hillel says: '. . . who creates the lights of fire [bore me'orei ha-esh].'  [7

6. They do not recite a blessing over the light or the spices of gentiles; nor over the light or spices used for the dead; nor over the light or spices which are in front of an idol.  [8

They do not recite a blessing over the light until they make use of its illumination.  [9

7. If a man ate and forgot to recite the blessing,[1] the House of Shammai says: 'He should return to his place and recite it.' The House of Hillel says: 'He may recite the blessing in the place where he remembers.'  [10

Until when is he obliged to recite the blessing? Until the food in his stomach is digested.  [11

8. If wine is brought to them after the food, and there is only that one cup, the House of Shammai says: 'He recites the blessing over the wine first, and then over the food.' The House of Hillel says: 'He recites the blessing over the food first and then over the wine.'  [12

They may respond 'Amen' after an Israelite who recites a blessing, but they may not respond 'Amen' after a Samaritan who recites a blessing, till they have heard the whole blessing.  [13

## 5.1.2 Babylonian Talmud, Shabbat 73a–75b and 49b. Work forbidden on the Sabbath

(73a) **Mishnah.**[2] The principal kinds of work[3] are forty minus one: (1) sowing, (2) ploughing, (3) reaping, (4) binding sheaves, (5) threshing, (6) winnowing, (7) sorting, (8) grinding, (9) sifting, (10) kneading, (11) baking; (12) shearing wool, (13) scouring, (14) or carding, (15) or dyeing it, (16) spinning, (17) warping, (18) making two heddle leashes, (19) weaving two threads, (20) unpicking two threads, (21) tying, (22) untying, (23) sewing two stitches, (24) tearing in order to sew two stitches; (25) catching a deer, (26) slaughtering, (27) or flaying, (28) or salting it, (29) tanning its hide, (30) or scraping it, (31) or cutting it up; (32) writing two letters, (33) erasing in order to write two letters; (34) building, (35) demolishing; (36) extinguishing, (37) kindling; (38) striking with a hammer; (39) transferring from one domain to another. These are the forty minus one principal kinds of work. [1

(49b) **Gemara.** Again they sat and posed the question: 'To what do the forty minus one principal kinds of work, about which we have learned, correspond?' Rabbi Hanina bar Hama said to them: 'To the kinds of work involved in the construction of the Tabernacle.' Rabbi Jonathan the son of Rabbi Eleazar said to them: 'Thus did Rabbi Simeon the son of Rabbi Yose of Laqonia say: They correspond to the words "work" [mela'khah], "his work" [mela'khto], and "the work of" [mele'khet], which occur forty minus one times in the Torah.' Rav Joseph asked: 'Is "He came into the house to do his work" [mela'khto] (Gen. 39:11) included in the number or not?' Abaye said to him: 'Let someone fetch a Torah Scroll and we will count!' Did not Rabbah bar Bar Hana say in the name of Rabbi Yohanan: 'They did not stir from there till they had brought a Torah Scroll and counted them'? He replied: 'I am faced with a dilemma. Is the verse "The work [mela'khah] was sufficient for them" (Exod. 36:7)[4] to be included in the number, and the other verse (Gen. 39:11) to be taken to mean: "He came into the house to satisfy his needs"? Or is the verse "He came into the house to do his work" to be included in the number, and the verse "The work was sufficient for them" to be explained as meaning: "The business was completed"?' The question remains unresolved. [2

The Tannaitic tradition agrees with the view that the number corresponds to the forms of work involved in the construction of the Tabernacle, for it was taught: 'Liability is incurred only for a work which is the same as that involved in the construction of the Tabernacle.' They sowed; you must not sow. They reaped; you must not reap. They lifted up the planks from the ground to the cart; you must not bring anything from a public to a private domain. They lowered the planks from the cart to the ground; you must not bring anything from a private domain to public domain. They transferred from one cart to another; you must not carry anything from one private domain to another. 'From one private domain to another' – what action is involved here? Abaye and Rava both said (or, according to some, Rav Adda bar Ahavah said): 'Transference from one private domain to another private domain through a public domain.' [3

(73b) **Gemara.** Why is the number stated? Rabbi Yohanan said: 'To indicate that if a man performs them all during a single period of unawareness, he is liable for each of them individually.' [4

*Sowing, ploughing.* Since ploughing is done first, should not ploughing be first mentioned and then sowing? The Tanna, however, speaks from the standpoint of the land of Israel, where they first sow and then plough. [5

A Tanna stated: 'Sowing, pruning, planting, layering, and grafting all count as one kind of work.' What do we learn from this? We learn that if anyone performs many separate tasks of a similar nature, he is liable for only one sin-offering. Rav Aha said in the name of Rav Hiyya bar Ashi, who said in the name of Rav Ashi: 'He who prunes is liable on account of planting; he who plants, or layers, or grafts is liable on account of sowing.' On account of sowing, but not on account of planting! Say: on account of sowing as well.                [6

Rav Kahana said: 'He who prunes and needs the wood for some purpose is liable for two sin-offerings, one on account of reaping and one on account of planting.' Rav Joseph said: 'He who cuts hay is liable for two sin-offerings, one on account of reaping and one on account of planting.' Abaye said: 'He who trims the top of growing beets is liable for two sin-offerings, one on account of reaping and one on account of sowing.'                [7

*Ploughing.* A Tanna stated: 'Ploughing, digging, and trenching all count as one kind of work.' Rav Sheshet said: 'If a man has a hummock inside his house and he removes it, he is liable on account of building; but if it is in his field, he is liable on account of ploughing.' Rava said: 'If a man has a hollow inside his house and he fills it in, he is liable on account of building; but if it is in his field, he is liable on account of ploughing.'                [8

Rabbi Abba said: 'He who digs a hole on Sabbath simply because he needs the soil from it is exempt.' Also Rabbi Judah, who rules that a man is liable for any work not necessary for its own sake, holds that this applies only when he effects an improvement; but a man who digs a hole causes an impairment.                [9

*Reaping.* A Tanna stated: 'Reaping, harvesting grapes, cutting dates, picking olives, and gathering figs all count as one kind of work.' Rav Pappa said: 'Whoever throws a lump of earth at a palm tree and dislodges dates from it is liable for two sin-offerings, one on account of pulling up the clod from the ground, the other on account of separating the fruit from the tree.' Rav Ashi said: 'Neither pulling up nor separating is normally done in this way.'                [10

*Binding sheaves.* Rava said: 'He who collects salt from a brine pit is liable on account of binding sheaves.' Abaye said: 'Binding sheaves applies only to the produce of the soil.'                [11

*Threshing.* A Tanna stated: 'Threshing, beating flax, and beating cotton all count as one kind of work.'                [12

*Winnowing, sorting, grinding, sifting.* But surely winnowing, sorting, grinding and sifting are the same? Abaye and Rava both said: 'All kinds of work involved in the construction of the Tabernacle (74a) are counted separately, even if they are similar to each other.' Why, then, is pounding grain not included in the list? Abaye said: 'Because a poor man eats his bread without pounding.' Rava said: 'This agrees with the view of Rabbi, who said: The principal kinds of work are forty minus one, but if pounding grain were included there would be forty.' Then let one of the other kinds of work be omitted and pounding grain inserted! However, it is clear that Abaye has explained it correctly.                [13

Our rabbis taught: 'If food of different kinds is lying in front of a man, he may sort and eat, or sort and put to one side; but he must not sort. If he does so, he is liable for a sin-offering.' What does this mean? Ulla said: 'This is what it means: he may sort and eat on the same day, and he may sort and put to one side for consumption on the same day, but he may not sort and put to one side for consumption on the morrow. If he does so, he is liable for a sin-offering.' Rav Hisda objected: 'Is it, then, permitted to bake for the same day, or is it permitted to cook for the same day? Rather,' said Rav Hisda, 'he may sort and eat less than the prescribed amount, but he must not sort out as much as the prescribed amount. If he does so, he is liable for a sin-offering.' Rav Joseph objected: 'Is it, then, permitted to bake less than the prescribed amount? Rather,' said Rav Joseph, 'he may sort by hand and eat, or he may sort by hand and put to one side, but he may not sort with a basket or a plate. If he does so, he is in fact exempt, though it is still forbidden. He may not sort with a sifter or a sieve; if he does so he is liable for a sin-offering.' Rav Hamnuna objected: 'Is anything said about a basket or a plate? Rather,' said Rav Hamnuna, 'he may sort and eat by separating the food from the refuse, and he may sort and put to one side by separating the food from the refuse, but he may not sort the refuse from the food. If he does so, he is liable for a sin-offering.' Abaye objected: 'Is anything said about separating food from refuse? Rather,' said Abaye, 'he may sort and eat at once, and he may sort and put to one side for immediate consumption, but he may not sort for later consumption on the same day. If he does so, he is regarded as one who sorts for the purposes of storage, and he is liable for a sin-offering.' The scholars reported Abaye's view to Rava. He said to them: 'Nahmani⁵ holds the correct opinion.'                                                [14

If two kinds of food are in front of a man, and he sorts and eats, or sorts and puts to one side – Rav Ashi learnt: 'He is exempt'; Rabbi Jeremiah from Difti learnt: 'He is liable.' Rav Ashi learnt: 'He is exempt'; but it was also taught: 'He is liable'! There is no difficulty. The one refers to sorting with a basket or a plate; the other to sorting with a sifter or a sieve.                                    [15

When Rav Dimi came he said: 'It was Rav Bevai's Sabbath, and Rabbi Ammi and Rabbi Assi happened to be present. He tossed before them a basket of fruit. I do not know whether he did this because he held the view that it is forbidden to sort the food from the refuse, or merely because he wanted to be generous.'  [16

Hezekiah said: 'He who sorts boiled lupines from their pods is liable.' Does this mean that Hezekiah holds the view that it is forbidden to sort the food from the refuse? No: lupines are a special case, (74b) because lupines have to be boiled seven times, and if they are not separated they go rancid; so it is like separating refuse from food.                                                        [17

*Grinding.* Rav Pappa said: 'He who chops up beets is liable on account of grinding.' Rav Manasseh said: 'He who cuts up wood chips is liable on account of grinding.' Rav Ashi said: 'If he is particular about obtaining a uniform size, then he is liable on account of cutting.'                                          [18

*Kneading, baking.* Rav Pappa said: 'Our Tanna leaves out the boiling of dyes, which *was* involved in the construction of the Tabernacle, and yet includes baking!' Our Tanna simply follows through the order of the steps in making bread.                                                                [19

D

Rav Aha the son of Rav Avira said: 'He who throws a tent peg into a stove is liable on account of cooking.' But surely that is obvious! You might, however, argue that the intention is to *harden* the peg. So the statement is meant to teach us that the peg first softens and then becomes hard. [20

Rabbah bar Rav Huna said: 'He who heats pitch is liable on account of cooking.' But surely that is obvious! You might, however, argue: Since the pitch hardens again, I might suppose that he is not liable. So the statement is meant to teach us that the contrary is the case. [21

Rava said: 'He who makes a pottery jar is liable for seven sin-offerings. He who makes an oven is liable for eight sin-offerings.' Abaye said: 'He who makes a wickerwork beehive is liable for eleven sin-offerings, and if he sews round its rim, he is liable for thirteen sin-offerings.' [22

*Shearing wool, scouring it.* Rabbah bar Bar Hana said in Rabbi Yohanan's name: 'He who spins wool straight off the animal's back on Sabbath is liable for three sin-offerings, one on account of shearing, one on account of carding, and one on account of spinning.' Rav Kahana said: 'Neither shearing, nor carding, nor spinning is normally done this way.' No? But surely it was taught in the name of Rabbi Nehemiah: 'It was washed while still on the goats, and spun while still on the goats' (cf. Exod. 35:26). Hence spinning direct from the animal's back is called spinning. However, such a special skill constitutes an exception. [23

Our Rabbis taught: 'He who pulls out a bird's feather, clips it, and plucks off the down is liable for three sin-offerings.' Rabbi Simeon ben Laqish said: 'For pulling out, he is liable on account of shearing; for clipping, he is liable on account of cutting; and for plucking, he is liable on account of scraping.' [24

*Tying, untying.* Where was tying involved in the construction of the Tabernacle? Rava said: 'They tied the tent pegs.' But this was tying with a view to subsequent untying. 'Rather,' said Abaye, 'when a thread snapped, the curtain weavers tied it again.' Rava said to him: 'You have explained tying, but what about untying? Should you say that if knots chanced to form in two adjacent threads, one knot was untied and the other left in place, then I would reply: Since they would not do such work for a king of flesh and blood, would they do it for the King of the kings of kings, the Holy One, blessed be he? Rather,' said Rava (or, as some say, Rabbi Eleazar[6]), 'those who caught the purple-fish tied and untied.' [25

*Sewing two stitches.* But they would soon come out. Rabbah bar Bar Hana said in the name of Rabbi Yohanan: 'Not if they were knotted.' [26

*Tearing in order to sew two stitches.* Was there any tearing during the construction of the Tabernacle? Rabbah and Rabbi Zera both say: (75a) 'They tore a curtain which had been attacked by a moth, and resewed it.' [27

Rav Zutra bar Toviyyah said in Rav's name: 'He who on Sabbath pulls taut the thread by which a seam is sewn is liable for one sin-offering. He who learns anything from a Magus deserves the death penalty. He who knows how to compute the cycles of the sun and the courses of the planets but does not do so —

no one should converse with him.'                                                    *[28*

Rav and Samuel differed as to what is Magianism: one took it as sorcery, the other as blasphemy. It may be proved conclusively that it was Rav who held that it was blasphemy, for Rav Toviyyah bar Zutra said in Rav's name: 'He who learns anything from a Magus deserves the death penalty.' Should you suppose that Magianism is sorcery, then observe that Scripture says: 'You shall not learn *to do* according to the detestable practices of those nations' (Deut. 18:9), implying that you may, nevertheless, learn in order to understand and to instruct. This proves it.'                                                    *[29*

Rabbi Simeon ben Pazzi said that Rabbi Joshua ben Levi said in the name of Bar Qappara: 'He who knows how to compute the cycles of the sun and the courses of the planets but does not do so – Scripture says of him: "They do not regard the work of the Lord, nor consider what his hands have done" ' (Isa. 5:12). Rabbi Samuel bar Nahmani said in Rabbi Yohanan's name: 'From where do we learn that we have a duty to compute the cycles of the sun and the courses of the planets? From the verse: "You shall observe and do them, for this is your wisdom and understanding in the sight of the peoples" (Deut. 4:6). What wisdom and understanding lies in the sight of the peoples? You must answer: The computation of the cycles of the sun and the courses of the planets.'   *[30*

*Catching a deer.* Our rabbis taught: 'He who catches a purple-fish and crushes it is liable only for one sin-offering.' Rabbi Judah says: 'He is liable for two sin-offerings,' for Rabbi Judah maintained that crushing belongs to the category of threshing. They said to him: 'Crushing does not belong to the category of threshing.' Rava said: 'What is our rabbis' reason? They hold that threshing applies only to the produce of the soil.' But surely he is also liable on account of taking life? Rabbi Yohanan said: 'He crushed it when it was already dead.' Rava said: 'You may even say he crushed it while it was still alive, since the taking of life was incidental to his primary purpose.' But Abaye and Rava both said: 'Rabbi Simeon admits liability if it is a case of "cut off his head, but let him not die!" Here, however, it is different, for the longer it lives, the better pleased he is – so that he may achieve a brighter colour.'   *[31*

*Slaughtering it.* On what account is slaughtering liable? Rav said: 'On account of dyeing'; Samuel said: 'On account of taking life.' (75b) On account of dyeing, but not on account of taking life! Say: on account of dyeing as well. Rav said: 'I will give you an explanation of what I have said, so that future generations may not come and ridicule me. Why should a butcher be interested in dyeing? He likes the throat of the slaughtered animal to be freshly stained with blood, so that people should see it and come and buy from him.'   *[32*

*Salting it, tanning it.* But salting and tanning are the same? Rabbi Yohanan and Resh Laqish both say: 'Omit one of these and include drawing the lines of the pattern.' Rabbah bar Rav Huna said: 'He who salts meat is liable on account of tanning.' Rav said: 'Tanning does not apply to comestibles.' Rav Ashi said: 'Even Rabbah bar Rav Huna only spoke of when a man requires meat for a journey, but for home consumption people do not cure their food till it is as hard as wood!' *[33*

*Scraping it, cutting it up.* Rabbi Aha bar Hanina said: 'He who on Sabbath rubs smooth a hide stretched between poles is liable on account of scraping.' Rabbi Hiyya bar Abba said: 'Rav Ashi reported three things to me in the name of Rabbi Joshua ben Levi: He who planes the tops of beams on Sabbath is liable on account of cutting. He who smears a poultice over a sore on Sabbath is liable on account of scraping. He who dresses a masonry block with a chisel on Sabbath is liable on account of striking with a hammer.' Rabbi Simeon ben Qisma said in the name of Resh Laqish: 'He who executes a design on a utensil and he who blows a new glass vessel is liable on account of striking with a hammer.' Rav said: 'He who picks superfluous threads out of clothes is liable on account of striking with a hammer.' This is the case only if he is particular about removing such threads. *[34*

*Writing two letters.* Our rabbis taught: 'If anyone writes one large letter in a space where there was room to write two, he is exempt. If he erases one large letter and so creates space enough to write two normal-sized letters, he is liable.' Rabbi Menahem the son of Rabbi Yose said: 'Thus erasing is treated more stringently than writing.' *[35*

*Building, demolishing, extinguishing, kindling, striking with a hammer.* Rabbah and Rabbi Zera both say: 'Whatever involves the finishing of work is liable on account of striking with a hammer.' *[36*

*These are the principal kinds of work.* 'These' is meant to exclude the opinion of Rabbi Eleazar, who imposed liability for a subsidiary kind of work when performed in conjunction with a principal kind of work.[7] *[37*

*Minus one.* This is meant to exclude the opinion of Rabbi Judah, for it was taught: 'Rabbi Judah adds evening up the warp yarns and beating in the weft.' They said to him: 'Evening up belongs to the category of warping, and beating in belongs to the category of weaving.' *[38*

## 5.2 THE *SHULHAN ARUKH*

### 5.2.1 *Shulhan Arukh*, Hoshen Mishpat 26:1–6. Prohibition against resorting to non-Jewish courts

1. It is forbidden to appear for trial before gentile judges[8] and in their law courts – *i.e. at fixed judicial sessions at which magistrates adjudicate* – even in a lawsuit that they would judge in accordance with the laws of Israel. Even should both parties agree to be tried before them, it is forbidden. Whoever appears for trial before them is a wicked man: it is as if he reviled, blasphemed and rebelled against the Torah of Moses our teacher. **Gloss.** *The Jewish court has the right to impose on such a one the lesser ban* [niddui], *or the greater ban* [herem], *till he instructs the gentile authorities to drop proceedings against his fellow litigant. So, too, they may impose a ban* [herem] *on anyone who encourages one who goes to law before a gentile court. Even if the plaintiff does*

*not go to law before a gentile court, but merely compels the defendant through the agency of the gentile court to appear with him for trial before a Jewish court – he deserves to be flogged. He who went before a gentile court and was found guilty under their laws, and then turned round and summoned the other party to appear before a Jewish court – some say his case should not be heard; others that it should be heard, unless he was the cause of some loss to his fellow litigant before the gentile court. The former opinion is, in my view, fundamental.* [1

2. If the power of the gentile courts is great, and the defendant a violent man, so that the plaintiff is unable to receive satisfaction from him through the Jewish courts, then he must first summon the defendant to appear before a Jewish court. Should he refuse, then the plaintiff may obtain permission from the Jewish court to seek redress through the gentile courts. **Gloss.** *The members of a Jewish court have the right to go before the gentile courts and give evidence that one party is culpable in respect of another. This whole ruling applies only when the defendant refuses to submit to the Jewish court. Otherwise the Jewish court is forbidden to grant anyone permission to appear before a gentile court.* [2

3. If anyone undertook by means of a *qinyan* [a symbolic way of making an agreement binding, in which one party hands over an object to another] to appear with his fellow litigant for trial before a gentile court, it has no legal validity, and he is forbidden to appear for trial before them. If he gave an undertaking that, should he not appear before them, he would be bound to give such-and-such a sum to the poor, he is still forbidden to appear with his fellow litigant before the gentile court, though he *is* obliged to give the poor whatever he undertook to pay them. There is one authority who states that the Jewish court may not exact this pledge from him, but should merely inform him that the vow is binding on him. [3

4. Even if the plaintiff possesses a document in which it is written that he may summon the defendant under gentile law – he is still not permitted to summon him before the gentile courts. If the plaintiff handed over the document to the gentile court so that it might summon the defendant under its laws, he is obliged to reimburse the defendant for any loss he caused him, in excess of whatever the defendant is liable to pay under the laws of Israel. **Gloss.** *This whole ruling applies only where one party can compel the other to appear before a Jewish court, but if a debtor proves violent, a creditor may hand over such a document to a gentile court.* [4

### 5.2.2 *Shulhan Arukh*, Yoreh De'ah 335:1–10. Laws regarding visiting the sick

1. It is a religious duty [*mizvah*] to visit the sick. Relatives and friends may call immediately, and strangers after three days. If, however, a man falls ill suddenly, both parties may call on him immediately. [1

2. Even an eminent person should visit a humble one, even many times a day, and even if he is of the same age as the invalid. Whoever visits often is

considered praiseworthy, provided he does not weary the sick person. **Gloss.** *Some say that an enemy may visit a sick person. However, this does not seem right to me. Rather a man should not visit a sick person or comfort a mourner who is his enemy, lest the latter think that he rejoices at his misfortune, and only be distressed. This seems to me to be the correct view.* [2

3. He who visits the sick may not sit on a bed, or on a chair, or on a stool, but must reverently wrap himself and sit in front of the invalid, for the Shekhinah is above the headboard of his bed. **Gloss.** *This applies only if the invalid lies on the ground so that the person sitting down will be higher than he; but if he lies on the bed, the visitor is permitted to sit on a chair or a stool. This is our custom.* [3

4. One should not visit the sick during the first three hours of the day, for every invalid's illness is less severe in the morning, and so one will not trouble one's self to pray for him. Nor should one visit during the last three hours of the day, for then his illness grows worse and one will despair of praying for him. **Gloss.** *He who visited a sick person and did not pray for him has not fulfilled the religious duty of visiting the sick.* [4

5. If one prays in the presence of the sick person, one may pray in any language one chooses. If, however, one prays not in his presence, then one should pray only in Hebrew. [5

6. One should combine him with the other sick of Israel by saying: 'May the Omnipresent One have compassion on you among the sick of Israel.' On Sabbath one should say: 'It is the Sabbath when it is forbidden to lament; healing will come soon.' [6

7. The invalid should be encouraged to give attention to his affairs – whether he has loaned or deposited anything with others, or others have loaned or deposited anything with him. And he should be told not to fear death because he is doing this. [7

8. One should not visit those suffering from diseases of the bowels, or of the eyes, or from headaches. So too, anyone gravely ill, to whom conversation would be injurious, must not be visited personally, but one may call at an outer room and make inquiries, and ascertain whether the invalid needs his room swept and sprinkled, or any similar service performed for him. And one should take an interest in his affliction and pray for him. [8

9. One should visit the sick of the gentiles for the sake of preserving peaceful relations. [9

10. In the case of those suffering from diseases of the bowels, the law is that a man must not nurse a woman, but a woman may nurse a man. **Gloss.** *Some say that whoever has a sick person in his home should go to the Sage of the city so that he should pray for the invalid. So too, it is our custom to recite blessings on behalf of the sick in the Synagogues, so as to give them a new name, for a change of name cancels a man's doom. Comforting of mourners takes precedence over visiting the sick.* [10

**5.2.3** *Qizzur Shulhan Arukh* **36:1–28. Laws regarding the salting of meat**

1. Before the meat is salted it must be well rinsed in water. It should be soaked entirely submerged in water for half an hour. Wherever blood is visible on the meat it must be rubbed in the water used for soaking till it is removed. In the case of fowl the place where the incision was made for slaughtering should also be rubbed thoroughly clean, as well as any place inside the fowl where blood is visible. Sometimes one finds in cattle or fowl a spot where blood has coagulated because of a blow: an incision must be made at such a place and the blood removed before soaking. When the water is very cold it should be left in a fairly warm place to take the chill off it before the meat is soaked in it, because the meat would be hardened by the coldness of the water and as a result the blood would not be drawn out by the salt.                                        [1

2. If one forgot and allowed the meat to soak for twenty-four hours, both the meat and the vessel in which it was soaked are forbidden. If liver was soaked in water for twenty-four hours, a competent authority should be consulted.     [2

3. On Sabbath eve when one is busy, or on any other occasion when time presses, it suffices to rub the meat well in water and let it soak for only a short while, and when the water no longer shows any redness, the meat may be salted.                                                                                 [3

4. If, after soaking, a piece of meat is cut in two, the freshly exposed surfaces must be well rinsed to remove any blood that may be on them.        [4

5. It is necessary to see that frozen meat has thawed out, but it should not be placed near a hot stove. In case of emergency it may be soaked in lukewarm water.                                                                                [5

6. The vessel specifically used for soaking meat may not be used for any other purpose in connection with food.                                           [6

7. After the meat has been soaked, the water must be drained from it, so that the salt should not be totally dissolved in the water and so fail to draw out the blood. Care should be taken to prevent the meat from completely drying out, so that the salt should not fall off it.                                            [7

8. The salt should not be as fine-grained as flour, so that it should not dissolve immediately on the meat and fail to draw out the blood. Nor should it be very coarse, for then it would fall off the meat. Rather it should be medium-sized, like the salt used for cooking; and it should be dry, so that it may be sprinkled easily.                                                              [8

9. The salt should be sprinkled on the meat on all sides so that no part is left unsalted. Fowl, therefore, should be opened up properly, so that they may be salted on the inside as well.                                                  [9

10. The salted meat should be put in a place where the blood can drain from it freely. So the draining-basket with the meat in it should not be stood on the ground, for this would impede the free flow of the blood. Even after the meat has remained in its salt for the required period of time prior to rinsing, it should not be put in a place where the blood cannot drain away freely. When it is salted on a board, the board must be set in a sloping position, so that the blood may

flow away freely, and the board should not contain any grooves where brine could collect. When one salts a fowl or a side of meat which has a cavity that forms a receptacle, the hollow side must be turned downwards, so that the blood can drain off freely.                                                                          [10

11. The meat should remain in its salt for one hour, or, in time of emergency, for twenty-four minutes.                                                    [11

12. After the meat has remained in its salt for the prescribed period of time, the salt should be thoroughly dispersed from it, and it should be rinsed three times in water very thoroughly. A God-fearing woman should personally supervise the rinsing of the meat, for sometimes the prohibition against eating blood may — heaven forbid! — be transgressed.                                      [12

13. Care must be taken to remove the heads of fowl before soaking. If the fowl was salted with its head still on, a competent authority should be consulted. Similar care must be taken with regard to cattle.                      [13

14. Meat which has not yet been salted should not be put in a place where there is sometimes salt. A special dish should be set aside solely for such meat, and vegetables or fruit or any such food, which is usually eaten without rinsing, should not be put in this dish, for blood from the meat adheres to the dish, and from the dish it would be transferred to the food.                              [14

15. The head should be split open before soaking, the brains removed and the membrane which covers them torn off. The head should be soaked and salted separately. It must be salted inside and out, but one may salt it with the hair still on it.                                                                                   [15

16. If bones containing marrow are still attached to the meat, they may be salted along with the meat just as they are; but if they are separated from the meat, they should be salted separately and not placed in their salt with the meat.                                                                                       [16

17. It is necessary to cut off the tips of the hooves before soaking the feet of animals, so that the blood can flow from them, and they should be placed in such a way that it can drain out. They may be salted with the hairs still on them.                                                                                       [17

18. The heart must be split open before soaking, so that the blood may be let out from it.                                                                              [18

19. It is likewise customary to cut into the lungs and to open the large tubes in them before soaking.                                                                     [19

20. Liver contains much blood; consequently, it follows directly that it should not be made *kosher* in the same way as other meat, but must be broiled over a fire. First, however, it should be cut open properly and placed with the cut downwards over the fire, so that the fire may draw out all the blood that is in it. It should be rinsed before it is set over the fire, and when it is in place over the fire it should be sprinkled lightly with salt. It should be broiled till it is fit to eat, and then well rinsed to remove the blood which has escaped. Care must be taken to rinse it three times, and after that it may be boiled.                            [20

21. Care must be taken to broil it directly over the fire and not in an oven

from which the coals have been swept out. So too, it may not be broiled while wrapped in paper, no matter how thin the paper may be. [21

22. Liver must not be salted before broiling in the way that meat is salted, and liver should certainly not be salted together with meat. [22

23. The law regarding the spleen is the same as for other meat, save that, prior to soaking, the membrane which is over it must be removed, because it is classed as forbidden fat. It is also necessary to porge it of sinews. The sinew is grasped by the head and pulled out along with the three cords that are in it. Care should be taken not to sever any of these cords; if one is severed, it must be pulled out by the roots. [23

24. The intestines and other entrails should be salted on the exterior surface to which the fat adheres. [24

25. The stomach of a calf must be emptied of any milk that it may contain before it is soaked, and it is then treated like other meat. [25

26. Eggs found in fowl, whether they are very small or fully developed with their shells, must be soaked, salted and rinsed. However, they should not be salted with the meat, but should be put in a place where blood from the meat will not flow on to them. It is forbidden to eat such eggs, even if they are fully developed, along with milk. [26

27. It is forbidden to boil meat which has been kept for three full days, unless it was soaked within that period of time. [27

28. It is customary to singe fowl after they are plucked, to remove the remaining hairs. Care must be taken to singe them only with a flame from burning straw or stubble. One may not make a large flame, and one should take care to move the fowl to and fro over the flame to prevent it from becoming heated. [28

# 6. ETHICAL LITERATURE

*See 1.5. 6.1 is from Pirqei Avot, by far the most popular ethical text in Judaism, and, though untypical of the Mishnah, the best-known Mishnaic tractate. (On the Mishnah in general see 1.4.) Pirqei Avot has been built into the liturgy, and is read at various points in the liturgical year. For this reason it is printed in full in traditional Siddurim. It is in the form of an unsystematic collection of moral maxims. The other two texts in this chapter, however, come from systematic ethical treatises. 6.2 dates from the eleventh century, and 6.3 from the eighteenth.*

### 6.1 MISHNAH, PIRQEI AVOT. MISCELLANEOUS MAXIMS[1]

2:2. Rabban Gamaliel, the son of Rabbi Judah the Prince, says: 'It is an excellent thing to combine the study of Torah with a secular occupation [derekh erez], for the labour necessary for both together puts sin out of mind. But any study of Torah which is not combined with secular employment comes in the end to nothing and brings sin in its train. Let all who work for the congregation do so for the sake of Heaven, for then the merit of their fathers will sustain them, and their righteousness will endure for ever. "And as for you," God will say, "I count you as worthy of a rich reward, as though you had done it all by yourselves." '   [1

2:5. Hillel used to say: 'A boor cannot fear sin, an ignorant man [am ha-arez] cannot be pious [hasid], a timid man cannot learn, a short-tempered man cannot teach, and a man who is too preoccupied with business cannot grow wise. Where there are no men, try to be a man!'   [2

2:9. Rabban Yohanan ben Zakkai said to his pupils: 'Go out and discover what is the good way to which a man should adhere.' Rabbi Eliezer says: 'A good eye.'[2] Rabbi Joshua says: 'A good companion.' Rabbi Yose says: 'A good neighbour.' Rabbi Simeon says: 'He who considers the consequences of his actions.' Rabbi Eleazar says: 'A good heart.' He said to them: 'I prefer the answer of Eleazar ben Arakh, for your answers are included in his.'   [3

2:10. Rabbi Eliezer says: 'Let your friend's honour be as dear to you as your own. Do not be easily provoked to anger. Repent one day before your death.'   [4

3:2. Rabbi Hananyah, the Prefect of the Priests, says: 'Pray for the welfare of the government, since, were it not for the fear it inspires, men would swallow each other alive.'   [5

3:7. Rabbi Simeon says: 'If a man is studying as he walks along the road, and breaks off from his study to exclaim, "How fine is this tree! How fine is this ploughed field!" Scripture regards him as though he were guilty of a mortal sin' (cf. Deut. 4:9).   [6

3:9. Rabbi Haninah ben Dosa says: 'He whose fear of sin comes before his wisdom, his wisdom endures; but he whose wisdom comes before his fear of sin, his wisdom does not endure.'   [7

3.13. Rabbi Aqiva says: 'Joking and frivolity accustom one to immorality. Tradition [masoret] is a fence around the Torah; tithes are a fence around riches; vows are a fence around abstinence; a fence around wisdom is silence.'[8

3:15. Everything is foreseen, yet freedom of choice is given. The world is judged with mercy, yet everything is according to the amount of work.   [9

3:16. Rabbi Aqiva used to say: 'Everything is given on pledge, and a net is spread over all the living. The shop is open, and the shopkeeper gives credit. The ledger lies open, and a hand writes: whoever wants to borrow may come and borrow. But the collectors make their rounds regularly, every day, and exact payment from man with or without his consent. Their claims are well founded, and the judgement is a true one. And everything is prepared for the feast.'   [10

3:17. Rabbi Eleazar ben Azaryah used to say: 'The man whose wisdom exceeds his works – to what may he be compared? To a tree which has many branches but few roots. The wind comes along, uproots it, and overturns it, as Scripture says: "He shall be like a juniper tree in the desert. When good comes, he shall not see it, but he shall dwell in the arid places of the wilderness, in a salt land, where no man can live" (Jer. 17:6). But the man whose works exceed his wisdom – to what may he be compared? To a tree which has few branches but many roots, so that even if all the winds in the world were to come and blow on it, they could not shift it from its place, as Scripture says: "He shall be like a tree planted by the waterside, that spreads out its roots along the stream." When heat comes, it shall not feel it, but its foliage shall stay green. It shall not be troubled in a year of drought, nor cease to bear fruit' (Jer. 17:8). *[11*

4:1. Ben Zoma says: 'Who is wise? The man who learns from all men, as Scripture says: "From *all* my teachers I have gained understanding" (Ps. 119:99). Who is mighty? The man who subdues his evil inclination [*yezer*], as Scripture says: "He who is slow to anger is better than a mighty man, and he who governs his temper than someone who captures a city" (Prov. 16:32). Who is rich? The man who is content with what he has, as Scripture says: "When you eat the fruit of your own labours, you shall be happy, and you shall prosper" (Ps. 128:2) – "you shall be happy" in this world, and "you shall prosper" in the world to come. Who is held in honour? The man who honours his fellow men, as Scripture says: "I will honour those who honour me, and those who despise me shall meet with contempt" (1 Sam. 2:30).' *[12*

4:5. Rabbi Zadoq says: 'Do not make the Torah a crown for self-aggrandisement, nor a spade with which to dig.' So too, Hillel used to say: 'He who puts the crown to his own use shall perish.' From this you learn that anyone who gains personal profit from the words of Torah destroys himself. *[13*

4:16. Rabbi Jacob says: 'This world is like a vestibule leading into the world to come. Prepare yourself in the vestibule, so that you may enter the inner chamber.' *[14*

5:7. The uncultured man has seven characteristics and the wise man seven. The wise man does not speak before someone who is his superior in wisdom. He does not interrupt his fellow when he is speaking. He does not rush to answer. He asks relevant questions and replies in accordance with halakhah. He speaks about first things first, and last things last. As to what he has not heard he says: 'I have not heard it.' He acknowledges the truth. The opposite characteristics are found in the uncultured man. *[15*

5:10. There are four types of men. The man who says: 'What is mine is mine, and what is yours is yours' – this is the average type (Some say it is the type of Sodom [cf. Ezek. 16:49].) The man who says: 'What is mine is yours, and what is yours is mine' – he is an ignoramus [*am ha-arez*]. The man who says: 'What is mine is yours, and what is yours is yours' – he is a saint [*hasid*]. The man who says: 'What is mine is mine, and what is yours is mine' – he is wicked. *[16*

5:11. There are four types of temperament. Easy to provoke and easy to appease – his loss is cancelled by his gain. Hard to provoke and hard to appease – his gain is cancelled by his loss. Hard to provoke and easy to appease

– he is a saint [*hasid*]. Easy to provoke and hard to appease – he is wicked. *[17*

5:13. There are four types of people who give to charity. The man who wants himself to give, but does not want others to give – he begrudges what belongs to others.[3] The man who wants others to give, but will not himself give – he begrudges what belongs to himself. The man who himself gives, and wants others to give as well – he is a saint [*hasid*]. The man who himself does not give, and does not want others to give – he is wicked. *[18*

5:15. There are four types among those who sit before the Sages: the sponge, the funnel, the strainer, and the sieve. The sponge soaks everything up. The funnel takes in at one end and lets out at the other. The strainer lets the wine pass through and retains the lees. The sieve lets out the coarse flour and retains the fine. *[19*

5:16. If love depends on a material cause, when the cause fails, the love fails too; but if love does not depend on such a cause, it will never fail. What love depended on a material cause? Amnon's love for Tamar (2 Sam. 13). What love did not depend on a material cause? The love of David and Jonathan (1 Sam. 18). *[20*

5:21. Judah ben Tema used to say: 'At five years of age – the study of Scripture; at ten – the study of Mishnah; at thirteen – fulfilment of the commandments [*mizvot*]; at fifteen – the study of Talmud; at eighteen – marriage; at twenty – pursuit of a livelihood; at thirty – physical maturity; at forty – understanding; at fifty – counsel; at sixty – old age; at seventy – grey hairs; at eighty – the special strength (Ps. 90:10); at ninety – bent over; at one hundred – as good as dead and gone from the world.' *[21*

## 6.2 BAHYA IBN PAQUDA, *THE DUTIES OF THE HEART*, GATE 5, CH. 5. THE FIGHT AGAINST THE EVIL INCLINATION

You should know, O man, that the greatest enemy you have in the world is your inclination,[4] which is woven into the powers of your soul and intertwined with the constitution of your spirit, sharing with you the direction of your bodily senses and mental faculties. He[5] rules over the secrets of your soul, over the thoughts you keep hidden away in your mind. He is your counsellor in all your actions – seen and unseen – which you perform out of free choice. He lies in wait for your moments of inattention: you may be asleep to him, but he is always awake to you; you may be unaware of him, but he is never unaware of you. He dons for you the robe of friendship, and bedecks himself with the guise of love for you. He becomes one of your confidants and counsellors, one of the sincerest of your friends. He subtly deceives you, going along with what you want with outward signs and gestures of agreement, but all the while he is shooting at you his deadly arrows in order to destroy you, after the fashion of the one of whom Scripture speaks: 'Like a madman shooting deadly darts and arrows, so is the man who deceives his fellow and then says, "I was only joking!" ' (Prov. 26:18–19). [1

The most powerful of his weapons with which he fights you in your innermost being is to try to make you doubt the truths you have accepted, to throw into confusion what you regard as certain, to perplex your soul with lying notions and false arguments, by which he would distract you from your true welfare and confound your firm faith and belief. If you keep on your guard against him and have at the ready the weapons of your mind with which to fight him and turn away his arrows from you, then, with God's help, you will be delivered and saved from him. But if you follow his lead and accept his direction, he will not leave you till he has destroyed you both in this world and the next, and uprooted you from both places, as the saint says of one of the inclination's agents, one of his soldiers: 'The wanton woman has mortally wounded many, the strongest of men have all been her victims. Her house is the way to the netherworld, the descent to the courts of death' (Prov. 7:26–7). So then do not let a conflict with anyone else distract you from your conflict [Arabic, *jihad*] with him, nor war against another prevent you fighting against him. The struggle against a distant foe should not draw you away from the struggle against an enemy who is engaging you at close quarters, and defence against one who cannot approach you without God's permission must not stand in the way of defending yourself against one who requires no permission to be with you. The story is told of a pious man who met some people returning from a campaign against their enemies, with the spoils they had taken after a fierce battle. He said to them: 'You are returning victorious, God be praised, from a little conflict. Prepare yourselves now for the greater conflict!' 'What is this greater conflict?' they asked him. 'The conflict [Arabic, *jihad*] against the inclination and his armies,' he replied. [2

It is indeed astonishing, O my brother, that every other enemy you have, when you have defeated him once or twice, leaves you alone: it never occurs to him to go on fighting you, since he knows your power is greater than his, and he is in despair of ever overcoming you or gaining a victory over you. The inclination, however, is never convinced – whether you defeat him once or a hundred times. You may defeat him or he may defeat you: if he defeats you, he will kill you, but if you defeat him once, he will lie in wait for you as long as you live to overcome you, as our ancient sages said: 'Do not trust yourself till the day of your death' (Mishnah, Pirqei Avot 2:4). [3

He does not regard the most trivial of your affairs as too insignificant a means of overcoming you. It serves him a stepping-stone, enabling him to vanquish you in more important matters. So you should always be on your guard against him. Indeed, you should regard as important your smallest victory, the least increase of your power over him, and use it as a stepping-stone to greater conquests. For he is quick to submit to you, and has not the strength to resist you, if you stand up to him, as Scripture says: 'To you shall be his desire, and you shall rule over him' (Gen. 4:7). So do not let his authority terrify you, even if his retinue is great, nor his high rank frighten you, even though his aides are many. For his chief aim is to make what is false seem true; it is his primary intention to establish the lie. And yet, how swift is his downfall, how soon he is destroyed, if you but realise his weakness! The sage well described him in the following verse: 'Once there was a small city, with few inhabitants in it, and a mighty king came against it, and besieged it, and built great bulwarks against it. But a poor, wise man was found in it, who by his wisdom saved the city' (Eccl. 9:14–15). /4

Man is described here as 'a small city', because he is a microcosm. The limbs of his body and the faculties of his soul are referred to in the phrase, 'few inhabitants'. The sage thinks little of them, because though man's ambition is great and his desires many in this world, he lacks strength and achieves little in it. The inclination is called 'a great king' because he commands large armies and his followers and servants are numerous. It says, 'he besieged it', because the inclination embraces all of a man's affairs, both secret and open alike. The phrase 'and built great bulwarks against it' refers to the evil imaginations, bad thoughts and improper suggestions with which the inclination strives to work the destruction of man, as we shall explain further on in this chapter. The saying 'but a poor, wise man was found in it' contains an allusion to the intellect which is described as 'poor' because its retinue is small and its aides few, as the text goes on to say: 'Yet no one remembered that same poor man. Now I say: Wisdom is better than strength, yet a poor man's wisdom is despised and his words are disregarded' (Eccl. 9:16). Since the inclination is weak, the text describes how quickly it capitulates to the intellect when it struggles with the intellect, and how easily the intellect shields man from being harmed by the inclination. For a little truth overcomes much falsehood, and a little light dispels great darkness. This should serve to spur us on to fight against our desires and to resist the inclination with energy and gusto, for we know that the inclination is too weak to stand up to the intellect and quickly capitulates to it, as Scripture says: 'The evil bow down before the good, the wicked at the gates of the righteous' (Prov. 14:19). /5

## 6.3 M. H. LUZZATO, *THE PATH OF THE UPRIGHT*, CH. 13. ON ABSTINENCE[6]

Abstinence [*perishut*] is the beginning of saintliness [*hasidut*]. Observe that all we have so far said explains what a man must do to be righteous [*zaddiq*]; now we must explain what he must do to be saintly [*hasid*]. Abstinence stands in the same relationship to saintliness as watchfulness does to zeal, for abstinence and watchfulness involve the avoidance of evil, whereas saintliness and zeal involve the positive performance of good. Our Sages laid down the basic principle of abstinence when they said: 'Sanctify yourself through that which is permitted to you' (Babylonian Talmud, Yevamot 20a). This is the meaning of the term itself: 'abstinence' denotes withdrawing and keeping away from things. It implies that one forbids oneself the enjoyment of things permitted, with the intention of avoiding contact with things in themselves forbidden. To practise abstinence means to shun and avoid anything that could become a cause of evil, even though at present it is not such a cause, and is not, indeed, intrinsically evil.                                                                              [1

Mark well and observe that three stages are involved here. We have, in the first place, the prohibitions laid down in the Torah; secondly, we have the 'fences' to those prohibitions, that is, the decrees and safeguards imposed by our Sages on all Israel; thirdly, we have the precautionary measures which should be taken by anyone who would be abstinent. Such a one must restrict his field of action and erect barriers for himself, that is he must deny himself and avoid things in themselves permitted and not normally forbidden to any Jew, in order to place himself at the farthest possible remove from evil. You will say, 'What right have we to go on adding to the prohibitions?' Our Sages have said: 'Are you so dissatisfied with what the Torah has prohibited that you want to impose yet further restrictions on yourself?' (Jerusalem Talmud, Nedarim 9:1, 41b). Our Sages have already instituted all the prohibitions and safeguards which in their wisdom they saw to be necessary. If they have allowed anything, it is because they considered it right to permit it, and not prohibit it. Why, then, should we impose new ordinances which they did not think it proper to impose? There is no end to this business. At this rate men will end up as tortured ascetics, deriving no enjoyment whatsoever from the world. Our Sages taught that a man will be held accountable before the Omnipresent One for refusing to enjoy whatever his eyes saw, even though it was permitted and he had opportunity to do so (Jerusalem Talmud, Qiddushin 4:12, 66d). And they can find direct support for this view in the verse: 'I denied my eyes nothing they desired' (Eccl. 2:10).                                                                          [2

My answer is that it is most emphatically necessary and obligatory to practise abstinence. The Sages warned us of this when they interpreted the commandment 'Be holy' (Lev. 19:2) as meaning 'Be abstinent' (Sifra to Lev. 19:2). They also said: 'Whoever observes a fast is called holy – *qal va-homer* than a Nazirite' (see below, 'Luzzato's sources', Text A). Again they said: 'The verse "The righteous man eats only to satisfy his hunger" (Prov. 13:25) applies to Hezekiah king of Judah. It was said of him that he ordered only two bunches of vegetables and a pound of meat to be set before him as his daily fare, and Israel ridiculed him for it and said: "This fellow calls himself a king!"' ' (Pesiqta deRav Kahana 6:2). Again the Sages reported that when our holy teacher [i.e. Rabbi Judah ha-Nasi] was on his deathbed, he raised his ten fingers and said: 'It is known and revealed before you, O God, that I have not derived any enjoyment from this world, even with my little finger!' (Babylonian Talmud, Ketubbot 104a). They further maintained that while a man should pray for the words of Torah to become part of him, he should pray that eating and drinking should not become part of him (cf. Yalqut Shim'oni, Deut. 830). All these sayings clearly teach that abstinence is both a necessity and a duty. On the other hand we must try to explain the sayings which teach the contrary view. The fact is that many fundamental distinctions are involved here. There is a form of abstinence which we are commanded to practice, and there is a form of abstinence against which we are warned, lest it should lead us into sin. It is to the latter that king Solomon referred when he said: 'Do not be over-righteous' (Eccl. 7:16). . . . 	[3

True abstinence means that we take from the world in whatever use we make of it only what is indispensable because of some natural need we have for it. That is why Rabbi [Judah ha-Nasi], in the saying I mentioned, gloried in the fact that he had not derived any enjoyment from this world, even with his little finger, although he was a prince of Israel and had to maintain a royal table in keeping with the dignity of his office. (According to the tradition of our Sages the verse 'Two nations are in your womb' (Gen. 25:23) refers to Rabbi and the emperor Antoninus, whose tables never lacked lettuces, cucumbers, and radishes, either in summer or in winter. The same was true of Hezekiah king of Judah [Babylonian Talmud, Avodah Zarah 11a].) All the other sayings I quoted affirm and teach that a man should abstain from all worldly pleasure so as to avoid falling into its dangers. 	[4

Perhaps you will ask and say: 'If, then, abstinence is necessary and obligatory, why have the Sages not enacted laws about it in the way they have enacted laws about the "fences" and the ordinances which they have instituted?' The answer is plain and simple. The Sages have enacted only such laws as the greater part of the community are able to obey. But the greater part of the community cannot be saints; it is enough for them to be righteous. However, the remaining few of the people who desire to be counted worthy to draw near to God, and by their own merit impute merit to the mass of the people dependent on them, are obliged to fulfil the special law for saints [mishnat hasidim], which the average person is unable to fulfil, that is, the rules of abstinence which I have described. God has so ordained it that, since it is impossible for a whole people to be at one and the same level of attainment (different people are at different stages of development, each in accordance with his intellectual capacity), at least a chosen few would be found who would submit themselves to a total discipline, and through their agency those not under such rigorous discipline would also merit God's love and the abiding of his Shekhinah. This accords with the Sages' symbolical explanation of the four species in the ceremony of the lulav [on the festival of Sukkot]: 'These shall come and make atonement for those' (see below, 'Luzzato's sources', Text B). We also find Elijah making the same point in the answer he gave to Rabbi Joshua ben Levi in the story about Ulla bar Qoshev. When Joshua defended his action by pleading, 'Is it not the law [mishnah]?' Elijah retorted: 'But is it the law for saints [mishnat hasidim]?' (see below, 'Luzzato's sources', Text C). 	[5

The wrong kind of abstinence is that practised by the foolish gentiles. They are not content with refusing to take from the world what is not essential, but deny themselves what is essential as well, and afflict their bodies with torments and strange practises such as the Lord abhors. The Sages, by way of contrast, maintained that it is forbidden for a man to afflict himself (Babylonian Talmud, Ta'anit 22b). With regard to charity they said: 'Anyone in need of charity who refuses to accept it sheds blood' (Jerusalem Talmud, Peah 8:9, 21b). They took the verse 'And man became a living soul' (Gen. 2:7) as implying that God commands man: 'Keep alive the soul which I have placed within you' (Babylonian Talmud, Ta'anit 22b). They said: 'He who observes a fast is called a sinner,' and they applied this dictum to 'one who is not able to bear self-affliction' (see below, 'Luzzato's sources', Text A). Hillel used to say that the verse 'The pious man [*ish hasid*] does good to his own soul' (Prov. 11:17) refers to eating a hearty breakfast. He used to wash his face and hands in honour of his Creator, arguing by *qal va-homer* from the practice of washing the royal images (see below, 'Luzzato's sources', Text D). So the true principle is that a man should abstain from any of the things of this world which are not essential to him; but if anything is essential to him for any reason whatsoever, he is counted a sinner, should he abstain from it, since it is indispensable. This is an invariable rule. However, the way this general principle is to be applied in concrete instances must be left to each man's discretion: 'a man deserves praise in proportion to his understanding' (Prov. 12:8). It is impossible to collect all the concrete instances: they are too numerous, and the human mind could not grasp them all together; rather it must deal with each separate case as it arises.                                                                                  [6

### Luzzato's sources

*Text A.* Samuel said: 'Whoever observes a fast is called a sinner.' He holds the same view as the Tanna who taught: 'Rabbi Eleazar ha-Qappar Berabbi says: What does Scripture mean when it says: "The priest shall make atonement for the Nazirite, since he sinned against the soul" (Num. 6:11)? Against whose soul did he sin? Against his own, in that he denied himself wine.' We can now reason by *qal va-homer*: If the Nazirite who denied himself only wine is called a sinner, how much more so someone who denies himself all life's pleasures. Rabbi Eleazar says: 'Whoever observes a fast is called holy, as Scripture says: "The Nazirite shall be holy; he shall let the locks of the hair on his head grow long" (Num. 6:5). If the Nazirite who denied himself only wine is called holy, how much more someone who denies himself all life's pleasures.' How can Samuel explain the fact that the Nazirite is called holy? By arguing that the term is applied to him only because he let his hair grow long. And how can Rabbi Eleazar explain the fact that the Nazirite is called a sinner? By arguing that this term is applied to him only because he defiled himself by contact with a corpse. But did Rabbi Eleazar really say this? Did he not say: 'A man should always consider himself as if the Holy One dwells within him, as Scripture says, "The Holy One in the midst of you" (Hos. 11:9)'? There is no contradiction here, for in the one instance he has in mind someone who is able to bear self-affliction, and in the other someone who is not. (Babylonian Talmud, Ta'anit 11a–11b)                                                 [7

*Text B. The fruit of goodly trees* (Lev. 23:40). This symbolises Israel: just as the *etrog* has taste as well as fragrance, so there are in Israel men who possess both Torah and good deeds. *Branches of palm trees.* This also symbolises Israel: just as the palm tree has taste but no fragrance, so there are in Israel men who possess Torah, but not good deeds. *Boughs of thick trees.* This also symbolises Israel: just as the myrtle has fragrance but no taste, so there are in Israel men who possess good deeds but not Torah. *Willows of the brook.* This also symbolises Israel: just as the willow has neither taste nor fragrance, so there are in Israel men who possess neither Torah nor good deeds. What, then, does the Holy One, blessed be he, do to them? To destroy them would be impossible. 'Rather,' says the Holy One, 'let them all be tied together in one bunch, and these will make atonement for those.' (Leviticus Rabbah 30:12)                [8

*Text C.* It was taught: A company of Jews were travelling along the road when some gentiles met them and said: 'Give us one of your number that we may kill him, otherwise we will kill all of you!' Even if all of them should be killed, they may not hand over one soul of Israel. But if the gentiles specified a particular person, as happened in the case of Sheva ben Bikhri (2 Sam. 20:21–2), they may hand him over to prevent everyone being killed. Rabbi Simeon ben Laqish said: 'They may do so only if the person was, like Sheva ben Bikhri, worthy of death.' Rabbi Yohanan said: 'They may do so, even if the person was not, like Sheva ben Bikhri, worthy of death.' Ulla bar Qoshev was wanted by the government. He fled for asylum to Rabbi Joshua ben Levi at Lod. The government forces came and surrounded the town. They said: 'If you do not surrender him to us, we will destroy the town.' Rabbi Joshua went up to Ulla bar Qoshev and persuaded him to give himself up. Elijah used to appear to Rabbi Joshua, but from that moment on he ceased to do so. Rabbi Joshua fasted many days, and finally Elijah revealed himself to him. 'Am I supposed to appear to informers?' he asked. Rabbi Joshua said: 'I followed the law [*mishnah*].' Elijah retorted: 'But is it the law for saints [*mishnat hasidim*]?' (Jerusalem Talmud, Terumot 8:10, 46b)[7]                [9

*Text D.* The verse 'The merciful man does good to his own soul' (Prov. 11:17) applies to Hillel the elder. Once when he had finished teaching his students he was walking along with them. His students said to him: 'Rabbi, where are you going?' He answered: 'To perform a religious duty [*mizvah*].' 'What duty is that?' they asked. He said: 'To wash in the bath-house.' They said: 'Is that a religious duty?' 'Yes,' he replied. 'If the official appointed to look after the statues of the emperors erected in the theatres and circuses scrubs and cleans them, and receives maintenance for so doing, and, indeed, is regarded as occupying an important office, how much more should I wash myself, seeing that I have been created in God's image and likeness, as Scripture says: "In the image of God he made man" (Gen. 9:6).' Another interpretation of 'The merciful man does good to his own soul' also applies it to Hillel the elder. Once when he had finished teaching his students, he was walking along with them. His students said to him: 'Rabbi, where are you going?' He answered: 'To bestow kindness on a guest in my house.' They said to him: 'Do you have a guest every day?' He replied: 'Is not the poor soul a guest in the body – here today and gone tomorrow!' (Leviticus Rabbah 34:3)                                    *[10*

# 7. PHILOSOPHY AND THEOLOGY

*See 1.6. All the texts quoted in this chapter belong to the classic medieval period of Jewish theology (tenth to twelfth centuries C.E.), when philosophical ideas entered mainstream Judaism for the first time. 7.3 is by far the most important single statement of Jewish theology, and is a good place to begin the study of this section. In shortened form it has been incorporated into the prayer books. 7.2 contains a useful, if rather technical, summary of the teachings of the philosophers. Sa'adiah, the author of 7.1, was the father of rabbinic theology. For a passage from Mendelssohn, the father of modern Jewish thought, see 9.3.1 below.*

## 7.1 SA'ADIAH GAON, *THE BOOK OF BELIEFS AND OPINIONS*, INTRODUCTION, SECTION 6. THE RELATIONSHIP BETWEEN FAITH AND REASON

The reader of this book should know that we inquire into and speculate on the teachings of our religion for two reasons: first, to find out for ourselves what we have learned as imparted knowledge from the prophets of God; and secondly, to be able to refute anyone who argues against us concerning anything to do with our religion. Our Lord has instructed us in all we need to know about the teachings of our religion through the agency of his prophets, having first confirmed by signs and miracles that they possessed the gift of prophecy. He commanded us to believe those teachings and keep them in mind. He also informed us that, when we engage in speculation and inquiry, true and complete inquiry will in every instance agree with what he has already told us through the words of his messengers; and he has given us an assurance that infidels will never be able to offer proof nor sceptics valid arguments against our religion. . . .                                                                      *[1*

In this way we engage in speculation and inquiry, so as to make our own what our Lord has taught us by way of imparted knowledge. This inevitably raises a point which we must now consider. It may be asked: 'If the teachings of religion can be discovered by correct inquiry and speculation, as our Lord has informed us, what prompted his wisdom to transmit them to us through prophecy and to confirm them by visible, miraculous proofs, rather than by rational demonstrations?' To this question, with God's help, we will give a complete answer. We say: God in his wisdom knew that the conclusions achieved by skill in reasoning can only be reached after the lapse of a certain interval of time. If, therefore, he had left us to depend on such conclusions for our religious knowledge, we would have remained for a time without religion, till the process of reasoning had been completed and our labour had come to an end. It is possible that many of us would never have completed the process because of our intellectual deficiencies, nor finished the work on account of impatience. Or doubts could have overwhelmed us, confusing and hindering us. That is why God saved us quickly from all these troubles by sending us his Messenger [Moses] through whom he transmitted the truths directly to us, and before our very eyes he confirmed those truths with signs and proofs which doubt could not assail and which we could not possibly reject, as Scripture says: 'You yourselves have seen that I talked with you from heaven' (Exod. 20:19). He spoke to his Messenger in our presence, and made it an obligation to believe his Messenger for ever, as Scripture says: 'So that the people may hear when I speak to you, and may also believe you for ever' (Exod. 19:9). *[2*

Thus we were obliged at once to accept the teachings of religion, together with all that they implied, because they had been verified by the testimony of the senses. (We are also obliged to accept them on the grounds that they have been passed on to us fully authenticated by reliable tradition, as we shall explain later.) But God commanded us to take our time with our rational inquiries till we should arrive by argument at the truth of religion, and not to abandon our quest till we have found convincing arguments in favour of it and are compelled to believe God's revelation by what our eyes have seen and our ears heard. In the case of some of us our inquiries may take a long time before they are completed, but that should not worry us; no one prevented by any hindrance from pursuing his investigations is left without religious guidance. Even women and children and those with no aptitude for speculation can attain to a complete religion, for all men are on an equal footing as far as knowledge derived from the senses is concerned. Praised be God who in his wisdom ordered things thus! This is why you often find in the Torah the women and the children included with the fathers when signs and miracles are mentioned. *[3*

To make this matter clearer we could compare it to the case of a man who out of a sum of 1,000 dirhems distributes the following: to five men, 20 dirhems each; to six men $16\frac{2}{3}$ dirhems each; to seven men $14\frac{2}{7}$ dirhems each; to eight men $12\frac{1}{2}$ dirhems each; to nine men $11\frac{1}{9}$ dirhems each. He now wishes to let his friends know quickly how much money he has left, so he tells them that the remainder amounts to 500 dirhems and proves his statement by weighing the money. When he has quickly weighed it and found it to be 500 dirhems, they are obliged to believe what he told them. They can now take as long as they like to reach the same conclusion by calculation, each according to his ability and understanding and the difficulties he may encounter. Or we could compare the matter to the case of a man who, on being told of an illness accompanied by certain pathological conditions, immediately identifies what the illness is from some characteristic symptom, and whose diagnosis is later confirmed by someone investigating the illness by means of an exhaustive inquiry.          [4

## 7.2 JUDAH HA-LEVI, *THE KUZARI*, 5:14–19. THE TEACHINGS OF THE PHILOSOPHERS AND THE THEOLOGIANS

14. *The Jewish scholar* [*haver*]. The ancient philosophers could justify their recourse to rational argument on the grounds that they did not have the benefit of prophecy or of the light of revelation. They brought the sciences concerned with proof to the highest pitch of perfection and devoted themselves single-mindedly to them. In these sciences there are no differences of opinion between them. But it is hard to find them agreeing in the subjects which come after these sciences – in metaphysics and, indeed, often in physics as well. Should you find a number of them agreeing on some particular point, it is not because of any independent investigation they have carried out, or because they have reached the same conclusion, but it is because they form the school of some philosopher whose views they blindly follow (such as the school of Pythagoras, or the school of Empedocles, or the school of Aristotle, or the school of Plato), or it is because they follow the Companions of the Porch [the Stoics], or the Peripatetics, who are a part of the school of Aristotle.          [1

On fundamental principles the philosophers hold opinions which are absurd to the intellect, and which the intellect treats with contempt. Such, for example, is their explanation of the revolution of the celestial sphere. They state that the sphere seeks for a perfection which it lacks, namely, to occupy all possible spatial positions. Since it cannot achieve such a state simultaneously in respect of each of its constituent parts, it attempts to achieve it by occupying each possible position in turn. Equally false is their opinion regarding the emanations which flow from the First Cause. They maintain that from an angel's knowledge of the First Cause there arises of necessity another angel, and from the angel's knowledge of itself there arises a sphere; and so the process of emanation advances step by step down through eleven stages till the emanations come to an end with the Active Intellect from which arises neither an angel nor a sphere. And they hold other views like these which are less convincing than those advanced in the *Sefer Yezirah*.[1] All these opinions are highly dubious, and it is impossible to find any two philosophers agreeing on them. However, we should not blame the philosophers for this. Rather, they deserve our praise for what they managed to achieve simply through the force of rational argument. Their intentions were good, they established the laws of thought, and they rejected the pleasures of this world. They may, in any case, be granted superiority, since they were not obliged to accept our opinions. We, however, are obliged to accept whatever we see with our own eyes, or any well founded tradition, which is tantamount to seeing for oneself.          [2

15. *The Khazar king*. Please give me a brief account of the views held by the

theologians whom the Qaraites call the 'Masters of the Science of Kalam'.    *[3*

16. *The Jewish scholar.* This would have no value – save as an exercise in dialectics, or as in aid to fulfilling the injunction of the Sages, 'Take care how to reply to an Epicurean' (Mishnah, Pirqei Avot 2:14). A simple, wise man, such as a prophet, can impart little to others by way of instruction, nor can he solve a problem by dialectic methods, whereas the Master of Kalam has such an aura of learning that those who hear him regard him as superior to the simple, pious man whose learning consists of beliefs which no one can induce him to abandon. Yet the supreme achievement for the Master of Kalam, in all that he learns and teaches, would be that there should enter into his own soul and into the souls of his students those very beliefs which are implanted naturally in the soul of the simple man. It can happen that the science of Kalam destroys many true beliefs in a man's heart by introducing him to doubts and conflicting opinions. The Masters of Kalam are like experts on poetic metres who investigate scansion. Such experts make a great fuss and use a lot of formidable terms to describe a skill which comes easily to the naturally gifted poet, who senses the metre and so never breaks in any way the rules of scansion. The ultimate achievement for the prosodic expert would be to acquire the skill of the natural poet, who appears ignorant of scansion because he cannot teach it, in contrast to the expert who can. As a matter of fact the naturally gifted person can teach someone as gifted as himself, by the merest hint. The same may be said about those who possess a natural aptitude for living in accordance with the divine law and for drawing near to God: through the words of the pious, sparks are kindled in their souls, which become rays of illumination in their hearts. A man not endowed with such a natural gift must resort, perforce, to the Kalam, which may not bring him any benefit, and may possibly cause him positive harm.    *[4*

17. *The Khazar king.* I do not want a lengthy exposition of the subject; rather all I ask for is a summary of the basic principles, to serve me as an *aide-mémoire*, for I have already heard something of them, and my soul desires to know more.    *[5*

18. *The Jewish scholar. First principle.* The first point to be established is that the world was originated. This may be demonstrated by refuting the contrary view that it is eternal. If the past were without beginning, then the number of individuals existing in the period stretching from the past down to our own time would be infinite. But that which is infinite can never become actual. How, then, did those individuals become actual, if they were so numerous as to be infinite? There can be no doubt, therefore, that the past had a beginning and that the number of individuals that have existed is finite. For although it is within the power of the intellect to count thousands and millions multiplied without end, this is possible only potentially; no one could achieve it in actuality. Anything that comes to actuality is counted as a single entity, and so too any number which has become actual must undoubtedly be finite, for how could that which is infinite ever have become actual? So the world had a beginning and the celestial sphere has performed only a finite number of

revolutions.                                                                        [6
Furthermore, neither division nor multiplication nor any numerical ratio can apply to that which is infinite. Yet we know that the revolutions of the sun are one-twelfth those of the moon, and that the other movements of the celestial spheres stand in similar relationships to each other, so that one can be expressed as a fraction of the other. But fractions cannot apply to what is infinite, so how could all these movements be infinite when some fall short of or exceed others, that is to say, are greater or less in magnitude?                                    [7
Furthermore, how could that which is infinite ever have reached us? If an infinite number of created beings preceded us, how could the number ever have terminated with us? That which reaches an end must have had a beginning, for were this not so, then every individual before coming into existence would have had to await the coming into being of an infinite series of individuals preceding him, and so no one would ever come into existence.                            [8

*Second principle.* The world is originated because it is a body. A body must be either in a state of motion or in a state of rest. The state emerging in the body is obviously originated, as may be seen from the simple fact of its emergence; the antecedent state which it replaces must also be originated, for had it been pre-existent it could never have suffered extinction. Both motion and rest, therefore, are originated attributes. But whatever is inseparable from originated attributes must itself be originated, since it could not have existed prior to those attributes, and if the attributes are originated, then it must be originated as well.                                                            [9

*Third principle.* Whatever is originated must have a cause which originated it, for whatever is originated must have come into being at a specific point in time. It would have been possible to have assigned it to an earlier or a later time, so the fact that it came into being when it did and not earlier or later, testifies to the existence of a cause which assigned it to that specific point in time.        [10

*Fourth principle.* God is pre-existent, and there never was a time when he was not; for had he been originated he would have required an originator, and so we would find ourselves caught in an infinite regress. But it is impossible that we should not come in the end to a pre-existent Creator who is the First Cause, and he is the one whom we seek.                                                    [11

*Fifth principle.* God is everlasting and will never pass away. A being whose pre-existence has been established cannot cease to be. The emergence of non-existence as much requires a cause as the emergence of existence. Nothing is annihilated through its own agency, but through the agency of an opposing force. God, however, can neither have an opposite nor a like. Anything like him in every respect would be identical to him and could not be conceived of as distinct from him. On the other hand, an opposing, annihilating force could not share pre-existence with him, for it has already been shown that God's existence is prior to that of everything else. Nor is it possible that the annihilating force could have been originated, for everything that is originated depends for its existence on the pre-existent Cause, and it is surely inconceivable that that which has been caused should annihilate the cause which brought it into being. [12

*Sixth principle.* God is not a body, for a body is inseparable from originated attributes, and whatever is inseparable from originated attributes is itself originated. So, too, it is false to regard God as an accident, for an accident can subsist only in the body which bears it: the accident depends for its existence on the body, adhering to it and being borne by it. Nor is God defined or delimited by any of the dimensions of space, for this is one of the characteristics of a body. [13

*Seventh principle.* God knows everything, both that which is universal and that which is particular. Nothing escapes his knowledge, for it has been shown that he created, ordered and arranged everything, as Scripture says: 'Is the one who planted the ear unable to hear? The creator of the eye unable to see?' (Ps. 94:9). Again it says: 'Darkness would not be dark to you' (Ps. 139:12). And again: 'It was you who created my innermost being' (Ps. 139:13). [14

*Eighth principle.* God is living. Since it has already been established that God possesses knowledge and power, then the fact that he possesses life has been established as well. His life, however, is not as our life which is defined by sensation and motion. Rather his life consists of pure thought, and his life is identical with him and he with it. [15

*Ninth principle.* God possesses will. With regard to everything that issues from before him, the possibility exists that its opposite could have issued, or that it might not have come into being at all, or that it could have issued earlier than it did or later. God's power encompasses equally the different possibilities. We need, therefore, to postulate the presence of a will directing God's power to one of the possibilities to the exclusion of the other. It is also possible to say that God's knowledge is alone sufficient, without speaking of power or will, since his knowledge is specific to one of the contrary possibilities. God's pre-existent knowledge, then, would be the cause of everything that happens. This agrees with the opinion of the philosophers. [16

*Tenth principle.* God's will is pre-existent and accords with his knowledge; therefore nothing new emerges in this will, nor does it undergo any change. God lives with the life of his own essence, not with an acquired life; so too he is powerful through his power and willing through his will, for it is impossible for a thing and that which negates it to coexist; hence one may not make the unqualified statement 'He is powerful without power'. [17

19. *The Khazar king.* This is sufficient to refresh my memory. Without doubt what you have related about the soul and the intellect and about these articles of belief comes from your recollection of what others have said. Now I would like to hear your own opinions and your own creed. You have already said to me that you intend to investigate these and similar matters. In my view you cannot avoid discussing the problem of predestination and freewill, since it is a question of such importance for human conduct. So tell me now your views on this point. [18

## 7.3 MAIMONIDES, *COMMENTARY ON THE MISHNAH*, SANHEDRIN 10 (HELEQ). THE THIRTEEN FUNDAMENTAL PRINCIPLES OF THE JEWISH FAITH

The basic tenets of our Torah and its fundamental principles are thirteen in number:

*The first fundamental principle* is the existence of the Creator. There is a being who exists in the most perfect mode of existence, and he is the cause of the existence of all other beings. In him is the source of their existence, and from him their continued existence derives. If we could imagine the elimination of his existence, then the existence of every other being would be annulled and nothing would remain in being. But if we could eliminate the existence of all other beings, then his existence would not be annulled or diminished, for he depends for his existence on none beside himself. Everything apart from him, the Intelligences (that is, the angels), the bodies of the spheres, and whatever is beneath them – all depend for their existence on him. This first fundamental principle is taught in the verse: 'I am the Lord your God' (Exod. 20:2).      [1

*The second fundamental principle* is the unity of God. The Cause of all things is one, not with the oneness of a genus or a species, nor with the oneness of a single composite human being who may be divided into many discrete elements. Nor is his oneness like that of a simple body which is numerically one, but capable of infinite subdivision and fragmentation. Rather he is one with a oneness that is absolutely unique. This second fundamental principle is taught in the verse: 'Hear, O Israel: the Lord our God, the Lord is One' (Deut. 6:4).      [2

*The Third fundamental principle* is the denial of corporeality to God. This One is neither a body nor a force in a body. None of the accidents of bodies, such as motion and rest, appertain to him either by essence or by accident. That is why the Sages denied to him composition and separation when they said: 'In heaven above there is neither sitting nor standing, neither *oref* nor *ippui*' (Babylonian Talmud, Hagigah 15a); that is to say, neither 'separation [*oref*], nor 'composition' [*ippui*], for the sense of *ippui* may be determined from the verse *Ve-afu be-khatef pelishtim* (Isa. 11:14), which means: 'They shall push them with their shoulders so as to mass them together'. The prophet said: 'To whom will you compare God?' (Isa. 40:18); and again: 'To whom will you compare me, whom do I resemble?' (Isa. 40:25). If God were a body, then he would be like other bodies. Wherever Scripture describes him as having the attributes of bodies, such as movement, standing, sitting, speaking and so on, it speaks metaphorically, as the Sages have said: 'The Torah speaks in the language of men' (Babylonian Talmud, Berakhot 31b). People have already had much to say on this subject. This third fundamental principle is taught in the verse: 'You saw no image' (Deut. 4:15), which means: 'You did not perceive him as having an image', for, as we have stated, he is neither a body nor a force in a body.      [3

*The fourth fundamental principle* is God's pre-existence. This One whom we have described precedes all things absolutely. No other being has pre-existence in relation to him. The proofs of this in Scripture are numerous. This fourth fundamental principle is taught in the verse: 'The pre-existent God [*Elohei qedem*]² is a refuge' (Deut. 33:27). *[4*

Know that one of the great principles of the Torah of Moses our Teacher is that the world is originated: God brought it into being and created it after absolute non-existence. The reason you see me dwelling so much on this question of the pre-existence of the world as taught by the philosophers, is to make possible the demonstration of God's existence, as I have explained and made clear in the *Guide of the Perplexed* [II 15–19]. *[5*

*The fifth fundamental principle* is that God is the one who should be worshipped and exalted, whose greatness should be proclaimed, and whom men should be called on to obey. We should not act thus towards anything beneath him in existence, whether angels, or stars, or spheres, or elements, or things compounded of them, for all these have been imprinted with their functions: they have no independent judgement or free-will, but only love for God. We should not adopt intermediaries through whom to approach God, but should direct our thoughts towards him and turn away from whatever is beneath him. This fifth fundamental principle is the prohibition against idolatry. The greater part of the Torah is taken up with forbidding idolatry. *[6*

*The sixth fundamental principle* is prophecy. It should be known that there exist in the human species certain persons of a vastly superior disposition and a high degree of perfection. If their souls are so trained that they receive the form of the intellect, then that human intellect will unite with the Active Intellect, from which a beneficent emanation will flow to it. Such people are prophets; this process is prophecy; this is the true meaning of prophecy. A full explanation of this principle would be very lengthy. It is not our intention to offer proofs for each of the principles or to explain in what ways they are to be understood, for that would involve the sum of all the sciences. Rather we shall state them in the form of simple assertions. The verses of the Torah testifying to the prophecy of the prophets are numerous. *[7*

*The seventh fundamental principle* is the prophecy of Moses our Teacher. We should believe that Moses was the father of all the prophets, both of those who came before him and those who followed him: all of them were inferior to him in rank. He was the one specially chosen by God out of the whole human species. He comprehended more of God than anyone in the past or the future ever comprehended or will comprehend. He reached such a state of exaltation beyond ordinary mortals that he attained angelic status and was included in the order of the angels. There remained no veil before him which he did not penetrate; no bodily hindrance stood in his way; no defect small or great marred him. The imaginative and sensual faculties in his perceptions were neutralised, his desiderative faculty was inoperative, and he remained pure intellect alone. It was for this reason it was said of him that he conversed with God without the mediation of an angel. *[8*

I had intended to explain here this extraordinary subject and to open up secrets locked away in the text of the Torah; to explain the meaning of the expression 'mouth to mouth' (Num. 12:8), and the rest of the verse where it occurs, as well as the other verses dealing with the same subject. But I saw that this subject is very subtle and would require extensive treatment with introductions and illustrations. It would be necessary first to make clear the existence of the angels and the difference between their ranks and that of the Creator. The soul and all its faculties would have to be explained. The circle would have to be widened to include a discussion of the images which the prophets attribute to the Creator and his angels. For this subject alone a hundred pages would not suffice, even if I confined the discussion within the narrowest possible bounds. For this reason I shall leave it to its proper place, either in the 'Treatise on the Explanation of the Midrashim [*derashot*]' which I have promised, or in the 'Treatise on Prophecy' which I have begun to compose,[3] or in a commentary which I shall write on these fundamental principles. [9

I shall now come back to the point of this seventh fundamental principle and say that the prophecy of Moses our Teacher differs from the prophecy of all other prophets in four respects.

The first difference: To every other prophet that ever was God spoke only through a mediator, but to Moses without a mediator, as Scripture says: 'Mouth to mouth I speak with him' (Num. 12:8). [10

The second difference: To every other prophet inspiration came only in a state of sleep, as Scripture says in various places: 'In a dream of the night' (Gen. 31:24); 'He had a dream' (Gen. 28:12); 'By dreams and visions that come in the night' (Job 33:15); and there are many other verses of similar import. Or if inspiration came during the day, it was only after a deep sleep had fallen upon the prophet and his condition had become such that all his senses were inoperative and his mind was as empty as in sleep. This condition is called 'vision' [*mahazeh*] and 'apparition' [*mar'ah*], and is referred to in the phrase 'Visions from God' [*mar'ot Elohim*] (Ezek. 8:3). But to Moses the word came in the daytime, when he was standing between the two cherubim, as God had promised him: 'There I will meet with you and speak with you' (Exod. 25:22). God also said: 'If there is a prophet among you, I the Lord will make myself known to him in a vision, and will speak with him in a dream. Not so with Moses my servant . . . with him I speak mouth to mouth' (Num. 12:6–7). [11

The third difference: When inspiration came to any other prophet, even if in a vision or through the mediation of an angel, his faculties grew weak, his body became agitated, and a very great terror fell on him, so that he was almost crushed by it. This may be illustrated from the case of Daniel. When Gabriel spoke with him in a vision Daniel said: 'No strength remained in me, my appearance was altered beyond recognition, what strength I had deserted me' (Dan. 10:8). He also said: 'I fell unconscious, face downwards on the ground' (Dan. 10:9). And again: 'At the vision my anguish overcomes me' (Dan. 10:16).

But it was not like this with Moses. The word came to him, but no agitation of any kind befell him, as Scripture says: 'The Lord spoke to Moses face to face, as a man speaks to his friend' (Exod. 33:11). That is to say, just as a man does not feel disquiet when his friend speaks to him, so Moses was not disquieted when God's words came to him, even though it was 'face to face'. This was so because of the strength of his union with the Active Intellect, as we have said.    [12

The fourth difference: To all other prophets inspiration came not by their own choice but by the will of God. Sometimes the prophet remained for a number of years without inspiration coming to him; sometimes the people asked the prophet to tell them something by inspiration, and he had to wait days or months to prophesy about it, or else he received no prophecy on the matter at all. We have seen cases where the prophet prepared himself by delighting his soul and by purifying his mind, as Elisha did when he said: 'Now bring me a minstrel!' (2 Kgs 3:15); and then inspiration came to him, though it was not inevitable that he would receive inspiration every time he prepared himself thus. But Moses our Teacher was able to say whenever he wished: 'Stand still and I will hear what the Lord commands you' (Num. 9:8). And God said: 'Tell Aaron your brother that he may not enter the santuary whenever he choses' (Lev. 16:2). The Sages commented: 'This prohibition against entering the sanctuary applied only to Aaron, but Moses was free to enter whenever he chose' (Sifra to Lev. 16:2).    [13

*The eighth fundamental principle* is that the Torah is from heaven. We should believe that the whole Torah which is in our possession today is the same Torah as was handed down to Moses, and that in its entirety it is from the mouth of the Almighty. That is to say, that the whole Torah came to him from God in a manner which is metaphorically called 'speaking', though no one knows the real nature of that communication save Moses to whom it came. He fulfilled the function of a scribe receiving dictation, and he wrote the whole Torah, its histories, its narratives and its commandments, and that is why he is called a 'copyist' [*mehoqeq* – Deut. 33:21].[4] There is no difference between such verses as 'The sons of Ham were Cush, Egypt, Put and Canaan' (Gen. 10:6) and 'His wife's name was Mehetabel, daughter of Matred' (Gen. 36:39), on the one hand, and such verses as 'I am the Lord your God' (Exod. 20:2) and 'Hear, O Israel' (Deut. 6:4), on the other. It is all from the mouth of the Almighty, it is all the Torah of the Lord which is perfect, pure, holy and true.    [14

The Sages regarded Manasseh as the greatest infidel and heretic that ever was, because he thought that there was both a kernel and a husk to the Torah, and that the histories and narratives have no value but were composed by Moses himself (Babylonian Talmud, Sanhedrin 99b). The Sages said that he who asserts that the *whole* Torah is from the mouth of the Almighty except for *one* verse which he claims was spoken not by God but by Moses himself, says, in effect, 'The Torah is not from heaven' (Babylonian Talmud, Sanhedrin 99a). To such a one may be applied the verse: 'He has despised the word of the Lord' (Num. 15:31). May God be exalted above all that infidels say! Rather, every letter of the Torah contains wisdom and wonders for him to whom God has granted understanding. You cannot comprehend the limit of its wisdom: 'Its length is longer than the earth, its breadth broader than the sea' (Job 11:9). Man has only to follow the example of the Anointed of the God of Jacob who prayed: 'Open my eyes that I may see wonders in your Torah' (Ps. 119: 18). *[15*

So too the interpretation of the Torah which we have received is from the mouth of the Almighty, and the form of the Sukkah we make today, the Lulav, the Shofar, the Zizit, the Tefillin, and so on, are the very same as the forms which God told to Moses and which Moses passed on to us. He was a messenger who was 'faithful' [*ne'eman*, cf. Num. 12:7] to his message. The verse of Scripture which teaches this eighth principle is: 'By this you shall know that the Lord has sent me to do all these works, and that I have not done them on my own initiative' (Num. 16:28). *[16*

*The ninth fundamental principle* is abrogation. This Torah of Moses will not be abrogated, nor shall another Torah come from God. Nothing may be added to it or taken from it, either from the written text or from the oral commentary, as Scripture says: 'You shall not add to it nor take away from it' (Deut. 13:1). In the introduction to this work we have already explained what needs to be explained of this principle. *[17*

*The tenth fundamental principle* is that God has knowledge of the deeds of men and does not disregard them. The view is not correct which says: 'The Lord has abandoned the earth' (Ezek. 8:12); rather, as Scripture says, God is 'great in counsel and mighty in deed, and his eyes are open to all the ways of men' (Jer. 32:19). Scripture also says: 'The Lord saw that the wickedness of man was great in the earth' (Gen. 6:5). And again it says: 'The cry of Sodom and Gomorrah is great' (Gen. 18:20). These verses teach this tenth fundamental principle. *[18*

*The eleventh fundamental principle* is that God rewards him who obeys the commands of the Torah and punishes him who transgresses its prohibitions. The greatest of God's rewards is the world to come [*ha-olam ha-ba*], and the severest of his punishments is 'cutting off' [*karet*]. In this chapter we have already said enough about this subject. The verse which teaches this principle is: 'And yet, if it pleased you to forgive this sin of theirs . . . ! But if not, erase me from the book that you have written'; and God replied: 'It is the man who has sinned against me that I shall erase from my book' (Exod. 32:32 f). This is evidence that God takes cognisance both of the obedient and of the rebellious, so as to reward the one and punish the other. *[19*

*The twelfth fundamental principle* concerns the Messianic Age. We should believe and affirm that the Messiah will come, and should not consider him as tardy: 'Should he tarry, wait for him' (Hab. 2:13). No date may be fixed for his appearance, nor may the Scriptures be interpreted in such a way as to derive from them the time of his coming. The Sages have said: 'May the wits of those who calculate the end be blasted!' (Babylonian Talmud, Sanhedrin 97b). We should have firm faith in him, honouring and loving him, and praying for his coming, in accordance with what has been said about him by all the prophets from Moses to Malachi. Whoever has doubts about him, or makes light of his authority, contradicts the Torah, which clearly promises his coming in the section [*parashah*] of Balaam (Num. 22:2–25:9),[5] and in the section *Nizzavim* (Deut. 29:9–30:20).[6] A general consequence of this principle is that Israel cannot have a king who is not descended from David, and, more particularly, from Solomon. Whoever disputes the authority of this dynasty denies God and the words of his prophets.                                               [20

The thirteenth fundamental principle is the resurrection of the dead. We have already explained this.

[The resurrection of the dead is one of the fundamental principles of the Torah of Moses our Teacher. He who does not believe it is devoid of religion, and has no bond with the Jewish people. However, resurrection is only for the righteous. As Bere'shit Rabbah says: 'The power of the rain is for both the righteous and the wicked, but the resurrection of the dead is for the righteous alone' (cf. Genesis Rabbah 13:6). How can the wicked come back to life when they are dead even during their lifetime? The Sages said: 'The wicked, even during their lifetime, are called dead, but the righteous, even when they are dead, are called alive' (Babylonian Talmud, Berakhot 18b). Know that man must assuredly die and be resolved into his consituent elements.][7]                                               [21

When all these principles are held as certain by a man and his faith in them is firm, then he belongs to the Community of Israel [*Kelal Yisra'el*], and there is an obligation to love him, to have compassion on him, and to perform for him all the acts of love and brotherhood which God has commanded us to perform one for another. Even if he has committed every possible sin because of lust, or because his lower nature got the better of him, though he will surely be punished to the extent of his rebellion, yet still he has a share in the world to come, and is regarded as 'a sinner in Israel'. However, if a man doubts one of these principles he has left the Community, has denied a basic principle, and is called a heretic, an Epicurean, and a 'cutter of plants' (Babylonian Talmud, Hagigah 14b). There is an obligation to hate and to destroy him, and of him Scripture says: 'Shall I not hate those who hate you, O Lord' (Ps. 139:21).   [22

# 8. MYSTICAL LITERATURE

*See 1.7. The Qabbalistic selections in 8.3 form the core of this chapter and should be studied first. All are taken from the* Zohar *(thirteenth century) — the most important text of Jewish mysticism. The doctrine of Torah expressed in 8.3.2 may profitably be compared with that implicit in the texts quoted in chapter 2 above. Cf. also 7.3.7–17. The background to the mystical doctrine of exile and redemption (8.3.5) may be found above in 3.1.2.7, 10,*

14, 15, 17, and in 3.3.1. For the Zionist reworking of this theme see below 10.1.1–2 and 10.2.1. The influence of the Qabbalah on Hasidism is evident from 9.1.2 below. 8.1.1 and 8.1.2 are pre-medieval in date and illustrate the two major concerns of the Jewish esoteric tradition prior to the rise of the Qabbalah – the secrets of nature, and the wonders of God's heavenly throne and palaces.

## 8.1 MA'ASEH BERE'SHIT

### 8.1.1 Sefer Yezirah. The mysteries of Creation[1]

1. Thirty-two wondrous paths were engraved by Yah, the Lord of hosts, the God of Israel, the living God, God Almighty, the 'High and Exalted One who inhabits eternity and whose name is holy' (Isa. 57:15). He created his world by three principles: by limit, by letter and by number.                    [1

2. There are ten primordial numbers [sefirot] and twenty-two fundamental letters.                                                                              [2

6. Ten primordial numbers: their end is already present in their beginning, and their beginning in their end, as the flame is linked to the coal. Know, count and form. For the Lord is unique and the Creator is one. He has no second, and before one what can you count?                                              [3

7. Ten primordial numbers: their measure is ten infinities: the dimension of beginning, the dimension of end; the dimension of goodness, the dimension of evil; the dimension of height, the dimension of depth; the dimension of east, the dimension of west; the dimension of north, the dimension of south. The Lord, the Unique One, God, the Faithful King, rules over them all from his holy dwelling to the eternity of eternities.                                        [4

8. Ten primordial numbers: in appearance they are like lightning, and as for their limit – they have no end. His word is in them when they 'run and return' (cf. Ezek. 1:14), and at his command they rush like a whirlwind and bow down before his throne.                                                            [5

10. Ten primordial numbers:
One. Spirit of the Living God.                                                       [6

12. Two. Air [ruah] from Spirit [ruah]: he engraved and hewed out in it the twenty-two fundamental letters: three mothers, seven double and twelve simple; and each of them has the same Spirit.                              [7

13. Three. Water from Air [ruah]: he engraved and hewed out in it chaos and disorder, mud and mire. He made them into a kind of a seed-bed; he raised them as a kind of wall; he wove them into a kind of roof. He poured snow over them and it became earth, as Scripture says: 'He said to the snow, "Be earth!" ' (Job 37:6).                                                                            [8

14. Four. Fire from Water: he engraved and hewed out in it the Throne of Glory, the Ofannim, the Seraphim, the Holy Creatures, and the ministering angels, as Scripture says: 'God makes winds his angels, and fiery flames his

ministers' (Ps. 104:4). *[9*

15. He chose three of the simple letters, Yod, He and Vav, and he fixed them into his great name. With them he sealed six extremities:

*Five.* He sealed height; he turned upwards and sealed it with Yod, He, Vav.

*Six.* He sealed depth; he turned downwards and sealed it with Yod, Vav, He.

*Seven.* He sealed east; he turned forwards and sealed it with He, Yod, Vav.

*Eight.* He sealed west; he turned backwards and sealed it with He, Vav, Yod.

*Nine.* He sealed south; he turned right and sealed it with Vav, Yod, He.

*Ten.* He sealed north; he turned left and sealed it with Vav, He, Yod. *[10*

17. There are twenty-two fundamental letters: three mothers, seven double and twelve simple. *[11*

18. Twenty-two fundamental letters: they are fixed in a wheel with two hundred and thirty-one gates. And the wheel rotates backwards and forwards. This is the sign of the matter: There is no good above pleasure [*'oneg*], and no evil below affliction [*nega'*]. *[12*

19. Twenty-two fundamental letters: he engraved them, he hewed them out, he weighed them, he set them as opposites, he combined them, and he formed with them the soul [*nefesh*] of everything that has been formed, and the soul of everything that will be formed. *[13*

23. Three mothers, Alef, Mem and Shin: their foundation is in the scale of merit and the scale of guilt, with the tongue of the law holding the balance between them. *[14*

27. Three mothers, Alef, Mem and Shin: from them were born the three fathers from which everything has been created. *[15*

25. Three mothers, Alef, Mem and Shin: fire, water and air – fire above, water below, and air the law which holds the balance between them. The sign of the matter is this: Fire carries off water. *[16*

31. Three mothers, Alef, Mem and Shin: He engraved them, he hewed them out, he combined them, and sealed with them – three mothers in the world; three mothers in the year; three mothers in the body [*nefesh*] of male and female. *[17*

28. Three mothers, Alef, Mem and Shin, in the world: air, water and fire. The heavens were created first from fire; the earth was created from water; air [*avir*] was created from air [*ruah*], and it holds the balance between the other two. *[18*

29. Three mothers, Alef, Mem and Shin, in the year: air, water and fire. Heat was created from fire; cold was created from water; temperateness was created from air, and it holds the balance between the other two. *[19*

30. Three mothers, Alef, Mem and Shin, in the body [*nefesh*]: air, water and fire. The head was created from fire; the belly was created from water; the chest

was created from air, and it holds the balance between the other two.     [20

37. Seven double letters, Bet, Gimel, Dalet, Kaf, Pe, Resh and Tav. Their foundation is life, well-being [shalom], wisdom, wealth, seed, gracefulness and dominion. They occur with two sounds, and this doubling indicates opposites: Bet–Bhet; Gimel–Ghimel; Dalet–Dhalet; Kaf–Khaf; Pe–Phe; Resh–Rhesh; Tav–Thav, a pattern of soft and hard, strong and weak. These are the opposites: the opposite of life is death; the opposite of well-being is disaster; the opposite of wisdom is folly; the opposite of wealth is poverty; the opposite of seed is desolation; the opposite of gracefulness is ugliness; the opposite of dominion is slavery.     [21

39. Seven double letters, Bet, Gimel, Dalet, Kaf, Pe, Resh, Tav: he engraved them, he hewed them out, he combined them, he weighed them, he set them as opposites, and he formed with them – seven stars in the world; seven days in the year; seven gates in the body [nefesh].     [22

40. How did he combine them? Two stones build two houses. Three stones built six houses. Four stones build twenty-four houses. Five stones build one hundred and twenty houses. Six stones build seven hundred and twenty houses. Seven stones build five thousand and forty houses. From here on go and compute what the mouth is unable to speak, what the eye is unable to see, and what the ear is unable to hear.     [23

43. These are the seven stars in the world: the Sun, Venus, Mercury, the Moon, Saturn, Jupiter, Mars. These are the seven days in the year: the seven days of creation. These are the seven gates in the body: two eyes, two ears, two nostrils, and the mouth.     [24

45. Twelve simple letters – He, Vav, Zayin, Het, Tet, Yod, Lamed, Nun, Samekh, Ayin, Zade, Qof. Their measure is the twelve borders of the diagonal which point in six directions and separate one side from another: the north-east border; the upper east border; the lower east border; the north-west border; the upper north border; the lower north border; the west-south border; the upper west border; the lower west border; the south-east border; the upper south border; the lower south border. They go on widening ad infinitum, and they are the arms of the world.     [25

49. Twelve simple letters – He, Vav, Zayin, Het, Tet, Yod, Lamed, Nun, Samekh, Ayin, Zade, Qof. He engraved them, he hewed them out, he combined them, he weighed them, he set them as opposites, and he formed with them – twelve constellations in the world; twelve months in the year; twelve organs in the body. The twelve constellations are: Aries, Taurus, Gemini, Cancer, Leo, Virgo, Libra, Scorpio, Sagittarius, Capricorn, Aquarius, Pisces. The twelve months are: Nisan, Iyyar, Sivan, Tammuz, Av, Elul, Tishri, Marheshvan, Kislev, Tevet, Shevat, Adar. The twelve organs of the body are: two hands, two feet, two kidneys, liver, gall-bladder, spleen, intestines, stomach, and maw.     [26

56. Three Mothers, seven double, and twelve simple: these are the twenty-two letters by which Yah, the Lord of Hosts, the God of Israel, the living God, God almighty, 'the high and exalted One who inhabits eternity and whose name

E

is holy' (Isa. 57:15), engraved.                                                    [27
57. The twelve are below, the seven are above, on top of them, and the three are on top of the seven, and from the three he founded his dwelling. All of them depend on the One and point to the One, to whom there is no second, a King unique in his world, for he is One and his name is One.                    [28
59. Command over the three, the seven, and the twelve is entrusted to the Dragon, the diurnal sphere, and the heart. The Dragon in the world is like a king on his throne. The diurnal sphere in the year is like a king in his domain. The heart in the body is like a king in battle.                             [29
58. Three Fathers and their offspring; seven stars and their hosts; twelve borders of the diagonal. The proof of the matter is given by faithful witnesses – the world, the year, and the body. The world, the year and the body are each composed of twenty-two constituents. In the world three, fire, water and air, and the seven stars, and the twelve constellations. In the year three, cold, heat and temperateness, and the seven days of creation, and the twelve months. In the body three, head, belly and chest, and the seven gates, and the twelve organs.                                                                      [30
53. He separated the witnesses and placed each on its own – the world on its own, the year on its own, and the body on its own.                        [31
61. When Abraham our father had come, observed, seen, investigated and understood, and had successfully engraved, combined, hewn and computed, then the Lord of all was revealed to him. He set Abraham in his bosom, kissed him on the head, called him his beloved, and designated him his son. He made a covenant with him and with his descendants for ever, 'And Abraham believed in the Lord, and he reckoned it to him for righteousness' (Gen. 15:6).      [32
64. This is the Book of the Alphabet of Abraham our Father which is known as 'The Laws of Creation'. Whoever looks into it, there is no limit to his wisdom.                                                                        [33

## 8.2 MA'ASEH MERKAVAH

### 8.2.1 Heikhalot Rabbati 15:1–22:2. The ascent to God's heavenly throne
15:1. Rabbi Ishmael said: When Rabbi Nehunyah ben Ha-Qanah saw that wicked Rome had taken counsel to destroy the mighty ones of Israel, he at once revealed the secret of the world, the measure that appears to one who is worthy of gazing on the King, on his Thone, on his majesty and his beauty, on the Holy Creatures, on the mighty Cherubim, on the Ofannim of the Shekhinah, on the swift lightning, on the terrible *Hashmal*, on Rigyon [the River of Fire] which surrounds his Throne, on the bridges, on the fiery flames that blaze up between one bridge and the next, on the dense smoke, on the bright wind that raises from the burning coals the pall of smoke which covers and conceals all the chambers of the palace [*heikhal*] of Aravot, the [seventh] heaven, on the fiery clouds, on Surya, the Prince of the Divine Presence, the servant of TVTRKY'EL YHVH,

the Majestic One. [1

2. To what may this measure of the Yoredei Merkavah be compared? It is like a man who has a ladder in his house which he ascends and descends, with none to say him nay. This is the case with everyone who is pure and purged of idolatry, sexual offences, bloodshed, slander, vain oaths, profanation of God's name, insolence and groundless enmity, and keeps every positive and negative commandment. [2

16:1. Rabbi Ishmael said: When my ears heard this warning, my strength ebbed. I said to Rabbi Nehunyah ben Ha-Qanah my teacher: 'If this is so, then there is no end to the matter, for there is no man in whom is the breath of life, who is pure and purged of these eight vices!' He said to me: 'Proud One, if not, then go and bring before me all the heroes of the fellowship [havurah], and all the distinguished members of the academy [yeshivah], so that I may tell them the mysteries that are hidden and concealed, the wonders of the weaving of the web on which depends the perfection and glory of the world, the axle of heaven and earth to which the extremities of the earth and the world, and the extremities of the heavens above are bound, sewn and joined, on which they hang and depend, the wonders of the path of the celestial ladder, one end of which rests on earth and the other by the right foot of the Throne of Glory.' [3

2. Rabbi Ishmael said: Immediately I arose and assembled every greater Sanhedrin and every lesser Sanhedrin at the third entrance of the House of the Lord. He [Nehunyah ben Ha-Qanah] was sitting on a bench of pure marble which my father Elisha had given to him from my mother's property, for it had been hers and she had brought it to him as part of her dowry. [4

3. Then came Rabban Simeon ben Gamaliel, Rabbi Eliezer the Great, Rabbi Eleazar ben Dama, Rabbi Eliezer ben Shammua, Rabbi Yohanan ben Dahavai, Hananyah ben Hakhinai, Yonathan ben Uzziel, Rabbi Aqiva and Rabbi Judah ben Bava. We came and sat before him. The mass of the members of the fellowship [haverim] remained standing, for they saw sparks[2] of fire and torches of blazing fire separating them from us. Rabbi Nehunyah ben Ha-Qanah sat and expounded in order all the matters of the Merkavah, both the descent and the ascent, how he who descends should descend, and how he who ascends should ascend. [5

4. When anyone wishes to descend to the Merkavah, he should invoke Suryah, Prince of the Divine Presence, and conjure him one hundred and twelve times by TVTRVSY'Y YHVH who is called TVTRVSYY ZVRTQ TVRTQ TVRTBY'EL TVPGR AShRVYLY'Y ZBVDY'EL VZHDRY'EL TNR'EL VShQRHVZY'Y RHBYRVN 'DYRYRVN V'DYRYRYRVN YHVH the God of Israel. [6

5. He should take care not to recite the invocation more or less than one hundred and twelve times (if he adds or subtracts – his blood is on his own head!), but as his mouth pronounces the names he counts one hundred and twelve on his fingers. At once he descends and achieves mastery over the Merkavah. [7

17:1. Rabbi Ishmael said: Thus said Rabbi Nehunyah ben Ha-Qanah, my teacher: TVTRVSY'Y YHVH the God of Israel dwells in seven palaces [*heikhalot*], one inside the other, and at the gate of each palace are eight Keepers of the Threshold, four to the right and four to the left of the lintel. *[8*

*Then follow lists of the magical names of the Guardians of palaces one to six.*

8. At the gate of the seventh palace all the Mighty stand, wrathful, ruthless, strong, harsh, terrible and frightening, taller than mountains and sharper than peaks. Their bows are strung and ready before them; their swords are sharpened and in their hands. Bolts of lightning shoot forth from the balls of their eyes, sparks of fire from their nostrils and fiery torches from their mouths. They are clad in helmets and coats of mail, and spears and javelins hang upon their arms. *[9*

18:1. Their horses are horses of darkness, horses of the shadow of death, horses of gloom, horses of fire, horses of blood, horses of hail, horses of iron, horses of mist. Their horses on which they ride stand beside mangers of fire full of juniper coals, and eat fiery coals from the mangers – forty bushels of coal at one gulp! The capacity of each horse's mouth is equal to three of the mangers of Caesarea. *[10*

2. Rivers of fire run beside their mangers and all the horses drink from them a quantity equivalent to the capacity of the water-channel in the Kidron Valley, which carries off and contains all the rainwater of all Jerusalem. And there was there above their heads a cloud dripping blood – above their heads and the heads of their horses. It is the sign and measure of the Gatekeepers of the seventh palace, and of the Gatekeepers of each of the palaces. *[11*

19:1. Rabbi Ishmael said: When you come and stand at the gate of the first palace take two seals in your two hands – one of them the seal of TVTRVSY'Y YHVH and the other the seal of Suryah, Prince of the Divine Presence. Show the seal of TVTRVSY'Y to those standing on the right, and the seal of Suryah, Prince of the Divine Presence, to those standing on the left. Immediately RHBY'EL, the Prince who is head Gatekeeper of the first palace and ruler of the first palace, and who stands to the right of the lintel, and TVPHY'EL the Prince who stands with him to the left of the lintel, sieze hold of you and conduct you, one on your right and one on your left, to hand you on and give notice of your coming to TGRY'EL the Prince who is the chief Gatekeeper of the second palace and who stands to the right of the lintel, and MTPY'EL the Prince who stands with him to the left of the lintel. *[12*

*The ascent continues in similar fashion through the gates of the next four palaces until the gate of the sixth palace is reached.*

6. Because the Gatekeepers of the sixth palace were destroying those who were of the Yoredei Merkavah but who were not among the Yoredei Merkavah who [descend] without permission,[3] they [the Gatekeepers] were bidden [to desist]; they were flogged and burned, and others were set in their place, but the

others who took their place behaved in the same manner: they neither fear nor does it enter their minds to say, 'Why are we being thus burned, or what does it profit us that we are destroying those who are of the Yoredei Merkavah but who are not among the Yoredei Merkavah who [descend] without permission?' The Gatekeepers of the sixth palace still behave in this way. *[13*

20:1. Rabbi Ishmael said: All the members of the fellowship [*havurah*] said to me: 'Proud One, since you are as much a master of the great light, the light of Torah, as is Rabbi Nehunyah ben Ha-Qanah, attract his attention, bring him back to sit with us from the vision which he beholds of the Merkavah, and let him tell us who is he who is of the Yoredei Merkavah, but not among the Yoredei Merkavah, whom the Gatekeepers of the sixth palace attack, though they used not to molest in any way the Yoredei Merkavah. What is the difference between these and those?' *[14*

2. Rabbi Ishmael said: At once I took a piece of fine white woollen cloth and gave it to Rabbi Aqiva, and Rabbi Aqiva gave it to the beadle [*shammash*], and the beadle gave it to a servant [*eved*] of ours, saying: 'Go and place this cloth beside a woman who has immersed herself, but whose immersion is invalid, and cause her to immerse herself [again], so that if that same woman should come and state the nature of her menstruation before the fellowship, it is well known that one scholar would declare her forbidden, whereas the majority would declare her permitted. Say to that woman: "Touch this cloth with the tip of your middle finger. Do not press on it with the tip of your middle finger, but, like a man removing a fleck of straw that has fallen in his eye, push it ever so gently." ' *[15*

3. They went and did so and laid the cloth before Rabbi Ishmael. He inserted into it a myrtle twig impregnated with *foliatum* [nard oil] and soaked in pure balsam. They then laid it on the knees of Rabbi Nehunyah ben Ha-Qanah. Immediately he was dismissed from before the Throne of Glory where he had been sitting and beholding

A marvellous majesty and strange dominion,
A majesty of exaltation and dominion of radiance,
Which is aroused before the Throne of Glory
Three times each day, in the height,
Ever since the world was created until now, for praise. *[16*

4. Then we asked him: 'Who is he who is of the Yoredei Merkavah but not among the Yoredei Merkavah?' He said to us: 'These are the men whom those Yoredei Merkavah take and place above them and, setting them before them, they say to them: "Observe, see, hear and write all that we say and all that we hear before the Throne of Glory." If these men are not worthy for the task, then the Gatekeepers of the sixth palace attack them. Be careful, therefore, to choose for yourselves fit men who are tried and tested members of the fellowship.' *[17*

5. When you come and stand at the gate of the sixth palace, show the three seals of the Gatekeepers of the sixth palace, two of them to QZPY'EL the Prince, whose sword is unsheathed in his hand and from it lightning bolts shoot

out, and it is drawn against anyone unworthy to gaze on the King and on the Throne, and none can stay his hand. His sword shouts 'Destruction!' and he stands to the right of the lintel. [18

6. Show one seal to DVMY'EL. Is DVMY'EL really his name? Is not ABYRGHYDRYHM⁴ his name? Why then is he called DVMY'EL? Rabbi Ishmael said: Thus said Rabbi Nehunyah ben Ha-Qanah, my teacher, to me: Every day a heavenly voice [bat qol] is heard in the heaven of Aravot, announcing in the Celestial Law Court: Thus states T'VS VBR MNZYH VPVKYG Sh'T YHVH⁵ the God of Israel: 'Call him DVMY'EL after my name. Just as I see and remain silent, so does he. His post was to the right of the lintel, but QZPY'EL the Prince thrust him aside, yet he feels neither enmity nor rivalry towards him; rather "both these and those are for my glory".' [19

21:1. ZHDRY'EL and P'LYP'LY – show these two seals to QZPY'EL, and show BRVNYH to DVMY'EL the Prince, a prince upright and humble. At once QZPY'EL the Prince strings his bow and draws his sword. He summons for you a whirlwind and seats you in a carriage of light, and blows before you a blast like the sound of eight thousand myriads of trumpets, three thousand myriads of horns, four thousand myriads of bugles, and DVMY'EL the Prince holds the gift [Greek: doron] and goes before you. [20

2. What is the gift? Rabbi Ishmael said: Thus said Rabbi Nehunyah ben Ha-Qanah: The gift which DVMY'EL the Prince holds in front of the carriage of the man who is worthy to descend to the Merkavah is not a gift of silver or of gold; rather it is that [on account of] which he was neither molested nor questioned either at the first palace, or at the second palace, or at the third palace, or at the fourth palace, or at the fifth palace, or at the sixth palace, or at the seventh palace, but he was showing the Gatekeepers seals and they were allowing him to enter. [21

3. At the gate of the sixth palace DVMY'EL the Prince, Keeper of the Theshold on the right of the gate of the sixth palace, sits on a bench of pure stone in which is [depicted] the splendour of the heavenly luminaries and the creation of the world. ADST'N VBNPYKZT ZMNSh'RGH YHVH the God of Israel.⁶ DVMY'EL the Prince receives him cordially and seats him on the bench of pure stone and sits beside him on his right. [22

4. DVMY'EL says to him: I testify and warn you of two things: He who descends does not descend to the Merkavah unless he has these two qualities: [either he has read] the Torah, the Prophets and the Writings, and he studies Mishnah, Halakhot, Haggadot, and the legal decisions concerning what is forbidden and what is permitted, or he has fulfilled every negative command that is written in the Torah, and keeps all the prohibitions of the statutes and judgements and teachings which were spoken to Moses on Sinai. [23

22:1. If the man says, 'I have one of these two qualities,' immediately DVMY'EL summons Gabriel the scribe who writes for the man a document and hangs it on the shaft of the carriage of that man. It says: 'Such and such is the learning of this person, and such and such are his deeds. He requests permission to enter before the Throne of Glory.'                                            [24

2. As soon as the Gatekeepers of the seventh palace see DVMY'EL, Gabriel and QZPY'EL proceeding in front of the chariot of that man who is worthy to descend to the Merkavah, they cover their faces and sit down (for they were standing erect). They loosen their strung bows and return their sharp swords to their sheaths. Nevertheless it is necessary to show them a great seal and a fearful crown – T'DS VBR MNVGYH VK'ShPTSh YHVH the God of Israel.[7] Then they enter before the Throne of Glory and bring out before him all kinds of melody and song, and, making music, they proceed before him till they lead him in and seat him with the Cherubim, the Ofannim and the Holy Creatures, and he sees wonders, powers, majesty, greatness, holiness, dread, humility, and righteousness in that hour.                                            [25

### 8.3 QABBALAH

#### 8.3.1 The Ein Sof and the ten Sefirot (*Zohar*, Bo, II 42b–43a [Ra'aya Meheimna])

Should anyone raise an objection on the grounds that Scripture says, 'You saw no kind of image of God' (Deut. 4:15), we would reply, We did indeed see a certain image, for Scripture says: 'The image of the Lord does Moses behold' (Num. 12:8). But the Lord was revealed only in that image which Moses saw and not in any other belonging to any creature formed by his signs. That is why Scripture states: 'To whom will you liken me, that I may be compared to him?' (Isa. 40:25); and 'To whom will you liken God, or what form will you give him?' (Isa. 40:18). Moreover, even that image was not an image of the Holy One as he is in his own place. Rather, when he descends to exercise sovereignty over his creatures, and discloses himself to them, he appears to each of them according to each one's capacity to see, envisage, and imagine him, as Scripture says: 'I speak through the prophets in similes' (Hos. 12:10). Therefore he says: 'Though I represent myself to you in your own image, to whom will you liken me, that I may be compared to him?'                                            [1

For before the Holy One, blessed be he, had created any image, or fashioned any form, he was alone without any likeness or form. Whoever seeks to apprehend him as he was, prior to creation, when he existed without image, is forbidden to represent him with any kind of form or image, whether it be with the letter He or with the letter Yod, or even with the Holy Name, or with a single letter or sign of any kind. Thus, 'You saw no kind of image' (Deut. 4:15) means, You did not see anything which possesses image or form.                                            [2

But after he had fashioned the image of the Chariot [*Merkavah*] of Supernal Man, he descended into it and was known under the image of YHVH, so that men might apprehend him through his attributes, through each of them severally, and he was called El, Elohim, Shaddai, Zeva'ot, and YHVH, so that men might apprehend him through each of his attributes and perceive how the world is governed by kindness [*hesed*] and by justice [*dina*] in accordance with men's deeds. For if his radiance had not been shed over all creation how could men have apprehended him, or how could the verse be true, 'The whole earth is full of his glory' (Isa. 6:3)? [3

Woe to the man who would equate the Lord with any single attribute, even with one that is truly his own. Still less should he compare the Lord with the form of the sons of men 'whose foundation is in the dust' (Job 4:19), whose existence is transient and who soon pass away. Rather, the one true image of him is of his sovereignty over some particular attribute, or even over creation as a whole, but beyond that attribute, the moment he is separated from it, he possesses neither attribute, nor likeness, nor form. It is like the sea. The waters of the sea in themselves cannot be grasped and have no form, but when they are poured into a vessel – the earth – they receive form. [4

On this basis we are able to make the following calculation. The source of the sea is one. A fountain issued from it when it was poured into the vessel with a revolution, which is Yod. The source is one, and the fountain which issued from it makes two. Next he made a large vessel, as a man would dig a vast hollow in the ground, and this filled with the waters which flowed from the fountain. This vessel is called 'Sea', and it is the third vessel. The great vessel divided into seven channels. The source, the fountain, the sea and the seven channels together make ten. If the Craftsman should break those vessels which he has established, the waters would return to the source and only broken vessels would remain, dry and devoid of water. [5

In like manner the Cause of causes formed ten Sefirot. He called Crown [*keter*] the source. In it there is no end to the flow of his radiance, and on this account he called himself Ein Sof [the Infinite]. He possesses neither shape nor form, nor does any vessel exist there to contain him or any means of knowing him. It is to this that the saying refers: 'Do not investigate things too hard for you, or inquire into what is hidden from you' [Babylonian Talmud, Hagigah 13a, quoting Ben Sira]. [6

Next he made a little vessel, which is Yod, and filled it from himself. He called it a 'fountain pouring forth wisdom', and he called himself wise on its account. He called that vessel Wisdom [*hokhmah*]. Then he made a great vessel and called it 'Sea'. He called it Understanding [*binah*], and he called himself understanding on its account. He is wise and understanding in and of himself, but wisdom cannot claim the title of wisdom on its own account but only in virtue of the fact that one who understands filled it from himself, for should he remove himself from it, it would be left dry. This is the meaning of the verse: 'The waters fail from the sea, the river wastes away and dries up' (Job 14:11). [7

After this 'he smote the sea into seven channels' (Isa. 11:15), and he made seven precious vessels. He called them: Greatness [*gedullah*], Power [*gevurah*], Beauty [*tif'eret*], Victory [*nezah*], Majesty [*hod*], Foundation [*yesod*], and Sovereignty [*malkhut*]. He called himself great in Greatness, powerful in

Power, beautiful in Beauty, 'the One Victorious in Battle' in Victory. In majesty he gave himself the name of 'the Majesty of our Maker'. In Foundation he gave himself the name of righteous [*zaddiq*] [cf. Prov. 10:25, 'The Righteous One (*zaddiq*) is the foundation (*yesod*) of the world']. All vessels and all worlds depend on Foundation. In Sovereignty he gave himself the name of king. To him belong the greatness, the power, the beauty, the victory, and the majesty, for all [*kol*] that is in heaven ('all' referring to Zaddiq[8]) and on earth is his, and to him belongs the kingdom (that is, Sovereignty) (cf. 1 Chiron. 29:11). All things are under his authority, whether it be to reduce the number of the vessels, or to increase or decrease the flow in them according to his pleasure, for above him exists no deity with power to increase or to lessen. *[8*

### 8.3.2 Torah (*Zohar*, Be-ha'alotkha, III 152a)

Rabbi Simeon said: Woe to the man who says that the Torah intends to set forth mere tales and common talk! If that were so, then we could at once compose a torah out of common talk, one of much greater worth. If the Torah intends to disclose everyday matters, then the princes of the world possess books of greater excellence. Let us seek those out and make a torah of them. However, all the words of Torah are sublime and supernal mysteries. Observe: the upper world and the lower world are in perfect balance – Israel below corresponding to the angels above. Of the supernal angels Scripture says: 'Who makes his angels spirits [*ruhot*]' (Ps. 104:4). When the angels descend into the world below they clothe themselves in garments appropriate to this world, for if they did not do so, they would not be able to remain in this world, nor could the world endure them. If it is thus with the angels, how much more so must it be with the Torah, which created the angels and all the worlds, and through which all the worlds are sustained. When it descended into this world, it put on the garments of this world, otherwise the world could not have endured it. So the stories of the Torah are only the Torah's outer garment. Perdition take the man who mistakes that garment for the Torah itself, and thinks that there is nothing else to it! He shall have no portion in the world to come. That is why David said: 'Open my eyes that I may see wondrous things out of your Torah' (Ps. 119:18) – that is to say, that I may perceive what is beneath the Torah's outer garment. Observe: A man's garments are visible to all, and foolish people, when they see someone clothed in fine raiment, look no further: they regard the clothing as if it were the body [*gufa*], and the body as if it were the soul [*nishmeta*]. In like manner the Torah has a body [*gufa*], viz., the commandments of the Torah which are called *gufei Torah* [literally, 'bodies', i.e. main principles, 'of the Torah'; see Mishnah, Hagigah 1:8]. This body is clothed in garments made up of earthly tales. Foolish people look only at those garments, the tales of the Torah: they know nothing more and do not look at what is beneath the garment. Those who are wiser look not at the garment, but at the body beneath. But the true Sages, the servants of the Most High King, those who stood at Mount Sinai, look only at the soul [*nishmeta*] of the Torah, which is the root principle of all, the true Torah, and in the world to come they are destined to look at the soul of the soul [*nishmeta de-nishmeta*] of the Torah.

### 8.3.3 The 'other side' [*sitra ahra*] (*Zohar*, Terumah, II 173a)

All those stars which shine in heaven sing and praise the Holy One, blessed be he, all the time that they are visible in the sky. And the angels above sing the praises of their Lord in successive watches during the three divisions of the night. By night various sides are active in different ways. At the beginning of the night, when evening draws in and it becomes dark, all the evil spirits and evil powers scatter abroad and roam through all the world, and the 'other side' [*sitra ahra*] sets forth and asks the ways to the house of the King from all the holy sides. As soon as the 'other side' is roused to activity, all the inhabitants of this world experience the taste of sleep, which is a sixtieth part of death, and death rules over them. When the impure power separates itself from the realm above and descends to begin its rule here below, three companies of angels are formed to praise the Holy One in the three watches of the night. While these sing hymns of praise to the Holy One, the 'other side' roams about here below through all the regions of the earth. But until the 'other side' has departed from the upper sphere, the angels cannot unite themselves with their Lord.      [1

This is a mystery comprehensible only to the wise. The angels above and Israel below both seek to oust the 'other side'. The supernal angels, when they desire to be united with their Lord, are unable to do so till they have expelled the 'other side' from the higher realms. What, then, do they do? Sixty myriads of holy angels descend to earth and bring sleep to all its inhabitants. As soon as the 'other side' descends — for the angels thrust it out and give into its power all this world through sleep — it begins to rule over men and they receive impurity from it, save in the Land of Israel, where the 'other side' has no power. As soon as the 'other side' has departed, the angels enter before their Lord and sing songs of praise and thanksgiving before him. In like manner, Israel here below cannot unite themselves with their Lord till they have pushed the 'other side' away from them, by giving it its due portion to keep it occupied, and they too approach their Lord, and thus the Accuser is finally found neither above nor below.      [2

You might say: That there is an accusation below is easy to understand, but what accusation can there be above? The truth is that in the realm above, since the 'other side' is a spirit of impurity and the holy angels are spirits too, they cannot approach their Lord till they have banished the spirit of impurity from their midst, for holiness cannot ever mix with impurity, just as here below Israel cannot mix with the heathen nations of the world. Thus both regions, the celestial and the terrestrial, when their inhabitants wish to approach the Holy King, must thrust out the 'other side'. Therefore when night falls and the holy supernal angels marshal themselves in ranks to approach their Lord, they first thrust out the 'other side' and then enter in holiness.      [3

A king once had certain very precious stones which he kept in his palace in an engraved casket. The king was wise, and, to prevent anyone who might so desire from approaching the casket of precious stones and pearls that was found there, he took in his wisdom a deadly serpent and wound it round the box. If anyone tried to stretch out his hand to the casket, the serpent leapt upon him and killed him. The king, however, had a dear friend. The king said to him: 'Whenever you wish to enter and avail yourself of the casket, do such-and-such to the serpent and you will be able to open the casket and to make use of my treasures.' In like manner the Holy One, blessed be he, wound a serpent round his holiness. When the supernal angels come to enter the sphere of holiness, they find the serpent and are afraid lest they should be defiled by it.                          [4

You might say: 'All the angels are formed of fire and fire cannot receive impurity.' Observe, however, that Scripture says: 'He makes his angels spirits, his ministers flaming fire' (Ps. 104:4). 'He makes his angels spirits' – these are the angels who stand without; 'his ministers flaming fire' – these are the angels who stand within the innermost circle of holiness. The serpent is a spirit of impurity and the angels who encounter it are also spirits. One spirit cannot enter another, nor can the spirit of impurity mix with the spirit of holiness. So those angels who are called spirits are unable to enter within on account of that spirit of impurity. However, those angels that are within are fire and that fire thrusts out the impurity so that it cannot enter within. Therefore all combine to push out the impurity and prevent it mingling with them. And so the supernal angels can only begin to praise the Holy One after they have banished the 'other side' from the heavenly courts.                          [5

### 8.3.4 Tiqqun (*Zohar*, Terumah, II 155a)

The Holy One created man through the mystery of wisdom [i.e. the Sefirot], fashioned him with great craftsmanship, and breathed into his nostrils the breath of life, so that he might understand the mysteries of wisdom, and know the glories of his Lord, as it is written: 'Everyone that is called by my name: I have created him [*bera'tiv*] for my glory, I have formed him [*yezativ*], yea, I have made him [*asitiv*]' (Isa. 43:7) . . . As to the inner sense of this verse, we have learned that the lower Glory, the mystery of the Holy Throne [= the Sefirah Malkhut], is only established in the realm above by acts of reparation [*tiqquna*] performed by the inhabitants of this world, when they are righteous and pious and know how to make reparation in the proper manner. This is the meaning of the phrase 'I have created him for my glory', i.e. I have created him for the sake of my Glory, to establish it on firm pillars, to provide it with adornment and completion from below, so that my Glory may be exalted through the merit of the righteous who are on earth. So 'I created him' after the pattern of the upper Glory [the Sefirot above Malkhut] in which are found the following three aspects: Creation [*beri'ah*] on the left side, and Formation [*yezirah*] on the right, as it is written: 'Who forms [*yozer*] light [*or* = the Sefirah Hesed], and creates [*bore*] darkness [*hoshekh* = the Sefirah Din/Gevurah]' (Isa. 45:7); and Making [*asiyyah*] in the middle, as it is written: 'I, the Lord, do [*oseh*] all things [*kol* = the Sefirah Tif'eret],' 'making [*oseh*] peace and creating [*bore*] evil' (Isa. 45:7), 'making [*oseh*] peace in his heights' (Job 25:2). Hence: 'I have created him, I have formed him, yea I have made him' according to the celestial pattern. . . . These three aspects have I placed in man so that he should be in the likeness of the upper Glory which completes and blesses the lower Glory. Thus God created man on earth after the pattern of the upper Glory, to establish that Glory [i.e. the lower Glory], and to make it complete on all sides. In the upper Glory are these three aspects, and in man are these three aspects as well, so that the lower Glory might be completed both from above and from below, and might be perfect on all sides.[9]

### 8.3.5. Exile and redemption
#### 8.3.5.1 *Zohar*, Aharei Mot, III 77b
In time to come the Holy One, blessed be he, will restore the Shekhinah to her place, so that all things shall be joined together in a single union, as it is written: 'In that day shall the Lord be one and his Name one' (Zech. 14:9). It may be said: Is he not One now? No, for now the sinners of the world have brought it about that he is not one. For the Matrona [= the Shekhinah or the Sefirah Malkhut] is removed from the King and they are no longer united, and the Supernal Mother [*Binah*] is removed from the King and does not give him suck. Because the King is without the Matrona, he is not invested with the crowns of the Mother [*Imma*], as he was before when he was joined to the Matrona, for the Mother crowned him with many resplendent crowns and supernal, holy diadems, as it is written: 'Go out, daughters of Zion, and look on King Solomon, at the crown with which his mother crowned him' (Song of Songs 3:11). When he was united with the Matrona, then the Supernal Mother crowned him in a fitting manner; but now that the King is not with the Matrona, the Supernal Mother takes her crowns and withholds from him the waters of the streams, and he is not united in a single bond. And so he is not, so to speak, one. But when the Matrona shall return to the place of the Temple and the King shall be wedded to her in a single union, then all things shall be joined together in one, without separation, and that is why it is written: 'In that day shall the Lord be one, and his Name one'.
#### 8.3.5.2 *Zohar*, Bo, II 40b (Ra'aya Meheimna)
It is obligatory for every Israelite always to recount the praises of the Exodus from Egypt. Thus we have established: Whoever relates the story of the Exodus and does so joyously, shall be found worthy to rejoice in the Shekhinah in the world to come. So there is joy on every side: the man is as one rejoicing in his Master, and the Holy One rejoices as the man recounts his tale. At once the Holy One calls together all his heavenly Family and says to them: 'Come and listen to the recital of my praises, which my children bring me as they rejoice at my redemption!' Then all the supernal beings assemble in the presence of Israel and listen to the recitation of the praise which Israel brings as they rejoice at the redemption of their Master. Then the supernal beings come and extol the Holy

One for all these miracles and wonders, and they magnify him because he has such a holy people on earth that rejoices with such joy at the redemption of their Master. Then is his power and might increased above, for Israel by its recitation gives strength to their Lord, just as an earthly king gains strength and power when his subjects praise his might and extol him, so that all fear him and his fame spreads through the whole world.

### 8.3.6 The spiritual constitution of man (*Zohar*, Lekh, I 83b)

The 'soul' [*nefesh*] is the lowest stirring. It supports the body and nourishes it. The body is bound intimately to the 'soul' and the 'soul' to the body. When the 'soul' has been perfected it becomes a throne on which the 'spirit' [*ruah*] may rest, when the 'soul' that is joined to the body is aroused, as Scripture says: 'Till the spirit be poured on us from on high' (Isa. 32:15). When 'soul' and 'spirit' have perfected themselves, they become worthy to receive the 'super-soul' [*neshamah*], for the 'spirit' acts as a throne on which the 'super-soul' resides. This 'super-soul' stands highest of all, hidden and utterly mysterious. So we find that there is a throne supporting a throne, and a throne for the highest which is over all. When you study these grades of soul you will discover therein the secret of divine Wisdom, for it is always wise to investigate hidden mysteries in this way.                                                                            [1

Observe that the soul, the lowest stirring, cleaves to the body, just as in a candle flame the dark light at the bottom clings to the wick, from which it cannot be separated and without which it could never be kindled. But when it has been fully kindled on the wick it becomes a throne for the white light above which resides upon that dark light. When both the dark and the white light have been fully kindled, the white light in its turn becomes a throne for a hidden light, for what it is that reposes on that white light can neither be seen nor known. Thus the light is fully formed. And so it is with the man who attains complete perfection, and, as a result, is called 'holy', as Scripture says: 'For the holy that are in the earth' (Ps. 16:3). We find, too, that there is an analogous process in the upper world.                                                                            [2

Observe that when Abraham entered the land, the Holy One, blessed be he, appeared to him, as Scripture says: 'To the Lord who appeared to him' (Gen. 12:7). He received there nefesh, and he built an altar to the corresponding grade [in the world of the Sefirot = Malkhut]. Then 'he went on and journeyed towards the south' (Gen. 12:8), that is to say, he received *ruah* [corresponding to Tif'eret]. Finally, he reached the summit of cleaving to God through neshamah, and so 'he built an altar to the Lord' (Gen. 12:8), that is, to that grade which corresponds to neshamah [Binah], and which constitutes the secret of secrets. Then he found that he must test himself and be protected on account of the grades, so without delay 'Abram descended to Egypt' (Gen. 12:10). There he preserved himself from being seduced by the impure essences, and having proved himself, he returned to his own place. After he had descended and been tried, without delay 'Abram went up from Egypt' (Gen. 13:1) – he ascended literally, returned to his own place and attained to the highest degree of faith in God, as Scripture says: 'He went up . . . to the south' (Gen. 13:1). [3

# 9. MODERN MOVEMENTS, MODERN THINKERS

*See 1.8. The Qabbalistic background to the Hasidic selections in 9.1 may be illuminated from 8.3 above. 9.1.1 should be read alongside the classic rabbinic tales quoted in chapter 4 above. Zechariah Mendel, the author of 9.1.2, was a follower of the Zaddiq Elimelech of Lyzhansk. His letter was addressed to his uncle, who had written to him criticising the behaviour of the Zaddiqim and their followers. 9.2.1 and 9.2.2 should be carefully compared and contrasted: they neatly illustrate the shifts in Reform thought between 1885 and 1937. 9.2.3 is a modern example of the ancient Jewish legal institution of the Responsum. A Responsum is the reply of a competent halakhic authority to a question addressed to him on a problem of religious law. For other types of legal text see chapter 5 above. Mendelssohn (9.3.1) was the father of the Jewish Enlightenment which so profoundly influenced modern Jewish thought. Hirsch (9.3.2) is the mentor of Neo-orthodoxy. Schechter (9.3.3) was one of the architects of Conservatism.*

## 9.1 HASIDISM

### 9.1.1 Shivhei ha-Besht. The Besht reveals himself to the sect of the Great Hasidim

When the time drew near for the Besht to reveal himself, it happened that one of the students of our master and teacher Rabbi Gershon was travelling to visit Rabbi Gershon. On Tuesday he called at the house of the Besht, who received him with great honour. When they had eaten a meal the guest said, 'Israel, make ready the horses for me, so that I can continue my journey without delay.' The Besht did so and hitched the horses to the cart. Then the Besht said: 'What would happen if your Honour were to stay here over Sabbath?' The visitor laughed at him. But he had only gone on his way about half a mile when a wheel on his cart broke. He returned to the Besht's, replaced the wheel and set off again. The second time something else broke, till he was delayed there on Wednesday and Thursday as well. On Friday, too, many things befell him and in the end he was forced to spend the Sabbath in the village. He was very sad about this, for what could he do there in the company of a peasant? [1

Meanwhile he was very surprised to see the Besht's wife preparing twelve loaves of *hallah* [bread specially baked for Sabbath]. He said to her: 'Why do you need twelve loaves of hallah?' She replied: 'What if my husband is uneducated [am ha-arez]? He is still observant. Ever since I saw my brother making Qiddush over three loaves of hallah, I have made twelve loaves like this for my husband.' He asked her: 'Do you have a bath-house?' 'Yes,' she replied, 'and a miqveh [ritual bath] as well.' He said; 'What use have you for a miqveh?' She answered: 'My husband is an observant man and goes every day to the miqveh.' Despite all this the guest was very despondent because of his delay there.                                                                                    [2

When the time came to recite the afternoon prayers he said: 'Where is your husband?' She replied: 'He is in the field with the sheep and the cattle.' So the guest recited the afternoon prayers, and the prayers for the inauguration of Sabbath, and the evening prayers all by himself, and still the Besht had not come, for he was praying in his house of seclusion. When he came home, he changed his behaviour, his dress and his manner of speaking. He wished them 'Good Sabbath!' He said to the guest: 'See, I said you would remain here for Sabbath, and so it has happened!' The Besht stood at the wall to make it appear as if he were praying. Then the Besht said to himself: 'If I myself make Qiddush in my usual fashion with intense devotion [devequt], he will see, and realise the truth.' So he honoured the guest by asking him to make Qiddush. They sat at the table to eat, and, in peasant fashion, the Besht's wife sat beside him. They ate the evening meal joyfully and with good feeling, but still the guest was not able to banish the sadness from his heart. The Besht said to him: 'Rabbi, tell us a word of Torah.' The Scriptural portion for that Sabbath was Shemot (Exod. 1:1–6:1), and so the guest told him the whole story of the exile in Egypt under the rule of Pharaoh, according to its simple interpretation [ki-fshuto]. Then they made up a bed for the guest beside the table, and the Besht slept next to his wife.                                                                                                    [3

At midnight the guest awoke and saw a large fire burning by the stove. He ran to the stove because he thought that the firewood had caught fire. He saw a great light. Then he was hurled backwards and fainted. They revived him, and the Besht said: 'You should not have looked at what was not permitted to you!' The guest was amazed at what had happened. In the morning the Besht went to his house of seclusion to pray there in his usual fashion. He returned home joyful and in good spirits, with his head held high. He walked backwards and forwards inside the house singing Asadder li-se'udta,[1] and he made Qiddusha Rabba in his customary manner with intense devotion [devequt]. During the meal he asked the guest to say a word of Torah, but the guest did not know what to say, for he was perplexed. He quoted a phrase and gave the simple interpretation [peshat] of it. The Besht replied: 'I have heard another interpretation of this phrase.' After the meal the Besht went to his house of seclusion, and after the time for afternoon prayers he returned and revealed himself. He spoke words of Torah, and revealed secrets from the Law, such as no ear had ever heard before. He recited the evening prayers and made Havdalah in his usual fashion. Then he commanded his guest to continue on his journey to our master and teacher Rabbi Gershon, but not to disclose to him what had happened. Rather, he was to go to the sect of the Great Hasidim in the town, and also to the rabbi of the community, and deliver the following message: 'There is a great light living near your community. It is fitting that you should seek him out and bring him to the town.' [4

When all the Hasidim and the rabbi heard this, they all decided that the Besht was the one referred to. They remembered all their perplexities about him, but now everything was clear and plain. They all went to the Besht's village to ask him to come to town. The Besht foresaw what would happen, and set off towards the town as they were coming out to meet him. When they met they all went to a certain spot in the forest and made a chair out of branches. They seated the Besht on the chair and accepted him as their rabbi. And the Besht spoke words of Torah to them. [5

### 9.1.2 Letter of Zechariah Mendel of Jaroslav. The spiritual exercises of the Zaddiqim

The first thought of the Zaddiqim is always to do the will of the Creator with a perfect heart, and to serve him in truth, without any regard to self-interest and without any pride or self-aggrandisement whatsoever. At all times they are busy studying the Torah of the Lord, for its own sake, learning in order to fulfil. They have a further motive in study, namely to refine and purify themselves and their thoughts, so as to be able to pray without being disturbed by any undesirable thought [mahashavah zarah], and because of this their prayers ascend on high with intense concentration [kavvanah]. Yet another reason for their studies is to purify themselves and their thoughts, so as to prevent any lustful thought entering their minds during the day, and thus to avoid suffering pollution at night, God forbid! When they study the Gemara they wrap themselves in fear, dread, trembling and tremendous awe of the Lord, and the Torah shines in their faces. When they mention a Tanna, or one of the other masters of the tradition, they imagine it as if that Tanna were actually standing before them, together with the source of his light in the Chariot [Merkavah], in keeping with the advice offered in the Jerusalem Talmud that when one mentions a master of the tradition one should picture him to oneself. As a result of this, dread and tremendous awe of the Lord falls on them without limit or measure, and love of the Torah and its light burns within them unceasingly. When they go from this kind of study, miracles and wonders are performed for them, like those performed in earlier generations, so that they can heal the sick and draw down the divine emanations on all Israel. They are called the 'Eyes of the Congregation', who always watch over the needs of the congregation and offer up supplication for all their wants, whether physical or spiritual. In short, they sanctify themselves to such a degree that they lose all physical desire, and they have neither desire nor longing for any worldly pleasure. [1

While I am speaking of this quality, let me mention to my dear uncle something I once heard from a certain great scholar, may his soul rest in peace. It was an explanation of the verse: 'If you walk in my statutes . . . then I will give you your rains in their season' (Lev. 26:3–4). Rashi explained that 'in their season' means on Sabbath nights. The scholar commented that a man should so constantly immerse himself in pure thoughts in the service of God that he reaches a stage where desire is utterly eliminated from his body and he loses all longing for the pleasures of this world, whether for food or drink, or for the other things from which men derive pleasure, such as honour. However, when a man reaches this stage he becomes incapable of performing the marital act which is enjoined upon him in the Torah as a positive duty. The solution to this problem is that the good Lord in his great mercies takes pity on such a man who has reached this stage, and, when it is absolutely necessary, endows him, for that occasion alone, with physical power and desire, so that he can do his duty. Thereafter the man returns to his former condition and remains in the state in which all physical desire and longing are negated, as he has achieved for himself by his pure deeds and holy thoughts. The interpretation of the verse is now self-evident. 'If you walk in my statutes' means, as I have said above, that the Zaddiq walks with his thoughts constantly on God, till he attains to that stage in which the power of desire is eliminated from him. 'Then I will give your rains in their season' means that God promises that he will give him renewed physical desire, when it is necessary for him to carry out his marital duty as laid down in the Torah. That is why Rashi comments that the rains are given on Sabbath nights, for that is the time when the scholars perform their marital duties. Could any explanation be finer than this? *[2*

The Zaddiqim study the Torah of the Lord day and night, and are constantly discovering new meanings in the Torah. They uncover the secrets of the Torah and its mysteries, and all their words are sweeter than honey or the honeycomb. Whenever they speak some word of Torah or of the fear of God, or offer some new interpretation, there falls on anyone who hears them fear and dread of the terror of the Lord. I cannot comprehend what they achieve during the night, or how far their influence extends with their mighty *yihudim* [devotional exercises aimed at bringing about the union of God with the Shekhinah] and their acts of worship from midnight onwards. However, their great holiness is plain for all to see, and they may be known from their works and deeds. In the first place, water stands ready beside their beds all night. As soon as it is midnight they rise from sleep in fear and great physical trembling. They wash their hands and purify and cleanse themselves, evacuating their bowels thoroughly in the manner laid down in the *Shulhan Arukh*, all in dread, fear and trembling. Then they sit on the ground, with ashes on their heads, and weep with a heart broken and torn into twelve shreds for the exile of the Shekhinah, for the afflictions of Israel, for the yoke of exile, and for the harsh decrees of the king. They pray that the good Lord will speedily take pity on his holy people, and dispose the hearts of the king, his counsellors and princes favourably towards them, to save them from all tribulation, from any kind of sickness, from afflictions and from evil hours. They pray that the holy people should not have to rely on each other's charity, or on the charity of the gentiles, but that their livelihood should be provided for them amply and without trouble before they are in need. They ask that the hearts of the people should be turned to the fear and love of God, and that the stoney heart should be removed from them, and that they should be given a heart of flesh, in order that they might all know and acknowledge the greatness of the Creator and his exalted majesty, and might serve him with joy.      *[3*

After this they study the Gemara and the Tosafot, together with the commentaries on the Mishnah, the earlier and later law codes, and the works of Maimonides. Next they busy themselves with the secret books, such as the *Zohar* and the writings of the Ari.[2] They also study the four sections of the *Shulhan Arukh*, taking a passage from each section, and the Bible. Then they begin to seclude themselves alone with their Maker, and to prepare themselves for prayer, for they see that day is approaching. They banish from their minds as vain the thought of any temporal needs, and fix themselves, their thoughts, their nefesh, ruah and neshamah with great love and fear on the majesty of God. They ponder on man's lowliness and on his latter end. They set before their eyes the day of their death, without prior knowledge. So strongly do they cling to God that they virtually reach the state where they are stripped of corporeality. In all this they follow what is written in the *Shulhan Arukh*, in the section dealing with prayer. Intense love for God so burns in their hearts that a light shines in their faces. All creatures stand in awe of them, and sinners flee from them, because of the extreme terror they inspire through their great holiness and fear of Heaven. You should believe these things, my dear uncle, for in our province they are already known to hundreds of people, thousands have learned of them, and we could demonstrate them with clear signs. When the Zaddiqim pray they effect through their prayers the sort of miracles that used to occur in former generations. Sometimes their word alone is sufficient, just as surely as if they had offered prayer, in the way Scripture speaks of: 'You shall decree something, and it shall be established for you' (Job 22:28). If God should allow my dear uncle to come here I would prove it all to him and he would see it for himself. In the meantime he may believe me with confidence, for I have not yet acquired a reputation as a liar – God forbid! He should believe me that there are among them Zaddiqim who are virtually able to raise the dead by their prayers. With my very own eyes I have seen how on numerous occasions invalids – all of them hopeless cases – were brought to them, and through the pure prayers of the Zaddiqim they were restored to their good health as before, according to the way of all the earth.      *[4*

## 9.2 REFORM

### 9.2.1 The Pittsburgh platform, 1885

In view of the wide divergence of opinion and of the conflicting ideas prevailing in Judaism today, we, as representatives of Reform Judaism in America, in continuation of the work begun at Philadelphia in 1869, unite upon the following principles: *[1*

First – We recognise in every religion an attempt to grasp the Infinite One, and in every mode, source or book of revelation held sacred in any religious system the consciousness of the indwelling of God in man. We hold that Judaism presents the highest conception of the God-idea as taught in our holy Scriptures and developed and spiritualized by the Jewish teachers in accordance with the moral and philosophical progress of their respective ages. We maintain that Judaism preserved and defended amid continual struggles and trials and under enforced isolation this God-idea as the central religious truth for the human race. *[2*

Second – We recognize in the Bible the record of the consecration of the Jewish people to its mission as priest of the One God, and value it as the most potent instrument of religious and moral instruction. We hold that the modern discoveries of scientific researches in the domains of nature and history are not antagonistic to the doctrines of Judaism, the Bible reflecting the primitive ideas of its own age and at times clothing its conception of divine providence and justice dealing with man in miraculous narratives. *[3*

Third – We recognize in the Mosaic legislation a system of training the Jewish people for its mission during its national life in Palestine, and to-day we accept as binding only the moral laws and maintain only such ceremonies as elevate and sanctify our lives, but reject all such as are not adapted to the views and habits of modern civilization. *[4*

Fourth – We hold that all such Mosaic and Rabbinical laws as regulate diet, priestly purity and dress originated in ages and under the influence of ideas altogether foreign to our present mental and spiritual state. They fail to impress the modern Jew with a spirit of priestly holiness; their observance in our days is apt rather to obstruct than to further modern spiritual elevation. *[5*

Fifth – We recognize in the modern era of universal culture of heart and intellect the approach of the realisation of Israel's great Messianic hope for the establishment of the kingdom of truth, justice and peace among all men. We consider ourselves no longer a nation but a religious community, and therefore expect neither a return to Palestine, nor a sacrificial worship under the administration of the sons of Aaron, nor the restoration of any of the laws concerning the Jewish state. *[6*

Sixth – We recognize in Judaism a progressive religion, ever striving to be in accord with the postulates of reason. We are convinced of the utmost necessity of preserving the historical identity with our great past. Christianity and Islam being daughter-religions of Judaism, we appreciate their mission to aid in the spreading of monotheistic and moral truth. We acknowledge that the spirit of broad humanity of our age is our ally in the fulfillment of our mission, and therefore we extend the hand of fellowship to all who co-operate with us in the establishment of the reign of truth and righteousness among men. *[7*

Seventh – We reassert the doctrine of Judaism, that the soul of man is immortal, grounding this belief on the divine nature of the human spirit, which forever finds bliss in righteousness and misery in wickedness. We reject as ideas not rooted in Judaism the belief both in bodily resurrection and in Gehenna and Eden (hell and paradise), as abodes for everlasting punishment or reward. *[8*

Eighth – In full accordance with the spirit of Mosaic legislation which strives to regulate the relation between rich and poor, we deem it our duty to participate in the great task of modern times, to solve on the basis of justice and righteousness the problems presented by the contrasts and evils of the present organisation of society. *[9*

### 9.2.2 The Columbus platform, 1937

In view of the changes that have taken place in the modern world and the consequent need of stating anew the teachings of Reform Judaism, the Central Conference of American Rabbis makes the following declaration of principles. It presents them not as a fixed creed but as a guide for the progressive elements of Jewry. *[1*

**A. Judaism and its foundations**

1. *Nature of Judaism.* Judaism is the historical religious experience of the Jewish people. Though growing out of Jewish life, its message is universal, aiming at the union and perfection of mankind under the sovereignty of God. Reform Judaism recognizes the principle of progressive development in religion and consciously applies this principle to spiritual as well as to cultural and social life. *[2*

Judaism welcomes all truth, whether written in the pages of scripture or deciphered from the records of nature. The new discoveries of science, while replacing the older scientific views underlying our sacred literature, do not conflict with the essential spirit of religion as manifested in the consecration of man's will, heart and mind to the service of God and of humanity. *[3*

2. *God.* The heart of Judaism and its chief contribution to religion is the doctrine of the One, living God, who rules the world through law and love. In Him all existence has its creative source and mankind its ideal of conduct. Though transcending time and space, He is the indwelling Presence of the world. We worship Him as the Lord of the universe and as our merciful Father. *[4*

3. *Man.* Judaism affirms that man is created in the Divine image. His spirit is immortal. He is an active co-worker with God. As a child of God, he is endowed with moral freedom and is charged with the responsibility of overcoming evil and striving after ideal ends. *[5*

4. *Torah.* God reveals Himself not only in the majesty, beauty and orderliness of nature, but also in the vision and moral striving of the human spirit. Revelation is a continuous process, confined to no one group and to no one age. Yet the people of Israel, through its prophets and sages, achieved unique insight in the realm of religious truth. The Torah, both written and oral, enshrines Israel's ever-growing consciousness of God and of the moral law. It preserves the historical precedents, sanctions and norms of Jewish life, and

seeks to mould it in the patterns of goodness and holiness. Being products of historical processes, certain of its laws have lost their binding force with the passing of the conditions which called them forth. But as a depository of permanent spiritual ideals, the Torah remains the dynamic source of the life of Israel. Each age has the obligation to adapt the teachings of the Torah to its basic needs in consonance with the genius of Judaism. [6

5. *Israel.* Judaism is the soul of which Israel is the body. Living in all parts of the world, Israel has been held together by the ties of a common history, and above all, by the heritage of faith. Though we recognize in the group loyalty of Jews who have become estranged from our religious tradition, a bond which still unites them with us. We maintain that it is by its religion and for its religion that the Jewish people has lived. The non-Jew who accepts our faith is welcomed as a full member of the Jewish community. [7

In all lands where our people live, they assume and seek to share loyally the full duties and responsibilities of citizenship and to create seats of Jewish knowledge and religion. In the rehabilitation of Palestine, the land hallowed by memories and hopes, we behold the promise of renewed life for many of our brethren. We affirm the obligation of all Jewry to aid in its upbuilding as a Jewish homeland by endeavouring to make it not only a haven of refuge for the oppressed but also a centre of Jewish culture and spiritual life. [8

Throughout the ages it has been Israel's mission to witness to the Divine in the face of every form of paganism and materialism. We regard it as our historic task to cooperate with all men in the establishment of the kingdom of God, of universal brotherhood, justice, truth and peace on earth. This is our Messianic goal. [9

**B. Ethics**

6. *Ethics and Religion.* In Judaism religion and morality blend into one indissoluble unity. Seeking God means to strive after holiness, righteousness and goodness. The love of God is incomplete without the love of one's fellowmen. Judaism emphasises the kinship of the human race, the sanctity and worth of human life and personality and the right of the individual to freedom and to the pursuit of his chosen vocation. Justice to all, irrespective of race, sect or class is the inalienable right and the inescapable obligation of all. The state and organised government exist in order to further these ends. [10

7. *Social Justice.* Judaism seeks the attainment of a just society by the application of its teachings to the economic order, to industry and commerce, and to national and international affairs. It aims at the elimination of man-made misery and suffering, of poverty and degredation, of tyrany and slavery, of social inequality and prejudice, of ill-will and strife. It advocates the promotion of harmonious relations between warring classes on the basis of equity and justice, and the creation of conditions under which human personality may flourish. It pleads for the safeguarding of childhood against exploitation. It champions the cause of all who work and of their right to an adequate standard of living, as prior to the riches of property. Judaism

emphasises the duty of charity, and strives for a social order which will protect men against the material disabilities of old age, sickness and unemployment. [11

8. *Peace.* Judaism, from the days of the prophets, has proclaimed to mankind the ideal of universal peace. The spiritual and physical disarmament of all nations has been one of its essential teachings. It abhors all violence and relies upon moral education, love and sympathy to secure human progress. It regards justice as the foundation of the well-being of nations and the condition of enduring peace. It urges organised international action for disarmament, collective security and world peace. [12

**C. Religious practice**

9. *The Religious Life.* Jewish life is marked by consecration to these ideals of Judaism. It calls for faithful participation in the life of the Jewish community as it finds expression in home, synagogue and school and in all other agencies that enrich Jewish life and promote its welfare. [13

The Home has been and must continue to be a stronghold of Jewish life, hallowed by the spirit of love and reverence, by moral discipline and religious observance and worship. [14

The Synagogue is the oldest and most democratic institution in Jewish life. It is the prime communal agency by which Judaism is fostered and preserved. It links the Jews of each community and unites them with all Israel. [15

The perpetuation of Judaism as a living force depends upon religious knowledge and upon the education of each new generation in our rich cultural and spiritual heritage. [16

Prayer is the voice of religion, the language of faith and aspiration. It directs man's heart and mind Godward, voices the needs and hopes of the community, and reaches out after goals which invest life with supreme value. To deepen the spiritual life of our people, we must cultivate the traditional habit of communion with God through prayer in both home and synagogue. [17

Judaism as a way of life requires in addition to its moral and spiritual demands, the preservation of the Sabbath, festivals and Holy Days, the retention and development of such customs, symbols and ceremonies as possess inspirational value, the cultivation of distinctive forms of religious art and music and the use of Hebrew, together with the vernacular, in our worship and instruction. [18

These timeless aims and ideals of our faith we present anew to a confused and troubled world. We call upon our fellow Jews to rededicate themselves to them, and, in harmony with all men, hopefully and courageously to continue Israel's eternal quest after God and His kingdom. [19

### 9.2.3 Solomon B. Freehof. Responsum concerning the use of an anaesthetic during circumcision

*A physician performing a circumcision insisted upon using an anaesthetic 'to prevent fuss and bother with the baby crying, etc.' Should this be permitted or even encouraged from the point of view of Jewish legal tradition?*

This question has been asked a number of times in recent years when the use of anaesthetics (even for minor surgery) has come into general use. The question is asked usually with regard to adult converts. Sometimes a convert will not consent to circumcision unless an anaesthetic be used. In one case the circumstances were reversed and the convert insisted that no anaesthetic be used because he wanted to feel pain, since he considered the pain to be sacrificial. Sometimes it is asked with regard to children. A Jewish child had not been circumcised in infancy (for reasons of ill health). Now at the age of five, he is to be circumcised and the mother insists that a local anaesthetic be used. Out of these various cases a general attitude has emerged as to the use of anaesthetics for adults and for children.                                    [1

The first discussion of the question was by Meir Arik, the great Galician authority in the past generation. In his Responsa *Imre Yosher*, II, 140, he decides definitely in the negative. His arguments are worth notice because they reveal the general mood of the authorities of the time to all new suggestions which may effect [*sic!*] the ceremonial laws. He calls attention to the Talmudic debate (in *Kiddushin* 21b) which deals with the piercing of the ear of a Hebrew slave who refuses to be set free. The Talmud there speaks of '*sham*' (an anaesthetic medicine). This proves, he said, that the Talmud was well acquainted with such medicines. Yet since the Talmud does not mention the use of anaesthetic medicines in circumcision, it clearly was opposed to their use. Furthermore, he says that the Midrash (Genesis *Rabba* 47:9) tells that Abraham was in pain because of his circumcision, and it was for that pain that God gave him additional reward. Then he concludes with a general statement in the nature of a warning, namely, that we have never used anaesthetics in the past and God forbid that we should introduce any novelties.               [2

This firm and indignant negative is not shared by the majority of the scholars who have dealt with the question. For example, Bezalel Shafran (Responsa *Rabaz* 125) refutes the prohibitory opinion found in the book *Sefer ha-Bris*, in which it was insisted that the circumcised must be awake, since the fulfillments of commandments require conscious intention (*kavvana*). Shafran proves that a child may be asleep during the operation and that fact would not impair the legal validity of the circumcision.                                         [3

The strongest opinion in favour of the use of anaesthetics comes from the famous Rabbi of Kishinev, Judah Lev Zirelsohn (who was martyred by the Nazis). It was he who dealt with the question of the five-year-old boy mentioned above. In his *Ma'arche Lev*, 53, after reviewing various arguments, he comes to the general conclusion that the Torah *nowhere requires pain* in the circumcision, and therefore he agrees in the case mentioned to the use of anaesthetics.                                                                   [4

Gedalia Felder of Toronto, who has done yeoman service in collecting and organising the Law and Customs in his four-volume work *Yesodey Yeshurun*, has now written a special work on adoption, conversion, etc. In this work (*Nachalas Z'vi*, p. 57) he summarises the various opinions on this question and also refutes the negative opinion of Meir Arik.                    [5

In the light of the above, we may conclude that there is no objection to anaesthetics. The law does not insist upon pain in the fulfillment of this commandment. However, to this extent Meir Arik is correct, that we should not introduce novelties unless there is good reason for them. If the child is likely to be naturally asleep during the operation (as often happens) the law does not require that he be wakened (cf. the opinion of Bezalel Shafran). However, if the operation is done by a doctor and he insists that an anaesthetic be used, then we assume that he has a good reason for it and we should not raise any objections. In general, *we* should not institute the use of anaesthetics as a regular procedure, but should permit them when the surgeon or the parent ask that they be used.                    [6

The inquirer subsequently asked about the popular idea that wine which is (sometimes) given the infant during circumcision is for the purpose of allaying the pain of circumcision.                    [7

It is customary for the *mohel* to give a drop or a touch of wine with his finger after the two blessings, when the phrase from Ezekiel is used, 'Live in thy blood.' This custom is mentioned by Joseph Caro in the *Shulchan Aruch* (*Yore Deah* 265:2). Of all the classic commentators, only the Spaniard, Abudraham, gives an explanation; but his explanation has to do with the sinful Israelites being given to drink the water into which their Golden Calf had been ground. A later commentator tries to connect it with the word 'live' in the Ezekiel quotation, and attempts to have the drop of wine symbolise eternal life.                    [8

These explanations are obviously forced. One may say that no explanation is given for the drop of wine. Nowadays they sometimes give the child a bit of cloth or cake soaked in wine. This would lend itself to the notion that it was for the purpose of allaying pain. But the texts only speak of a 'drop' or a finger touch. This could hardly have any pain-allaying effect and, therefore, this could not be the reason.                    [9

For completeness' sake, it might be added that another taste of wine is sometimes given the child on fast-days at the blessing. The *mohel* recites the blessing but since it is a fast-day, he may not taste the wine. Therefore (in order that the blessing not be a 'vain blessing') a taste of the wine is given to the child (cf. Isserles to *Yore Deah* 265:4, *Orah Hayyim* 621:3). But Abudraham quotes Ibn Gayyat and Maimonides, who object to the practice and who prefer that on fast-days the wine blessing be omitted entirely. There is a wide variance in the *minhagim* about this practice. Some say: Give it to the *sandek* to taste. Some say: Give it to the young boys present to taste. Some say: Give it to the mother (*Mishna Berura*, The '*Chofetz Chaim*' to 621) and some say: Give it to the child. For a fuller discussion see *Eduth L'Yisroel* by Jacob Werdiger (Bnai Brak, 1963) page 127, 3.                    [10

The present custom of giving the child a wine-soaked object to suck and which leads to the notion of allaying pain, is not authentic. Only a drop was used and of this no pain alleviation is either mentioned or is possible.        *[11*

## 9.3  THREE MODERN THINKERS

### 9.3.1  Moses Mendelssohn. Judaism as revealed legislation

It is true: I recognise no eternal truths, other than those which can not only be comprehended by human reason, but also demonstrated and verified by the human faculties. However, he[3] is misled by a serious misconception of Judaism if he supposes that I cannot maintain this position without deviating from the religion of my forefathers. On the contrary, I hold that this is an essential point of the Jewish religion, and I believe that this doctrine constitutes a characteristic difference between Judaism and Christianity. To put it in one word: I believe that Judaism knows nothing of revealed religion [*geoffenbarte Religion*], in the sense in which this is understood by Christians. The Israelites possess divine legislation [*göttliche Gesetzgebung*] – laws, commandments, statutes, rules of conduct, instruction in God's will and in how they are to behave in order to attain temporal and eternal felicity. It was these laws and commandments that were revealed to them by Moses in a miraculous and supernatural way, but not dogmas, or saving truths, or universal propositions of reason. These the Eternal reveals to us, as to all other men, at all times through nature and events, never through the spoken or written word. . . .        *[1*

Judaism does not claim to possess the exclusive revelation of eternal truths which are necessary for man's happiness. It does not claim to be revealed religion in the sense in which this term is usually understood. Revealed religion [*geoffenbarte Religion*] is one thing, revealed legislation [*geoffenbarte Gesetzgebung*] another. The voice which was heard at Sinai on that day did not announce: 'I am the Eternal, your God, the necessary, self-existent Being, who is omnipotent and omniscient, and who rewards men in a future life according to their deeds!' This is general religion for all mankind, not Judaism; and the universal religion of mankind, without which men can be neither virtuous nor happy, should not – indeed, fundamentally could not – have been revealed at Sinai. For whom could the thunder-claps and the trumpet-blasts have convinced of these saving doctrines? Certainly not the unthinking animal man who had not yet been led by his own meditations to recognise the existence of an invisible Being who rules the visible world. The thunder-claps would have imparted no concepts to such a person, and so could never have convinced him. Still less would they have convinced the Sophist who has so many doubts and difficulties roaring in his ears that he no longer perceives the voice of sound common sense. He demands rational proofs, not miracles. And even if some great religious teacher were to resurrect from the earth all the dead who ever walked on it, in order to confirm some eternal truth, the sceptic would still say: 'The Teacher has, indeed, raised many dead, but I still know no more about eternal truth than I did before. All I know is that someone is able to perform and to make us hear extraordinary things, but there may exist other, similar beings who simply do not chose to reveal themselves at this moment.' And how far is all this still removed from the infinitely sublime idea of a unique, eternal Deity, who rules this whole universe according to his own absolute will, and who looks into men's innermost thoughts, in order to recompense their works according to their merit, if not here, then in the hereafter! – Anyone who did not already know all this, who was not already convinced of these truths which are necessary for human happiness, and approached the holy mountain unprepared, might have been stunned and overwhelmed by the great and wonderful happenings there, but he would still not have been enlightened as to the truth. No! all this was supposed to be already known; probably during the days of preparation it had been taught and explained, and through human arguments placed beyond all doubt. And now the divine voice announced: 'I am the Eternal, your God, who brought you out of the land of Egypt and freed you from slavery' (Exod. 20:2). It was an historical fact on which the legislation of this particular people was to be founded, and it was laws that were to be revealed there, commandments and ordinances, not eternal truths of religion. 'I am the Eternal, your God, who made a covenant with your forefathers, Abraham, Isaac and Jacob, and swore to them to form from their seed a nation special to myself. The time has at last come when this promise must be fulfilled. To this end I have redeemed you from slavery in Egypt, redeemed you with unheard-of miracles and signs. I am your Redeemer, your Sovereign and King. I now make with you a covenant, and give you laws by which you must live and become a fortunate people in the land which I shall bestow on you.' All these are historical truths which, by their very nature, rest on historical evidence, which must be validated by authority, and can be corroborated by miracles.          [2

According to Judaism miracles and extraordinary signs cannot furnish proof for or against the eternal truths of reason. Hence we are instructed by Scripture itself not to listen to a prophet if he teaches or advises things which are contrary to established truths, even if he confirms his mission by miracles. Indeed, we are bidden to condemn the wonder-worker to death, if he seeks to entice us into idolatry. For miracles can only verify testimonies, support authority, confirm the reliability of witnesses and of those who transmit traditions. But there is no testimony or authority that can overthrow an established truth of reason, or put a doubtful notion beyond doubt or question.          [3

Although that divine book which we have received from Moses is essentially a lawbook, and so contains ordinances, rules of conduct and regulations, it also includes, as is well known, an inexhaustible store of rational truths and religious doctrines, which are so closely bound up with the laws as to constitute with them a single unity. All laws refer to, or are based upon, the eternal truths of reason, or they recall those truths, or arouse us to reflect on them, so that our Rabbis rightly said: 'The laws and the doctrines are related to each other as the body to the soul.' I shall have occasion to say more about this later on. For the moment I shall rest content with simply asserting it as a fact which anyone can verify for himself who examines the laws of Moses, even if only in translation. The experience of many centuries also teaches that this divine lawbook has become for the great part of the human race a source of knowledge from which they derive new ideas, or correct old ones. The more you delve into it, the more astonished you will be at the insights which lie hidden within it. At first glance, indeed, truth presents itself in this book in the plainest garb without any pretension. But the nearer you approach her, and the purer, more innocent, more loving and longing is the look with which you gaze at her, the more she will disclose to you her divine beauty, which she covers with a thin veil, so that it may not be profaned by vulgar and unholy eyes. But all these excellent propositions are addressed to our understanding and laid before us for consideration, without being forced upon our belief. Among all the precepts and ordinances of the Mosaic law there is not one which demands: 'You shall believe!'; or, 'You shall not believe!' Rather, they all say: 'You shall do!'; or, 'You shall not do!' Faith cannot be commanded, for faith accepts no commands other than those which come to it by way of conviction. All the commands of the divine law are addressed to man's will, to his capacity to act. Indeed, the word in Hebrew which is usually translated 'belief', in most cases really means 'trust', 'confidence', 'firm reliance on a pledge or promise': 'Abraham trusted [*he'emin*] the Eternal and it was reckoned to him for righteousness' (Gen. 15:6); 'The Israelites saw . . . and trusted [*vayya'aminu*] the Lord and his servant Moses' (Exod. 14:31). Where it is a question of the eternal truths of reason, the text speaks not of 'believing' but of 'understanding' and 'knowing': 'That you might know [*la-da'at*] that the Eternal is the true God; there is none other beside him' (Deut. 4:35); 'Know [*ve-yada'ta*], therefore, and lay it to heart, that the Lord is God in heaven above and on the earth beneath: there is none other beside him' (Deut. 4:39); 'Hear, O Israel, the Lord our God, the Lord is One' (Deut. 6:4). Nowhere does it say: 'Believe, O Israel, and you will be blessed! Do not doubt, O Israel, or you will suffer this or that punishment!' Command and prohibition, reward and punishment, apply only to acts, whether of commission or omission, in which a man can exercise free choice, and these acts are affected by our notions of good and evil, and hence also by our hopes and our fears. Belief and doubt, assent and dissent, on the other hand, are governed neither by our volition nor by our hopes and fears, but by our knowledge of what is true or false. *[4*

It is for this reason that ancient Judaism has no symbolic books, no articles of faith. No one has to swear to creeds, or give his solemn consent to articles of faith. Indeed, we lack any real concept of what are called 'affirmations of faith', and we must regard such affirmations as incompatible with the spirit of true Judaism. Maimonides was the first to whom the idea occurred of reducing the religion of his forefathers to a fixed number of principles, so that, as he himself explained, religion, like all the other sciences, might have its axioms from which everything else could be deduced. From this purely casual idea arose the thirteen articles of the Jewish catechism to which we are indebted for the morning hymn *Yigdal*, and some fine writings of Hasdai [Crescas], [Joseph] Albo and [Isaac] Abrabanel. But these are the only results which till now Maimonides' articles have produced. They have not yet, thank God!, been forged into fetters for faith. Hasdai disputes some of them and proposes alterations. Albo reduces the number and would recognise only three basic principles, which agree fairly well with those proposed at a later date by Herbert of Cherbury for the catechism. Yet others, particularly [Isaac] Luria and his disciples, the modern Qabbalists, are unwilling to recognise any fixed number of tenets, maintaining that everything in our teaching is fundamental. However, this controversy was conducted, as all such controversies should be, with earnestness and zeal, but without bitterness and rancour. And although Maimonides' Thirteen Principles have been accepted by the large majority of our people, no one, as far as I know, has ever condemned Albo as a heretic, because he reduced their number and wanted to carry them back to more universal axioms. In this matter we have not disregarded the important dictum of our Sages: 'Though this one permits and this one prohibits, nevertheless both teach the words of the living God' [Babylonian Talmud, Eruvin 13b].  *[5*

Here too everything comes down in the end to the distinction between believing and knowing, between religious doctrine and religious law. All human knowledge can, of course, be reduced to a few basic concepts which are absolutely fundamental. The fewer these are, the stronger will be the superstructure that rests upon them. But laws can tolerate no abridgement. In their case everything is fundamental, and, since this is so, we have good grounds for saying: 'To us all the words of Scripture, all God's commandments and prohibitions, are fundamental.' Should you, nevertheless, wish to know the quintessence of these laws, then listen to how one of our great teachers, Hillel the Elder, who lived before the destruction of the second Temple, defined it. A heathen once said to him: 'Rabbi, teach me the whole law while I stand on one foot!' Shammai, to whom he had previously made this unreasonable request, dismissed him with contempt; but Hillel, famed for his unshakable composure and gentleness, said: 'My son, love your neighbour as yourself. This is the text of the law; all the rest is commentary. Now go and study!' [Babylonian Talmud, Shabbat 31a].  *[6*

### 9.3.2 S. R. Hirsch. The dangers of updating Judaism

But above all what kind of Judaism would that be, if we were allowed to bring it up to date? If the Jew were actually permitted at any given time to bring his Judaism up to date, then he would no longer have any need for it; it would no longer be worthwhile speaking of Judaism. We would take Judaism and throw it out among the other ancient products of delusion and absurdity, and say no more about Judaism and the Jewish religion!  *[1*

If the Bible is to be for me the word of God, and Judaism and the Jewish law the revealed will of God, am I to be allowed to take my stand on the highway of the ages and the lands and ask every mortal pilgrim on earth for his opinions, born as they are between dream and waking, between error and truth, in order to submit the word of the living God to his approval, in order to mould it to suit his passing whim? And am I to say: 'See here modern, purified Judaism! Here we have the word of the living God, refined, approved and purified by men!' [2

If the Bible is to be for me God's word, and Judaism and the Jewish law God's revealed will, am I to be allowed to consult my belly, my sensuality and convenience, my casual advantage, to see whether it is also sweet and easy, whether it is also reasonable and pleasant? Am I to be allowed to take religion, my religion which God has given me as the yardstick by which to measure myself, my times and all my actions, and first measure it and adjust it to suit the pettiness, the sensuality and the narrow-mindedness of my passing desires? Am I to be allowed to falsify the divine yardstick in accordance with my passing needs, and then to brag and say: 'See now, up-to-date, purified Judaism. Here we have the word of almighty God, cut down to fit my own weaknesses? See how much in tune with it we are, my times and I!' [3

Let us not delude ourselves. The whole question is quite simply this. Are the words 'And God spoke to Moses as follows,' with which the laws of the Jewish Bible begin, true or false? Do we really and truly believe that the omniponent, holy God spoke thus to Moses? Are we speaking the truth when, in the presence of our brethren, we lay our hand upon the Torah Scroll and say that God has given us this teaching, his teaching, the teaching of truth, and in so doing has planted eternal life in our midst? If this is to be more than lip service, more than verbiage and deception, then we must keep this Torah and fulfil it without abridgement, without fault-finding, under all circumstances and at all times. This word of God must be for us the eternal rule, superior to all human judgement, to which at all times we must conform ourselves and all our actions, and, instead of complaining that it is not in tune with the age, our one complaint should be that the age is not in tune with it! [4

And if in fulfilling this word of God we choose to follow the teachings and precepts that have come down to us from the Rabbis, then once again we may and indeed must do so only if and because those teachings (passed down as they are to us by those selfsame generations from whose hand we are prepared to receive as authentic the written word of God) are regarded by us as a tradition *orally* transmitted by God, the selfsame omnipotent, holy God, to Moses, and from Moses to each succeeding generation – a tradition established for the purpose of regulating the practical observance of God's word. This tradition, on the other hand, is for us nothing more than tradition, the word of God passed on *orally*, as Rabbinic Judaism has always taught through the long centuries of its history. [5

But if this tradition is for us no tradition, but only a mask, a pious fraud by which a priestly caste has foisted its own views on the people as the transmitted word of God; if, in consequence, the fathers have deceived their sons and grandsons, allowing them to live and suffer, to endure and die, for the sake of a deception and delusion; if each of us can be his own oracle and mould the Biblical laws to suit his own views and opinions, then that law is no longer and ought no longer to be God's word; then God did not speak to Moses; then what we have in our hands is not divine teaching; then we, and the whole of humanity whose hopes of salvation are rooted in this word, are all deceivers and deceived, and it is high time openly and freely to get rid of the whole miserable business.                                                                                             [6

These are the alternatives; there are no others. If Judaism has been established by God, then its business is to teach the age, but not to let itself be taught by the age.                                                                                             [7

From the beginning God placed Judaism and its adherents in opposition to the age. For thousands of years Judaism was the only protest against a totally pagan world. And if this opposition grew less as the centuries wore on, this was not because Judaism changed to suit the non-Jewish conditions, but because more and more seeds of the Jewish spirit, sparks from the Jewish word of God, found a home in the bosom of the non-Jewish world, and the Jewish word of God more and more fulfilled its silent mission in the world.                                   [8

For two thousand years at the dawn of history, as the Jewish word of God tells us, things went from bad to worse, the times became ever more godless. Then God spoke to the first Jew, Abraham: 'Dare not to conform to the spirit of the age. Go your own way, far from your native land, your family, your father's house, and let my approval, the approval of the All-Sufficient, be sufficient for you! [cf. Gen. 12:1].' And so among the most cultivated peoples of his time, the Egyptians and the Phoenicians, Abraham wandered alone – with God.           [9

And when the descendants of Abraham had grown in the bitter school of suffering into a people who could be the bearers of God's laws, God placed them once again amongst the most cultured nations of their time, pointed to the Egyptian culture on their left and to the culture of central Asia on their right, and said: 'I have separated you from these peoples; do not walk in their ways. Follow my laws and remain true!'                                                                 [10

And when the Jewish state fell in ruins, because Jeroboam in his cleverness had introduced for the first time the principle of adapting Judaism to conform to the times, and Judah once again wandered into strange lands, God addressed to them through the mouth of his prophets this warning valid for all time: 'But what you have in mind will never come to pass, when you say, "We shall be like the peoples of all other lands, worshipping wood and stone" ' [Ezek. 20:32]. 'Remember the teaching of Moses my servant which I commanded to him on Horeb for all Israel, even statutes and ordinances' [Mal. 4:4].            [11

All this is abundantly clear from the beginning to the end of the Biblical record, and yet today we make the amazing discovery that Judaism segregates its adherents and makes them appear to the superficial children of every age so out of step with their times!                                                                                   [12

Yet this segregation is only superficial. There is nothing so well suited as Judaism to inspire in its adherents an all-embracing love, to implant in them a spirit and a heart to which nothing human in the whole wide world is alien, which always shows the most open interest in all human suffering and well-being, which perceives in the darkest events of history God's eternal providence at work. It is the Jew who plants at the grave of the most degenerate profligacy the banner of hope for a future resurrection and return to God, and whose whole strength lies in the consciousness that all men are travelling with him towards the kingdom of God on earth, in which truth and love, justice and salvation will everywhere dwell. [13

Consider Abraham, the first and most isolated Jew on earth. Was any isolation ever like this? He was unique and alone with God on earth, unique and alone in conflict with the whole of his age. Yet what a heart he carried in his bosom – full of modesty, full of kindness, full of compassion and love for all, even for the most depraved men of his time! When the judgement of God threatened Sodom and Gomorrah, the greatest cess-pit of human depravity ever known, it was Abraham who prayed for Sodom and Gomorrah. [14

God concluded with him and with his descendants the most separatist of covenants and sealed this covenant with the most separatist of signs, marked on his body and the bodies of his descendants. Yet see how, with this painful sign of separation still fresh on his body, Abraham sits outside his tent in the heat of the sun, keeping watch for weary travellers, inviting wayfarers – strangers and idolators – into his house, and showing compassion and kindness, and the all-embracing love of God, to his fellow men without distinction. [15

How could it have been any different. Was not this universalism, this broad sympathy, those good deeds done to all without distinction, the essence and object, the reason and meaning of his separation? Was it not this very universalism which set him apart? According to the profound words of our Sages, it was when men, to perpetuate their own fame, had begun to build a tower reaching up to heaven, that God called Abraham to himself. *They* were motivated by selfish pleasure-seeking and ambition. They said: '*Na'aseh lanu shem* – Let us make *for ourselves* a name' [Gen. 11:4]. Their famous monument separated and divided men from each other, though it *seemed* to unite them. It was then God said to Abraham: 'You must go another way. Desire nothing for yourself, for your own blessing, for your own fame. In my name call men together, *qara ba-shem* [Gen. 12:8], and be a blessing to them, *heyeh berakhah* [Gen. 12:2], for see, I have destined you to be the father of mankind. Let this be *your* blessing, this *your* fame!'⁴ [16

This remained the fundamental character of Judaism. Abraham was set apart for the sake of mankind, and for the sake of mankind Judaism has to follow its separate path through the ages. [17

Judaism is the one religion which does *not* say: 'Outside me there is no salvation!' It is Judaism – a religion decried for its supposed particularism – which teaches that the upright of all peoples are journeying towards the same blessed destination. It is the very same Rabbis, so often disparaged for their alleged particularism, who point out that when the prophets and poets predict a glorious new day for humanity they say nothing about priests, Levites and Israelites, but speak only of 'the righteous', 'the just', and 'the honest', and so the righteous, the just and the honest of all peoples are included in the most glorious blessing. And in the darkest hours when the frenzied mob destroyed the Jewish synagogues and tore up the Jewish books, the persecuted, derided Jew always turned to his God and consoled himself by looking forward to the time when even this frenzy would disappear and the name of the one and only God would have implanted justice, truth and peace in every human breast. . . .    *[18*

But long before this goal is reached, in all his wandering through the ages and the lands, his Judaism has not brought the Jew into such sharp conflict with the ages and the lands. Rather this very Judaism has shown him how to adapt to every age and land through which he has wandered, and taught him to form the friendliest and closest ties with every age and every land.    *[19*

For he knows that the just and the pure of all societies are working with him for the kingdom of God on earth. He knows, too, that especially during the last two thousand years or so, not only the seeds of a purer humanity which were preserved even in the midst of heathenism, but also the seeds of genuinely Jewish thought, have been germinating and sprouting, and in a variety of spiritual endeavours have contributed to the salvation of mankind. And it is his Judaism – guiding him as it does through the garden of nature and the galleries of history, and summoning him to use his powers fully in the service of God – that encourages him to perceive in each newly discovered truth a welcome contribution to the clearer revelation of God in nature and in history, and to recognise in each new art and science a welcome addition to the means for rendering perfect service to God.    *[20*

Hence the Jew will not shy away from any science, any art or education, provided that it is truly genuine, truly moral, and truly promotes the good of mankind. He has to test everything by the eternally inviolable touchstone of his divine law. Whatever fails this test, he totally disregards. But the firmer he stands upon the rock of his Judaism, the more thoroughly he is umbued with the consciousness of his Judaism, the more inclined will he be to accept and thankfully appropriate whatever is really true and genuinely good, provided it conforms to the truths of Judaism. No matter in whose mind it originated, no matter who uttered it, he will always be ready *le-qabbel ha-emet mimmi she-amarah* [to accept the truth no matter who speaks it]. Nowhere will he ever sacrifice so much as a thread of his Judaism, nowhere will he ever shape his Judaism to suit the times, but, whenever his age offers him anything consonant with his Judaism, he will gladly make it his own. In every age he will regard it as his duty, from the standpoint of his Judaism, to seek to appreciate the age and its conditions, so that in every age, with whatever new means the age provides and in whatever new circumstances the age creates, he may unfold in every greater richness the spirit of his ancient Judaism, and fully and totally fulfil the task of his ancient Judaism, in every greater fulness and with ever-increased fidelity.    *[21*

### 9.3.3  Solomon Schechter.  The faith of Catholic Israel

Some years ago when the waves of the Higher Criticism of the Old Testament reached the shores of this country, and such questions as the heterogeneous composition of the Pentateuch, the comparatively late date of the Levitical Legislation, and the post-exilic origin of certain Prophecies as well as of the Psalms began to be freely discussed by the press and even in the pulpit, the invidious remark was often made: What will now become of Judaism when its last stronghold, the Law, is being shaken to its very foundations?                    [1

Such a remark shows a very superficial acquaintance with the nature of an old historical religion like Judaism, and the richness of the resources it has to fall back upon in cases of emergency.                    [2

As a fact, the emergency did not quite surprise Judaism. The alarm signal was given some 150 years ago by an Italian Rabbi, Abiad Sar Shalom Bazilai, in his pamphlet *The Faith of the Sages*. The pamphlet is, as the title indicates, of a polemical character, reviewing the work of the Jewish rationalistic schools, and after warming up in his attacks against heterodox views, Bazilai exclaims: 'Nature and simple meaning, they are our misfortune.' By 'nature and simple meaning' Bazilai, who wrote in Hebrew, understood what we would call Natural Science and Philology. With the right instinct of faith, Bazilai hit on the real sore points. For though he mostly argues against the philosophical systems of Aristotle and his commentators, he felt that it is not speculation that will ever seriously endanger religion. There is hardly any metaphysical system, old or new, which has not in the course of time been adapted by able dialecticians to the creed which they happened to hold. In our own time we have seen the glorious, though not entirely novel, spectacle of Agnosticism itself becoming the rightful handmaid of Queen Theology. The real danger lies in 'nature' (or Natural Science) with its stern demand of law and regularity in all phenomena, and in the 'simple meaning' (or Philology) with its inconsiderate insistence on truth. Of the two, the 'simple meaning' is the more objectionable. Not only is it very often at variance with Tradition, which has its own code of interpretation, but it is constantly increasing the difficulties raised by science. For if words could only have more than one meaning, there would be no objection to reading the first words of Genesis, 'In *a* beginning God *evolved*.' The difficulties of science would then be disposed of easily enough. Maimonides, who was as bold an interpreter as he was a deep metaphysician, hinted plainly that were he as convinced of the eternity of matter as he was satisfied of the impossibility of any corporeal quality in the deity, he would feel as little compunction in explaining (figuratively) the contents of the first chapter of Genesis as he did in allegorising the anthropomorphic passages of the Bible. Thus in the end all the difficulties resolve themselves into the one great difficulty of the 'simple meaning'. The best way to meet this difficulty was found to be to shift the centre of gravity in Judaism and to place it in the secondary meaning, thus making religion independent of philology and all its dangerous consequences.                    [3

F

This shifting work was chiefly done, perhaps not quite consciously, by the historical school which followed upon that of Mendelssohn and his first successors. The historical school, which is still in the ascendant, comprises many of the best Jewish writers who either by their learning or by their ecclesiastical profession as Rabbis and preachers in great communities have acquired some important position among their brethren. The men who have inaugurated this movement were Krochmal (1785–1841), Rapoport (1790–1867), and Zunz (1794–1886).                                      [4

It is not a mere coincidence that the first representatives of the historical school were also the first scholars who proved themselves more or less ready to join the modern school of Bible Criticism, and even to contribute their share to it. The first two, Krochmal and Rapoport, early in the second quarter of this century accepted and defended the view about second Isaiah, the post-exilic origin of many Psalms, and the late date of Ecclesiastes; whilst Zunz, who began (in 1832) with denying the authenticity of Ezekiel, concluded his literary career (1873) with a study of the Bible (*Gesammelte Schriften*, i. pp. 217–290), in which he expressed his view 'that the Book of Leviticus dates from a later period than the Book of Deuteronomy, later even than Ezekiel, having been composed during the age of the Second Temple, when there already existed a well-established priesthood which superintended the sacrificial worship.' But when Revelation or the Written Word is reduced to the level of history, there is no difficulty in elevating history in its aspect of Tradition to the rank of Scripture, for both have then the same human or divine origin (according to the student's predilection for the one or the other adjective), and emanate from the same authority. Tradition becomes thus the means whereby the modern divine seeks to compensate himself for the loss of the Bible, and the theological balance is to the satisfaction of all parties happily readjusted.                       [5

Jewish Tradition, or, as it is commonly called, the Oral Law, or, as we may term it (in consideration of its claims to represent an interpretation of the Bible), the Secondary Meaning of the Scriptures, is mainly embodied in the works of the Rabbis and their subsequent followers during the Middle Ages. Hence the zeal and energy with which the historical school applied itself to the Jewish post-Biblical literature, not only elucidating its texts by means of new critical editions, dictionaries and commentaries, but also trying to trace its origins and to pursue its history through its gradual development. To the work of Krochmal in this direction a special essay is devoted in this volume. The labours of Rapoport are more of a biographical and bibliographical nature, being occupied mostly with the minor details of the lives and writings of various famous Jewish Rabbis in the Middle Ages; thus they offer but little opportunity for general theological comment. Of more importance in this respect are the hints thrown out in his various works by Zunz, who was just as emphatic in asserting the claims of Tradition as he was advanced in his views on Bible criticism. Zunz's greatest work is *Die Gottesdienstlichen Vorträge* – an awkward title, which in fact means 'The History of the Interpretation of the

Scriptures as forming part of the divine service.' Now if a work displaying such wide learning and critical acumen, and written in such an impartial spirit, can be said to have a bias, it was towards bridging over the seemingly wide gap between the Written Word (the Scriptures) and the Spoken Word (the Oral Law or Tradition), which was the more deeply felt, as most of Zunz's older contemporaries were men grown up in the habits of the eighteenth century – a century distinguished both for its ignorance of and its power of ignoring, the teachings of history. Indeed it would seem that ages employed in making history have no time for studying it. 			[6

Zunz accomplished the task he set himself, by showing, as already indicated, the late date of certain portions of the Bible, which by setting the early history of Israel in an ideal light betray the moralising tendency of their authors, and are, in fact, little more than a traditional interpretation of older portions of Scripture, adapted to the religious needs of the time. Placing thus the origin of Tradition in the Bible itself, it was a comparatively easy matter for Zunz to prove its further continuity. Prophecy and Interpretation are with him the natural expressions of the religious life of the nation; and though by the loss of Israel's independence the voice of the prophets gradually died away, the voice of God was still heard. Israel continues to consult God through the medium of the Scriptures, and He answers his people by the mouth of the Scribes, the Sages, the Interpreters of the Law; whilst the liturgy of the Synagogue, springing up at the time when the Psalms were still being composed, expands its later stages through the work of the Poets of the Synagogue into such a rich luxuriance 'that it forms in itself a treasure of history, poetry, philosophy; and prophecy and psalms are again revived in the hymnology of the Middle Ages.' This is in brief the lesson to be learned from Zunz's *Gottesdienstliche Vorträge* as far as it deals with the significance of Tradition; and it is in the introduction to this work that Zunz expresses himself to the following effect: Indispensable is the free Spoken Word. Mankind has acquired all its ideal treasures only by Word of Mouth; an education continuing through all stages of life. In Israel, too, the Word of Instruction transmitted from mouth to mouth was never silenced. 	[7

The historical school has never, to my knowledge, offered the world a theological programme of its own. By the nature of its task, its labours are mostly conducted in the field of philology and archaeology, and it pays but little attention to purely dogmatic questions. On the whole, its attitude towards religion may be defined as an enlightened Scepticism combined with a staunch conservatism which is not even wholly devoid of a certain mystical touch. As far as we may gather from vague remarks and hints thrown out now and then, its theological position may be thus defined: – It is not the mere revealed Bible that is of first importance to the Jew, but the Bible as it repeats itself in history, in other words, as it is interpreted by Tradition. The Talmud, that wonderful mine of religious ideas from which it would be just as easy to draw up a manual for the most orthodox as to extract a vade-mecum for the most sceptical, lends some countenance to this view by certain controversial passages – not to be taken seriously – in which 'the words of the scribes' are placed above the words of the Torah. Since, then, the interpretation of Scripture or the Secondary Meaning is mainly the product of changing historical influences, it follows that the centre of authority is actually removed from the Bible and placed in some *living body*, which, by reason of its being in touch with the ideal aspirations and the religious needs of the age, is best able to determine the Secondary Meaning. This living body, however, is not represented by any section of the nation, or any corporate priesthood, or Rabbihood, but by the collective conscience of Catholic Israel as embodied in the Universal Synagogue. The Synagogue 'with its long continuous cry after God for more than twenty-three centuries,' with its unremitted activity in teaching and developing the word of God, with its uninterrupted succession of Prophets, Psalmists, Scribes, Assideans, Rabbis, Patriarchs, Interpreters, Elucidators, Eminences, and Teachers, with its glorious record of saints, martyrs, sages, philosophers, scholars, and mystics; this Synagogue, the only true witness to the past, and forming in all ages the sublimest expression of Israel's religious life, must also retain its authority as the sole true guide for the present and the future. And being in communion with this Synagogue, we may also look hopefully for a safe and rational solution of our present theological troubles. For was it not the Synagogue which even in antiquity determined the fate of Scripture? On the one hand, for example, books like Ezekiel, the Song of Songs, and Ecclesiastes, were only declared to be Holy Writ in virtue of the interpretation put upon them by the Rabbis: and, on the other hand, it was the veto of the Rabbis which excluded from the canon the works that now pass under the name of Apocrypha. We may, therefore, safely trust that the Synagogue will again assert its divine right in passing judgment upon the Bible when it feels called upon to exercise that holy office. It is 'God who has chosen the Torah, and Moses His servant, and Israel His people.' But indeed God's choice invariably coincides with the wishes of Israel; He 'performeth all things' upon which the councils of Israel, meeting under promise of the divine presence and communion, have previously agreed. As the Talmud somewhere expresses itself with regard to the Book of Esther, 'They have confirmed above what Israel has accepted below.'               [8

Another consequence of this conception of Tradition is that it is neither Scripture nor primitive Judaism, but general custom which forms the real rule of practice. Holy Writ as well as history, Zunz tells us, teaches that the law of Moses was never fully and absolutely put into practice. Liberty was always given to the great teachers of every generation to make modifications and innovations in harmony with the spirit of existing institutions. Hence a return to Mosaism would be illegal, pernicious, and indeed impossible. The norm as well as the sanction of Judaism is the practice actually in vogue. Its consecration is the consecration of general use, – or, in other words, of Catholic Israel. It was probably with a view to this communion that the later mystics introduced a short prayer to be said before the performance of any religious ceremony, in which, among other things, the speaker professes to act 'in the

name of all Israel.'                                                  *[9*
It would be out of place in an introductory essay to pursue any further this interesting subject with its far-reaching consequences upon Jewish life and Jewish thought. But the foregoing remarks may suffice to show that Judaism did not remain quite inactive at the approach of the great religious crisis which our generation has witnessed. Like so many other religious communities, it reviewed its forces, entrenched itself on the field of history, and what it lost of its old devotion to the Bible, it has sought to make up by a renewed reverence for institutions.                                              *[10*
In this connection, a mere mention may suffice of the ultra-orthodox party, led by the late Dr. S. R. Hirsch of Frankfort (1808–1889), whose defiance of reason and criticism a Ward might have envied, and whose saintliness and sublimity even a Keble might have admired. And, to take an example from the opposite school, we must at least record the name of that devout Jew, Osias Schoor (1816–1895), in whom we have profound learning combined with an uncompromising disposition of mind productive of a typical champion of Radicalism in things religious. These men are, however, representative of two extremes, and their followers constitute mere minorities; the majority is with the historical school.
How long the position of this school will prove tenable is another question.
*[11*

# 10. RELIGION AND POLITICS

*See 1.9. The 'secular' Zionism of Herzl (10.1.1) and Ahad Ha-Am (10.1.2) should be compared with the 'religious' Zionism of the prayer book (see 3.1.2.7, 10, 14, 15, 17; and cf. 8.3.5). The texts quoted in 11.1–4 below provide the background to Herzl's and Ahad Ha-Am's remarks on antisemitism and the attitude of host societies towards Jewish minorities. 10.2.1 throws light on the ideals of the Jewish State. 10.2.3 defines the status of the rabbinical courts and halakhah (on which see 1.4) within the Israeli legal system. 10.2.4 shows how conflicts can arise between Jewish and Israeli law, even over such a fundamental question as the definition of who is a Jew. 10.2.2 provides the necessary background to the verdict contained in 10.2.4. For examples of religious law see chapter 5 and 9.2.3 above.*

## 10.1 ZIONIST THINKERS

### 10.1.1 Theodor Herzl. The idea of the Jewish State
Previous attempts to solve the Jewish question
The artificial means which have been used up till now to overcome the

troubles of the Jews have either been too petty, such as the various attempts at colonisation, or mistaken in principle, such as the attempts to make Jews into peasants in their present homelands.　　　　　　　　　　　　　　　　　*[1*

What is achieved by transporting a few thousand Jews to another country? Either they prosper, and with their prosperity antisemitism arises, or they come to grief at once. We have already discussed the previous attempts to divert poor Jews to new lands. This diversion is clearly inadequate and futile, if it does not actually defeat its own ends, for it merely postpones and protracts a solution, and may even hinder one.　　　　　　　　　　　　　　　　　　　　　　*[2*

Anyone who tries to turn Jews into peasants is making an extraordinary mistake. For the peasant is an anachronistic type, as may be clearly seen by his costume, which in most countries is centuries old, and by his implements, which are exactly the same as those used in the time of his forefathers. His plough is unchanged; he sows his seed from the apron, mows with the time-honoured scythe, and threshes with the flail. But we know all this can now be done by machinery. America must conquer Europe in the same way as large estates absorb small ones.　　　　　　　　　　　　　　　　　　　　　　　　　*[3*

The peasant is, consequently, a type doomed to extinction. If he is artificially preserved, it is because of political interests which he is meant to serve. To create new peasants on the old pattern is an impossible and absurd enterprise. No one is wealthy or powerful enough to force civilisation to take a single, retrograde step. The mere preservation of obsolete institutions is a gigantic task for which all the means available to a totalitarian state scarcely suffice.　　*[4*

Will anyone, then, seriously suggest to the Jews, who are an intelligent people, that they should become peasants of the old stamp? That would be tantamount to saying to a Jew: 'Here is a crossbow; now go to war!' What? With a crossbow, while others have small arms and Krupp canon? In these circumstances the Jews are perfectly justified in refusing to budge when people try to make peasants of them. The crossbow is a pretty weapon, which inspires me with poetic feelings – when I can spare the time. But it belongs to the museum.　　　　　　　　　　　　　　　　　　　　　　　　　　　　*[5*

Now, there certainly are regions where desperate Jews go and work in the fields, or at any rate are willing to do so. And it turns out that these areas – such as the enclave of Hesse in Germany and certain provinces in Russia – are hotbeds of antisemitism.　　　　　　　　　　　　　　　　　　　　　　　*[6*

For the world's reformers who send the Jews out to plough the fields forget a very important person, who has a great deal to say on this subject. That person is the peasant. And the peasant is absolutely in the right. For the tax on land, the risks involved in growing crops, the pressure from the large landowners who produce more cheaply, and above all American competition, all combine to make life difficult enough for him. Besides, the duties on corn cannot go on increasing indefinitely. Nor can the factory workers be allowed to starve; his political influence is, in fact, in the ascendant, and he must therefore be treated with ever-increasing respect.　　　　　　　　　　　　　　　　　　　*[7*

All these difficulties are well known; so I refer to them only briefly. I want merely to indicate how worthless have been the deliberate attempts in the past — most of them well-intentioned — to solve the Jewish Question. Neither migration to other lands, nor an artificial lowering on the intellectual level of our proletariat can be of any help. And we have already dealt with the infallible expedient of assimilation. [8

Antisemitism cannot be overcome by any of these means. It cannot be eliminated until its causes have been removed. But can we remove those causes? [9

**Causes of antisemitism**

We are no longer speaking of the irrational causes, ancient prejudice and narrow-mindedness, but of the political and economic causes. Our modern antisemitism is not to be confused with the religious persecution of the Jews in former times, though it still does have a confessional tinge in some countries. The main characteristic of the anti-Jewish movement today is different. In the principle countries were antisemitism prevails it is a result of Jewish emancipation. When civilised nations became aware of the inhumanity of discriminatory legislation and enfranchised us, our enfranchisement came too late. Legislation alone no longer sufficed to emancipate us in the places where we had lived till then. For we had, strange to say, developed in the ghetto into a middle-class group, and we emerged from the ghetto as a formidable rival to the middle class. And so after emancipation we found ourselves thrust into the circle of the bourgeoisie, and there we come under a double pressure, from within and from without. The Christian bourgeoisie would not be loath, indeed, to cast us as a peace-offering to socialism, though little good would it do them. [10

At the same time, the equality before the law which Jews enjoy cannot be withdrawn, once it has been granted, not only because to do so would be contrary to the spirit of our age, but also because such an act would immediately drive us into the ranks of the revolutionary parties. [11

No serious harm can really be done us. In earlier times our jewels were taken from us, but how is our movable property to be seized today? It consists of printed papers which are locked up somewhere or other, perhaps in the strongboxes of Christians. It is, of course, possible by taxation to get at shares and bonds in railways, banks and industrial undertakings of all kinds; and where progressive income tax is in force, it would be possible eventually to lay hands on all our movable property. But all such efforts cannot be directed against Jews alone, and, even if they were attempted, the immediate outcome would be a series of economic crises which would spread far beyond the Jews who were first to feel the pinch. This impossibility of getting at the Jews only intensifies and deepens hatred of them. Antisemitism increases day by day and hour by hour among the nations; indeed, it is bound to increase, because the fundamental causes of its growth persist and cannot be removed. Its remote cause is our loss of assimilability during the middle ages; its immediate cause is our over-production of mediocre intellectuals, who have no outlet downward or upward – that is to say, no wholesome outlet downward or upward. When we sink, we become a revolutionary proletariat, the corporals of every revolutionary party; on the other hand, when we rise, there rises with us our terrifying financial power. [12

**Effects of antisemitism**

The pressure applied to us does nothing to improve us. We are no different from other men. It is quite true that we do not love our enemies; but he alone who has complete mastery of himself dares reproach us with that. Oppression naturally engenders hostility against our oppressors, and our hostility in turn increases the pressure. It is impossible to escape this vicious circle. [13

'No!' some soft-hearted visionaries will say. 'No! It is possible – through the perfectibility of man.'

Is it really necessary for me to show what sentimental drivel this is? He who would base his hopes for an improvement of conditions on the goodness of mankind would indeed be writing a Utopia! [14

I referred originally to our 'assimilation'. I do not for a moment wish to imply that I want this to happen. Our national character is historically too glorious, and, in spite of every degradation, too noble to make destruction desirable. We might, perhaps, be able to disappear without a trace into the surrounding peoples if they would leave us in peace for just two generations. But they will not leave us in peace. After brief periods of toleration, their hostility breaks out again and again. They find our prosperity unbearably irritating, for the world for many centuries has been accustomed to regard us as the most contemptible of the poor. And so out of ignorance or narrow-mindedness they have failed to observe that it is prosperity that weakens us as Jews; it is only pressure that drives us back to our tribal roots, only the hostility of our environment that turns us into strangers. [15

Thus we are now, and shall remain, whether we like it or not, a historic group of unmistakable cohesiveness.

We are one people – our enemies have made us one whether we liked it or not, as has repeatedly happened in history. In affliction we stand together, and, thus united, we suddenly discover our strength. Yes, we are strong enough to form a State, and, indeed, a model State. We possess all the human and material resources necessary for this purpose. [16

This would, accordingly, be the appropriate place to speak about our 'human material', to use a rather crude expression. But first we must give the broad outlines of the plan on which everything else depends. [17

**The plan**

The whole plan is basically quite simple, as it must be if it is to be comprehensible to all.

Let sovereignty be granted us over a portion of the globe adequate to meet our rightful national requirements; we ourselves will see to everything else.

To create a new sovereign state is neither ridiculous nor impossible. We have seen it happen in our own day, among peoples who were not largely middle-class as we are, but poorer, less educated, and hence weaker than ourselves. The governments of countries plagued by antisemitism will be keenly interested in obtaining this sovereignty for us.                                                                  [18

The task, simple in design but complicated in execution, will be carried out by two agencies: the Society of Jews and the Jewish Company.

The Society of Jews will establish the theoretical and political basis of the new state, and the Jewish Company will put their ideas into practice.

The Jewish Company will be the liquidating agent for all the business interests of departing Jews, and will organise trade and commerce in the new country.                                                                                                                  [19

We must not visualise the departure of the Jews as a sudden one. It will be a gradual process extending over a number of decades. The poorest will go first and bring the land under cultivation. According to a predetermined plan, they will build roads, bridges and railways, establish telecommunications, regulate rivers, and provide themselves with homesteads. Their labour will create trade, trade will create markets, and markets will attract new settlers – for every man will go voluntarily, at his own expense and his own risk. The labour invested in the soil will enhance the value of the land. The Jews will soon perceive that a new and permanent sphere has opened up for that spirit of enterprise which has till now earned them only hatred and abuse.                                                      [20

If we wish to found a state today, then we should not set about it in the way which a thousand years ago would have been the only one possible. It is foolish to revert to older stages of civilisation, as many Zionists propose to do. Supposing, for example, we were obliged to clear a country of wild beasts, we should not set about it in the manner of the fifth-century Europeans. We should not take spear and lance and set out singly in pursuit of bears. Rather, we would organise a great, merry hunting party, drive the animals together, and throw a melinite bomb among them.

If we want to erect buildings, we shall not plant a few shaky stilt-huts on the shore of some lake, but will build as men build now. Indeed, we shall build more boldly and grandly than has ever been done before; for we now have means which were not available in the past.                                                               [21

Emigrants of the lowest economic class will be followed gradually by those of the next highest grade. Those now in desperate straits will go first. They will be led by the intellectual mediocrities whom we produce so abundantly and who are persecuted everywhere.                                                                             [22

This pamphlet should serve to open the question of Jewish migration to general discussion. This does not mean, however, that the question should be put to a vote. Such an approach would ruin the cause from the outset. Whoever will not come with us may stay behind. The opposition of a few individuals is quite immaterial.

Whoever would go with us, let him take his stand beneath our banner and fight for the cause with voice and pen and deed.                                                    [23

The Jews who agree with our idea for a state will rally round the Society of Jews. In this way it will acquire the authority to speak and to negotiate with governments in the name of the Jews. To put it in the language of international law, the Society will be recognised as a state-creating power. And through this recognition the State will, in effect, be created.                    [24

Should the Powers show themselves willing to grant to the Jewish people sovereignty over some neutral land, then the Society would enter into negotiations for the purchase of this land. Here two regions come under consideration – Palestine and Argentina. Significant experiments in colonisation have been made in both these countries, though on the mistaken principle of a gradual infiltration of Jews. Infiltration is always bound to end badly, for there comes the inevitable moment when the government, under pressure from the native populace which feels itself threatened, puts a stop to any further influx of Jews. Immigration, consequently, only makes sense if it is based on a guaranteed autonomy.                    [25

The Society of Jews will negotiate with the present authorities in the land, under the sponsorship of the European powers, if the plan seems reasonable to them. We could offer enormous advantages to the present authorities in the land: we could assume part of their national debt, build highways, which we ourselves would also require, and do many other things. The neighbouring countries would benefit by the creation of the Jewish State, since the cultivation of a strip of land, whether on a large or small scale, always increases the value of the surrounding districts.                    [26

**Palestine or Argentina?**

Is Palestine or Argentina to be preferred? The Society will take whatever it is given and whatever the public opinion of the Jewish people favours. The Society will determine both these points.                    [27

Argentina is one of the most fertile countries in the world, covers a vast area, is sparsely populated, and has a mild climate. The Republic of Argentina would derive very great benefit from ceding to us a portion of its territory. The present infiltration of Jews has certainly produced some discontent there. It would be necessary to explain to the Argentinians the essentially different character of the new Jewish immigration.                    [28

Palestine is our unforgettable historic homeland. This name alone would be a powerfully emotive rallying cry for our people. If His Majesty the Sultan were to give us Palestine, we could, in return, undertake the complete management of the finances of Turkey. As for Europe, we would form an integral part of its defensive wall in Asia; we would function as an outpost of civilisation against barbarism. As a neutral state we would remain in contact with all Europe, which would have to guarantee our existence. For the holy places of Christendom some form of international extra-territoriality could be devised. We would form a guard of honour about these holy places, and answer for the fulfilment of this duty with our existence. This guard of honour would be the great symbol of the solution of the Jewish question after what were for us eighteen centuries of suffering. *[29*

## 10.1.2 Ahad Ha-Am (Asher Ginsberg). The deficiencies of Western Zionism

The truth is bitter, but with all its bitterness it is better than illusion. We must admit to ourselves that the 'ingathering of the exiles' is unattainable by natural means. By natural means we may one day establish a Jewish State, and Jews may multiply and increase in it till 'the land is filled with them', but even then the greater part of our people will remain scattered and divided in alien lands. 'To gather our scattered ones from the four corners of the earth' is impossible. Only religion can promise this – through a miraculous redemption. *[1*

But if this is so, if the Jewish State, too, means not an 'ingathering of the exiles' but the settlement of a small part of our people in the land of Israel, then how will this alleviate the physical distress of the Jewish masses living in the lands of the Diaspora? . . . *[2*

The physical distress will not be brought to an end by the founding of a Jewish State, nor, broadly speaking, does it lie in our power to put an end to it (though we could ease it more or less straight away by various means, such as encouraging more of our people to become farmers and artisans wherever they live). Whether or not we found a Jewish State, the material situation of the Jews will always depend essentially on the economic condition of each country, and the cultural level of each nation, which plays host to the Jewish people. *[3*

So we are driven to the conclusion that the only true basis of Zionism is to be sought in another problem, the moral one.

But the moral problem takes on two different forms, one in the west and one in the east, and it is this fact which gives rise to the fundamental differences between western 'Zionism' and eastern '*Hibbat Ziyyon*'. Nordau spoke only about the Jewish problem in the west, apparently knowing nothing about the problem in the east; and even the Congress as a whole concentrated on the first, and paid little attention to the second. *[4*

The western Jew, who has left the life of the ghetto and tried to attach himself to the gentile majority where he lives, is unhappy because his hope that the gentiles would receive him with open arms has been dashed. He returns, perforce, to his own people and seeks to find within the Jewish community that life for which he yearns – he seeks but does not find it: the life and concerns of the Jewish community no longer satisfy him. He has already grown accustomed to the broader social and political life, and, on the more spiritual side, our national cultural endeavour does not attract him, because from his earliest days Jewish culture has played no part in his education; he does not know it or understand it. In this dilemma he turns to the land of his ancestors and imagines how good it would be if a Jewish State were re-established there – a State just like other states, with all their forms and trappings. Then he could live a full and complete life among his own people, and he could find at home all that he now sees outside, dangled before his eyes but out of reach. Of course, not all Jews will be able to pack their bags and go to their State; but the very existence of the Jewish State will increase the prestige of those who remain in exile, and their fellow citizens will no longer despise them and keep them at arms' length, as though they were humble menials, dependent upon the hospitality of others. As he continues to contemplate this vision, it suddenly dawns on his inner consciousness that even now, before the Jewish State is established, the mere idea of it almost solves his problems. It provides an opportunity for communal work and political excitement; he finds his *métier* without having to truckle to non-Jews; and he feels that, thanks to this ideal, he stands once more spiritually erect and has regained his personal dignity, without too much trouble and without any external help. So he devotes himself to the ideal with all his ardour; he gives free reign to his fancy and lets it soar at will – beyond reality and the limitations of human power. For it is not the attainment of the ideal that he needs; its pursuit alone is sufficient to cure him of his moral sickness, his profound feeling of inferiority, and the loftier and more remote the ideal, the greater is its power to elevate his soul.      [5

This is the basis of western Zionism and the secret of its attraction. But eastern *Hibbat Ziyyon* originated and developed in a different manner. It, too, began as a political movement; but, because it was born out of material distress, it could not rest content with activity consisting only of outbursts of feeling and fine phrases which satisfy the heart but not the belly. So *Hibbat Ziyyon*, right from its inception, expressed itself in concrete activities – in establishing colonies in the Land of Israel. This practical work soon clipped the wings of fancy and demonstrated conclusively that *Hibbat Ziyyon* could not alleviate the material distress of the Jews one jot. One might, therefore, have supposed that, when this fact became apparent, the *Hovevei Ziyyon* would have abandoned their work and stopped wasting their time and energy on activities which brought them no nearer their goal. But no: they remained true to their banner and continued to work with their former enthusiasm, even though most of them did not understand in their own minds why they did so. Deep down in their hearts they felt they must go on. However, since they did not clearly appreciate the nature of this feeling, their efforts were not always effectively directed towards the real goal, towards which their hearts drew them without their conscious knowledge.      [6

For at the very time when the material distress in the east was at its height, the heart of the eastern Jews was afflicted by another kind of distress as well – a moral one; and when the *Hovevei Ziyyon* began to work for a solution of the material distress, the national instinct of the people felt that in this work it would find the remedy for its moral distress. Hence the people took up this work and refused to abandon it, even after it had become obvious that it would not cure the material distress of the Jews. This moral problem in the east takes on a very different form from what it has in the west. In the west it is the problem of the Jews; in the east it is the problem of Judaism. The former weighs heavily on the individual; the latter on the nation. The one is felt by Jews who have had a non-Jewish education; the other, by Jews whose education has been Jewish. The one is a product of antisemitism, and is dependent on antisemitism for its existence; the other is the natural outcome of a genuine bond with a thousand years of Jewish culture, and it will retain its hold even if the troubles of the Jews all over the world cease, together with antisemitism, and Jews in every land are admitted to the honourable professions, welcomed by their neighbours, and allowed to participate with them, on terms of absolute equality, in all branches of political and social life. [7

It is not only the Jews who have come out of the ghetto; Judaism has come out too. The Jews have attained emancipation only in certain countries, thanks to the toleration of the inhabitants; but Judaism, of its own accord, has come out (or is coming out) of the ghetto whenever it has come into contact with modern culture. The stream of modern culture, when it mingles with Judaism, destroys Judaism's defences from within, so that Judaism can no longer remain isolated and live a life apart. The spirit of our people strives for further development; it wants to absorb the basic elements of general culture which reach it from the outside world, to digest them and make them part of itself, as it has done in the past at different periods of its history. But the conditions of its life in exile are not conducive to this. In our time culture everywhere clothes itself in the national spirit of each people, and any alien who wants to participate in that culture must annihilate his individuality and be swallowed up by the dominant ethos. Hence Judaism in exile cannot develop its individuality in its own way. When it leaves the ghetto walls, it is in danger of losing its own essential life, or, at the very least, its national unity, of being split up into many kinds of Judaism, each with its different character and life, as there are countries where the Jews are dispersed. [8

When Judaism sees that it can no longer sustain the role of exile which its will-to-live forced it to assume when it left its own land, but that, if it abandons that role, its life is in danger, it seeks to return to its historic centre, to live there a life which will develop in a natural way, to apply its powers to every department of human culture, to broaden and perfect those national assets which it has acquired up till now, and thus to contribute to the treasury of mankind, in the future as in the past, a great national culture, the fruit of the free enterprise of a people living by its own spirit. For this purpose Judaism can, for the present, be content with little. It does not need an independent State, but only the creation in its native land of conditions favourable to its development: a fair-sized settlement of Jews working without hindrance in every branch of culture, from farming and handicrafts to science and literature. This settlement, which will grow little by little, will become in the fullness of time the centre of the nation, wherein its spirit will find its purest expression and develop in all its aspects to the highest degree of perfection of which it is capable. Then, from this centre, the spirit of Judaism will radiate to the great circumference, to all the communities of the Diaspora, to revitalise them and to preserve the overall unity of our people. When our national culture in the Land of Israel has attained this stage of development, we may be sure that it will raise up some of its own sons who will be well-qualified to seize the right moment for establishing a State there – one which will not merely be a State of Jews but a truly Jewish State. [9

This *Hibbat Ziyyon* which is concerned to preserve Judaism at a time when Jews are suffering so much, is something strange and incomprehensible to the 'political' Zionists of the west, just as Rabban Yohanan ben Zakkai's request for Yavneh was strange and incomprehensible to the politically minded people of his day. So political Zionism cannot satisfy those Jews who are loyal to Judaism; they see in its growth a danger to their own aspirations and aims. . . . [10

To sum up: *Hibbat Ziyyon*, no less than 'Zionism', wants a Jewish State and believes in the possibility of founding a Jewish State in the future. But while 'Zionism' looks to the Jewish State to provide a remedy for poverty, as well as complete tranquility and national glory, *Hibbat Ziyyon* knows that our State will not give us these things until 'universal righteousness sits enthroned and holds sway in the life of nations and states'. *Hibbat Ziyyon* looks to a Jewish State to provide a 'secure refuge' for Judaism and a cultural bond to unite our nation. 'Zionism', therefore, begins its work with political propaganda; but *Hibbat Ziyyon* begins with the national culture, because only through that culture and for its sake can a Jewish State be established in a way that will be acceptable and beneficial to the spirit of the Jewish people. [11

## 10.2 LAWS OF THE STATE OF ISRAEL

### 10.2.1 The Declaration of the State of Israel (1948)

*Eretz-Israel* was the birthplace of the Jewish people. Here their spiritual, religious and political identity was shaped. Here they first attained to statehood, created cultural values of national and universal significance and gave to the world the eternal Book of Books. [1

After being forcibly exiled from their land, the people kept faith with it throughout their Dispersion and never ceased to pray and hope for their return to it and for the restoration in it of their political freedom. [2

Impelled by this historic and traditional attachment, Jews strove in every successive generation to re-establish themselves in their ancient homeland. In recent decades they returned in their masses. Pioneers, *ma'pilim* [immigrants coming to Erez Israel in defiance of restrictive legislation] and defenders, they made the deserts bloom, revived the Hebrew language, built villages and towns, and created a thriving community, controlling its own economy and culture, loving peace but knowing how to defend itself, bringing the blessings of progress to all the country's inhabitants, and aspiring towards independent nationhood. [3

In the year 5657 (1897), at the summons of the spiritual father of the Jewish State, Theodor Herzl, the First Zionist Congress convened and proclaimed the right of the Jewish people to national rebirth in its own country.    [4

This right was recognised in the Balfour Declaration on the 2nd November, 1917, and reaffirmed in the Mandate of the League of Nations which, in particular, gave international sanction to the historic connection between the Jewish people and Eretz-Israel and to the right of the Jewish people to rebuild its National Home.    [5

The catastrophe which recently befell the Jewish people – the massacre of millions of Jews in Europe – was another clear demonstration of the urgency of solving the problem of its homelessness by re-establishing in Eretz-Israel the Jewish State, which would open the gates of the homeland wide to every Jew and confer upon the Jewish people the status of a fully privileged member of the comity of nations.    [6

Survivors of the Nazi holocaust in Europe, as well as Jews from other parts of the world, continued to migrate to Eretz-Israel, undaunted by difficulties, restrictions and dangers, and never ceased to assert their right to a life of dignity, freedom and honest toil in their national homeland.    [7

In the Second World War, the Jewish community of this country contributed its full share to the struggle of the freedom- and peace-loving nations against the forces of Nazi wickedness and, by the blood of its soldiers and its war effort, gained the right to be reckoned among the peoples who founded the United Nations.    [8

On the 29th November, 1947, the United Nations General Assembly passed a resolution calling for the establishment of a Jewish State in Eretz-Israel; the General Assembly required the inhabitants of Eretz-Israel to take such steps as were necessary on their part for the implementation of that resolution. This recognition by the United Nations of the right of the Jewish people to establish their State is irrevocable.    [9

This right is the natural right of the Jewish people to be masters of their own fate, like other nations, in their own sovereign State.    [10

*Accordingly we, members of the People's Council* [Mo'ezet ha-Am], *representatives of the Jewish community of Eretz-Israel and of the Zionist movement, are here assembled on the day of the termination of the British mandate over Eretz-Israel and, by virtue of our natural and historic right, and on the strength of the Resolution of the United Nations General Assembly, hereby declare the establishment of a Jewish State in Eretz-Israel, to be known as the State of Israel* [Medinat Yisra'el].    [11

*We declare* that, with effect from the moment of the termination of the Mandate, being tonight, the eve of Sabbath, the 6th Iyar, 5708 (15th May, 1948), until the establishment of the elected, regular authorities of the State in accordance with the Constitution which shall be adopted by the Elected Constituent Assembly not later than the 1st October, 1948, the People's Council shall act as a Provisional Council of State [*Mo'ezet Medinah*

*Zemannit*], and its executive organ, the People's Administration [*Minhelet Ha-Am*], shall be the Provisional Government of the Jewish State [*Ha-Memshalah Ha-Zemannit shel Ha-Medinah Ha-Yehudit*], to be called 'Israel'. *[12*

The State of Israel will be open for Jewish immigration and for the Ingathering of the Exiles; it will foster the development of the country for the benefit of all inhabitants; it will be based on freedom, justice and peace as envisaged by the prophets of Israel; it will ensure complete equality of social and political rights to all its inhabitants irrespective of religion, race or sex; it will guarantee freedom of religion, conscience, language, education and culture; it will safeguard the Holy Places of all religions; and it will be faithful to the principles of the Charter of the United Nations. *[13*

The State of Israel is prepared to cooperate with the agencies and representatives of the United Nations in implementing the resolution of the General Assembly of the 29th November, 1947, and will take steps to bring about the economic union of the whole of Eretz-Israel. *[14*

We appeal to the United Nations to assist the Jewish people in the building-up of its State and to receive the State of Israel into the comity of nations.

We appeal – in the very midst of the onslaught launched against us now for months – to the Arab inhabitants of the State of Israel to preserve peace and participate in the upbuilding of the State on the basis of full and equal citizenship and due representation in all its provisional and permanent institutions. *[15*

We extend our hand to all neighbouring states and their peoples in an offer of peace and good neighbourliness, and appeal to them to establish the bonds of cooperation and mutual help with the sovereign Jewish people settled in its own land. The State of Israel is prepared to do its share in common effort for the advancement of the entire Middle East. *[16*

We appeal to the Jewish people throughout the Diaspora to rally round the Jews of Eretz-Israel in the tasks of immigration and upbuilding and to stand by them in the great struggle for the realisation of the age-old dream – the redemption of Israel. *[17*

*Placing our trust in the Almighty* [be-Zur Yisra'el], *we affix our signatures to this Proclamation at this session of the Provisional Council of State, on the soil of the homeland, in the city of Tel-Aviv, on this Sabbath eve, the 5th day of Iyar, 5708 (14th May, 1948).* *[18*

### 10.2.2 The Law of Return (1950/1954/1970)

1. Every Jew has the right to come to this country as an *oleh* [immigrant]. *[1*
2. (a) *Aliyah* [immigration] shall be by *oleh*'s visa.

(b) An *oleh*'s visa shall be granted to every Jew who has expressed his desire to settle in Israel, unless the Minister of Immigration [1954: Minister of the Interior] is satisfied that the applicant – (1) is engaged in an activity directed against the Jewish people; or (2) is likely to endanger public health or the security of the State; [1954: or (3) is a person with a criminal past liable to endanger public welfare.] *[2*

3. (a) A Jew who has come to Israel and subsequent to his arrival has expressed his desire to settle in Israel may, while still in Israel, receive an *oleh*'s certificate.

(b) The restrictions specified in section 2(b) shall apply also to the grant of an *oleh*'s certificate, but a person shall not be regarded as endangering public health on account of an illness contracted after his arrival in Israel. *[3*

4. Every Jew who has immigrated into this country before the coming into force of this Law, and every Jew who was born in this country, whether before or after the coming into force of this Law, shall be deemed to be a person who has come to this country as an *oleh* under this Law. *[4*

[1970: 4A. (a) The rights of a Jew under this Law and the rights of an *oleh* under the Nationality Law, 5712–1952, as well as the rights of an *oleh* under any other enactment, are also vested in a child and a grandchild of a Jew, the spouse of a Jew, the spouse of a child of a Jew and the spouse of a grandchild of a Jew, except for a person who has been a Jew and has voluntarily changed his religion. *[5*

(b) It shall be immaterial whether or not a Jew by whose right a right under subsection (a) is claimed is still alive and whether or not he has immigrated to Israel. *[6*

(c) The restrictions and conditions prescribed in respect of a Jew or an *oleh* by or under this Law or by the enactments referred to in subsection (a) shall also apply to a person who claims a right under subsection (a). *[7*

4B. For the purposes of this Law, 'a Jew' means a person who was born of a Jewish mother or has become converted to Judaism and who is not a member of another religion.] *[8*

5. The Minister of Immigration [1954: Minister of the Interior] is charged with the implementation of this Law and may make regulations as to any matter relating to such implementation and also as to the grant of *oleh*'s visas and *oleh*'s certificates to minors up to the age of 18 years. *[9*

[1970: Regulations for the purposes of sections 4A and 4B require the approval of the Constitution, Legislation and Judicial Committee of the Knesset.] *[10*

### 10.2.3 The Rabbinical Courts Jurisdiction (Marriage and Divorce) Law (1953)

1. Matters of marriage and divorce of Jews in Israel, being nationals or residents of the State, shall be under the exclusive jurisdiction of rabbinical courts. *[1*

2. Marriages and divorces of Jews shall be performed in Israel in accordance with Jewish religious law. *[2*

3. Where a suit for divorce between Jews has been filed in a rabbinical court, whether by the wife or by the husband, a rabbinical court shall have exclusive jurisdiction in any matter connected with such a suit, including maintenance

G

for the wife and for the children of the couple. [3

4. Where a Jewish wife sues her Jewish husband or his estate for maintenance in a rabbinical court, otherwise than in connection with divorce, the plea of the defendant that a rabbinical court has no jurisdiction in the matter shall not be heard. [4

5. Where a woman sues her deceased husband's brother for *chalitza* in a rabbinical court, the rabbinical court shall have exclusive jursidiction in the matter, also as regards maintenance for the woman until the day on which *chalitza* is given. [5

6. Where a rabbinical court, by final judgement, has ordered that a husband be compelled to grant his wife a letter of divorce or that a wife be compelled to accept a letter of divorce from her husband, a district court may, upon expiration of six months from the day of the making of the order, on the application of the Attorney General, compel compliance with the order by imprisonment. [6

7. Where a rabbinical court, by final judgement, has ordered that a man be compelled to give his brother's widow *chalitza* [Deut. 25:9–10], a district court may, upon expiration of three months from the day of the making of the order, on application of the Attorney General, compel compliance with the order by imprisonment. [7

8. For the purpose of sections 6 and 7 a judgement shall be regarded as final when it is no longer appealable. [8

9. In matters of personal status of Jews, as specified in article 51 of the Palestine Orders in Council, 1922 to 1947, or in the Succession Ordinance, in which a rabbinical court has not exclusive jurisdiction under this Law, a rabbinical court shall have jurisdiction after all parties concerned have expressed their consent thereto. [9

10. A judgement given by a rabbinical court after the establishment of the State and before the coming into force of this Law, after the case had been heard in the presence of the litigants, and which would have been validly given had this Law been in force at the time, shall be deemed to have been validly given. [10

11. The Minister of Religious Affairs is charged with the implementation of this Law. [11

### 10.2.4 Judge Silberg's verdict in the 'Brother Daniel' case (1962)

The question of law before us is very simply the meaning of the expression 'Jew' as used in the Law of Return, 1950. Does it also include a Jew who has changed his religion and been baptised as a Christian but who still feels and regards himself as a Jew in spite of his conversion? [1

At this point I do not propose to decide this question or to give it an unequivocal answer. I wish to examine first the various alternatives which it involves. But I will say at once that were I to agree with the second or alternative submission of counsel for the petitioner, that the expression 'Jew' as used in the Law of Return bears the identical religious connotations which it bears in the Rabbinical Courts Jurisdiction (Marriage and Divorce) Law, 1953, I would then propose making the order nisi absolute and ordering the Minister of the Interior to grant the petitioner an immigration certificate under section 3(a) of the Law of Return. I would do so however strange and anomalous it may seem that a man who has renounced one creed in favour of another should rely on the doctrines of the faith he has abandoned, and in spite of my aversion for an argument so inconsistent and confused. *[2*

According to the prevailing opinion in Jewish law, so it seems to me, a Jew who is converted or becomes an apostate continues to be treated as a Jew for all purposes save perhaps as to certain 'marginal' laws which have no real importance with regard to the central problem. I shall not rely here on the well-known dictum that 'A Jew, even if he has sinned, remains a Jew' (*Sanhedrin* 44a), since, as some writers have already pointed out, it may well be that this dictum is more in the nature of a homily (aggada) than a rule of law (halachah). Be that as it may it has, however, served throughout the ages as a corner stone for judicial decision and ministered as authority, binding or persuasive, in nearly all cases decided in favour of converts being considered Jews (or, in traditional language, members of the people of Israel). For Jewish law is the law not only *of* the people of Israel but also *for* the people of Israel, and if the principle is, as will be seen in due course, that this law is binding on the convert, then he too is of the people of Israel, i.e. a Jew. *[3*

'To what does this rule refer? If he [a proselyte] renounces the Jewish faith and then marries a Jewish girl, we regard him as a non-conforming Jew and his marriage is legally binding' (*Yevamot* 47b). . . . *[4*

'If a Jew who has converted [to another religion] is married, though he may knowingly practise idolatry, his marriage is wholly binding and [should his wife wish to end the marriage] she will require to obtain a divorce [from him]' (Maimonides, *Laws of Marriage* IV, 15). *[5*

t1 '. . . for although he sinned, he is still a Jew' (*Migdal Oz*, Commentary on Maimonides, ibid.). *[6*

'If a Jew has converted [to another religion] and married, his marriage is valid [and should the wife wish to end the marriage] she requires to obtain a divorce from him' (*Tur, Even ha-Ezer* 44). *[7*

'For even though he has converted to another religion, he none the less remains a Jew, as it is written, "Israel has sinned"; though he has sinned, he remains a Jew' (*Prisha*, Commentary on *Tur*, ibid. note 22). . . . *[8*

'If a Jewish husband dies without issue, leaving a brother who was a convert [to another religion] there is some authority for saying that the widow is exempt from *halitza* [Deut. 25:9–10], if at the time of her marriage the brother was already converted. But this ruling is not to be relied upon' (*Shulchan Aruch, Even ha-Ezer* 157,4). . . . *[9*

All these considerations, together with the basic concept expressed above, leads to the conclusion that the Jewishness of a convert, which finds striking legal expression in the laws of marriage and divorce and *Yibbum* [the law

requiring a brother to marry his deceased brother's widow] constitutes a status
which is indivisable and absolute. [10

As I said at the beginning of the last section, were I of the opinion that the
term 'Jew' in the Law of Return is identical in meaning with the same term in
the Rabbinical Courts Jurisdiction (Marriage and Divorce) Law, that is to say,
*a Jew according to the rules of Jewish law*, I would grant the application of the
petitioner and make the order nisi absolute. The difficulty is, however, that the
term 'Jew' is not used in the same sense in both these Laws. In the Rabbinical
Courts Jurisdiction (Marriage and Divorce) Law, it bears a religious
connotation according to its precise meaning in Jewish law, whereas in the Law
of Return the term has a secular meaning, as it is usually understood in
common parlance – and this I emphasise – by the ordinary, simple Jew. [11

The reason for this is so clear that it need hardly be mentioned. The
Rabbinical Courts Jurisdiction (Marriage and Divorce) Law was enacted for
the purpose of extending rabbinical jurisdiction. It is an open secret that the
extension of this jurisdiction was sought and granted in order to broaden the
application of Jewish religious law to Jews. Hence the further question who is a
Jew for the purposes of this Law must be answered according to Jewish law. If it
were to be answered on the basis of other considerations, extrinsic, secular or
outside the framework of Jewish law, then the law applicable would no longer
be Jewish religious law. [12

It is otherwise with the Law of Return. For all its immense historical
importance, this Law is a secular Law, and in the absence of definition either in
the statute itself or in the decided cases, we must interpret its terms according to
their ordinary meaning, taking into consideration, when departing from the
ordinary sense, the legislative purpose behind its provisions. And because the
Law of Return is an Israel statute, originally enacted in Hebrew and not
translated, the term 'Jew' must be interpreted in the sense that it is understood
by the Jews, for they are nearest to the subject matter of the Law, and who
better than they know the essential content of the term 'Jew'? [13

Once more the question must be asked, what is the ordinary meaning of the
term 'Jew', and does it include a Jew who has become a Christian?

The answer to this question is, in my opinion, sharp and clear – a Jew who
has become a Christian is *not* deemed a 'Jew'. [14

It is not my purpose to preach religion, nor to present any particular point of
view as to the most desirable course for the future development of the Jewish
people. I know full well that opinion in Israel as to what is and what should be is
divided into all the various shades of the spiritual rainbow – from the extreme
orthodox to the total agnostic. But there is one thing that is shared by *all* Jews
who live in Israel (except a mere handful) and that is that we do not cut
ourselves off from our historical past nor deny our ancestral heritage. We
continue to drink from the original fountains. The shape has changed, the
channels have been altered, but we have not sealed the wells, for without them
we would be but 'as the poor that are cast out'. Only the simple believe or think

that we are creating a *new* culture; for this it is much too late. A people which is almost as old as the human race cannot start *ab ovo*, and our new culture in this land – at its highest – is merely a *new version* of the culture of the past.    *[15*

Whether he is religious, non-religious or anti-religious, the Jew living in Israel is bound, willingly or unwillingly, by an umbilical cord to historical Judaism from which he draws his language and its idiom, whose festivals are his own to celebrate, and whose great thinkers and spiritual heroes – not the least of whom are the martyrs of 1096 and those who perished at the stake in Spain – nourish his national pride. Would a Jew who has become a Christian find his place in all this? What can this national sentiment mean to him? Would he not see in a different light and appraise by other standards our draining to the dregs the bitter cup from which we drank so deeply in those dark Middle Ages? Certainly, Brother Daniel will love Israel. This he has proved beyond all doubt. But such love will be from without – the love of a distant brother. He will not be a true inherent part of this Jewish world. His settling in Israel in the midst of the Jewish community and his sincere affection for it cannot take the place of absolute inner identification which is absent. . . .

I am of the opinion therefore that the order nisi must be discharged.    *[16*

# 11. SOCIETY AND THE JEWS

*See 1.10. The first three texts in this chapter are medieval in origin and are intended to throw light on the attitude of the State (11.1), the Church (11.2) and the common people (11.3) towards the Jews. 11.4 gives some insight into the pressures which political emancipation brought to bear on the Jewish community. This text provides useful background to the rise of the Reform movement (9.2 above), which can be seen as a response to the challenge of emancipation. The Holocaust, to which the documents in 11.5 relate, was the supreme expression of European antisemitism. For some Jewish reflections on the phenomenon of antisemitism see 10.1.1–2 above.*

## 11.1 RICHARD I'S CHARTER TO CERTAIN JEWS IN ENGLAND (1190)

Richard, by the grace of God, King of England, Duke of Normandy . . . to his archbishops, bishops . . . greeting.

Know that we have granted, and by our present charter confirmed to Ysaac, son of Rabbi Joce, and to his children and to their men, all their customs and all their liberties, just as the Lord King Henry, our father granted them and by his charter confirmed to the Jews of England and of Normandy; namely: to reside in our land freely and honourably; to hold from us all those things which the aforesaid Ysaac and his children held in the time of King Henry our father, in lands, fiefs, pledges, gifts and purchases, viz., Hame, which King Henry our father gave to them in return for their service, and Thurroc, which the said Ysaac bought from the Count of Ferrars; to hold all the houses, messuages and pledges, which the same Ysaac and his children held in our land in the time of King Henry our father.                                                                            *[1*

And if a quarrel arises between a Christian and Ysaac, or any of his children or heirs, he who appeals the other to determine his quarrel shall have witnesses, viz., a lawful Christian and a lawful Jew.                                                       *[2*

And if the said Ysaac, or his heirs or children, has a writ concerning that quarrel, the writ shall serve them for testimony; and if a Christian has a quarrel against the aforementioned Jews it shall be adjudicated by the peers of the Jews [pares Judeorum].                                                                                        *[3*

And if any of the aforesaid Jews should die, let not his body be kept above ground, but let his heir have his money and debts, so that he be not disturbed therefrom, if he has an heir who can answer for him and do what is right in the matter of his debts and his forfeits; and let the aforesaid Jews receive and buy without impediment whatever is brought to them, except those things which belong to the Church and blood-stained garments.                                       *[4*

And if they are appealed by anyone without witnesses, let them be quit of that appeal on their own oath [solo sacramento] upon their Book; and let them be likewise quit from any appeal of those things which pertain to our crown on their own oath [solo sacramento] upon their Scroll.                                            *[5*

And if there be any dissension between a Christian and any of the aforesaid Jews or their children concerning the loan of any money, the Jew shall prove his capital and the Christian the interest.                                                          *[6*

And the aforesaid Jews are allowed to sell their pledges freely, after it is certified that they have held them for one full year and a day; and they shall not enter into any plea except before us, or before those who guard our castles, in whose bailiwicks they reside.                                                                  *[7*

And wherever they are,[1] they are allowed to go whithersoever they wish, with all their chattels, just like our own goods, and let no one retain them or prohibit this to them.[2]                                                                                 *[8*

And if a Christian debtor dies who owes money to a Jew, and the debtor has an heir, during the minority of the heir let not the Jew be disturbed from his debt, unless the land of the heir is in our hand.                                              *[9*

And we decree that the Jews shall be free of all customs, tolls, and modiation of wine, just like our own chattels; and we command and order you to ward, defend and protect them; and we forbid anyone, against this charter concerning the abovementioned persons, to put the said Jews into plea upon our forfeiture.                                                                                               *[10*

Witnesses: Will. de Hum. Constable of Normany. . . .

Given by the hand of William de Longchamp, our Chancellor, Bishop of Ely, at Rouen, 22nd day of March, in the first year of our reign.            *[11*

## 11.2  THE FOURTH LATERAN COUNCIL, 1215, DECREES
## CONCERNING THE JEWS

### LXVII.  On Jewish usury

The more the Christian religion refrains from exacting interest [*usura*], the more does the perfidy of the Jews in this practice increase, so that, in a short time, they exhaust the wealth of Christians. Desiring, therefore, to protect the Christians in this matter from being immoderately burdened by the Jews, we ordain by synodal decree that if, on any pretext, Jews extort heavy and excessive interest from Christians, all relationships with Christians shall be withdrawn from them, until they make adequate restitution for their exorbitant exactions. The Christians also shall be compelled, if need be, by ecclesiastical punishment against which no appeal will be heard, to abstain from business dealings with the Jews.            *[1*

Moreover, we enjoin princes not to be hostile to the Christians on this account, but rather to endeavour to restrain the Jews from so great an oppression.            *[2*

And under threat of the same penalty we decree that the Jews shall be compelled to make good the tithes and offerings owed to the Churches, which the Churches were accustomed to receive from the houses and other possessions of Christians, before these came, by whatever entitlement, into the hands of the Jews, in order that the Churches may be preserved against loss.            *[3*

### LXVIII.  That Jews should be distinguished from Christians in dress

In certain provinces a difference in dress marks off the Jews and the Saracens from the Christians, but in certain others there has arisen such confusion that Jews and Saracens cannot be distinguished from Christians by any differentiating mark. Thus it sometimes happens that by mistake Christians have intercourse with Jewish or Saracen women, and Jews or Saracens with Christian women. Therefore, to prevent these people in future finding an excuse for the sin of such forbidden intercourse under the cloak of an error, we decree that Jews and Saracens of both sexes, in every Christian province and at all times, shall be clearly and visibly differentiated from other peoples by the character of their dress, especially since such legislation is imposed upon them also by Moses [cf. Num. 15:37–41; Deut. 22:12].            *[4*

Moreover, during the Days of Lamentation and of the Passion of our Lord, they shall not show themselves in public at all, for the reason that, on those very days (as we have heard), some of them are not ashamed to go about more splendidly attired than usual, and are not afraid to mock the Christians who, in preserving the memory of the most holy Passion, display the signs of mourning.            *[5*

Moreover, we most strictly forbid that anyone should so far presume as to break forth into insults against the Redeemer. And, since we ought not to ignore any insult offered to Him who blotted out our transgressions, we command that secular princes should restrain such impudent persons by imposing on them fitting punishment, lest they should so far presume as to blaspheme Him who was crucified for us. [6

**LXIX. That Jews should not be appointed to public office**

Since it is altogether absurd that a blasphemer of Christ should exercise authority over Christians, we, on account of the boldness of transgressors, renew in this article [in hoc capitulo] what was prudently decreed on this matter by the Council of Toledo: we forbid Jews to be given preferment in public office, since this affords them a pretext under which they can vent their hostility towards Christians. Moreover, should anyone entrust such an office to them, he shall be restrained from doing so by the Provincial Council (which we order to convene every year). Due warning having been given, the Council shall impose whatever punishment it deems fit. Association with Christians, whether in commerce or in other matters, shall be denied to such a Jewish official until all that he has acquired from Christians through the office that he held is turned over for the use of the Christian poor under the direction of the diocesan bishop, and he relinquishes the office which he has impiously assumed, in disgrace. We extend this law also to pagans. [7

**LXX. That those Jews who have converted to the faith should not continue to observe Jewish rites**

We have heard that certain people who have come of their own free will to the waters of holy baptism, have not altogether put off the old man, in order to put on more perfectly the new, since they retain remnants of their former rites, and tarnish the beauty of the Christian religion by such an admixture. Since it is written, 'Woe to the man who treads two paths' [Eccl. 2:12/14], and since it is forbidden to wear a garment woven both of linen and wool [Lev. 19:19; Deut. 22:11], we decree that the prelates of the Churches should restrain by every means such persons from observing their old religious rites; for it is necessary for their salvation that those whom the exercise of free will has brought to the Christian religion should be subjected to compulsion, in order to keep them loyal to Christian observance, since it is a lesser evil never to have acknowledged the way of the Lord, than, having acknowledged it, to backslide. [8

**Expedition for the recovery of the Holy Land**

If any of those setting out thither [i.e. for the Holy Land] are bound by oath to pay interest, we command that their creditors shall be compelled by the same judicial authority [i.e. by ecclesiastical censure] to release them from the oath which they have taken upon themselves, and to desist from the exaction of interest. But if any of their creditors shall force them to pay interest, we order that he shall be forced by similar punishment to remit the interest. [9

We command that the secular powers shall compel the Jews to remit their interest, and, until they have done so, all the faithful of Christ shall, under pain of excommunication, refrain from any association with them. Moreover, for those who are unable to pay their debts to the Jews at the present time, the secular princes shall procure the requisite moratorium, so that, from the time they begin their journey [to the Holy Land] until their death or their return is known for certain, they may not suffer the inconvenience of [accruing] interest. The Jews shall be compelled, after deducting any necessary expenses, to count the income which they receive from the mortgaged property in the interim towards the repayment of the principal, since a concession of this kind, which postpones payment but does not cancel the debt, does not appear to involve much loss. Further, let those prelates of the Churches who show themselves slack in granting justice to the crusaders know that they will be severely punished.                                                                    [10

## 11.3 THE BALLAD OF HUGH OF LINCOLN

Four and twenty bonny boys / Were playing at the ba; / And by it came him, sweet Sir Hugh, / And he playd oer them a'.

He kicked the ba with his right foot, / [5] And catchd it wi his knee; / And throuch-and-thro the Jew's window, / He gard [made to, caused to] the bonny ba flee.

He's doen him [betaken himself] to the Jew's castell, / And walkd it round about; / [10] And there he saw the Jew's daughter / At the window looking out.

'Throw down the ba, ye Jew's daughter, / Throw down the ba to me!' / 'Never a bit,' says the Jew's daughter, / [15] 'Till up to me come ye.'

'How will I come up? How can I come up? / How can I come to thee? / For as ye did to my auld father, / The same ye'll do to me.'                                     [20

She's gane till her father's garden, / And pu'd an apple, red and green; / 'Twas a' to wyle him, sweet Sir Hugh, / And to entice him in.

She's led him in through ae dark door, / [25] And sae has she thro nine; / She's laid him on a dressing table, / And stickit him like a swine.

And first came out the thick, thick blood, / And syne came out the thin; / [30] And syne came out the bonny heart's blood; / There was nae mair within.

She's row'd him in a cake o lead, / Bade him lie still and sleep; / She's thrown him in Our Lady's draw-well, / [35] Was fifty fathom deep.

When bells were run, and mass was sung, / And a' the bairns came hame, / When every lady gat hame her son, / The lady Maisry gat nane.                               [40

She's taen her mantle her about, / Her coffer by the hand; / And she's gane out to seek her son, / And wanderd oer the land.

She's doen her [betaken herself] to the Jew's castell, / [45] Where a' were fast asleep; / 'Gin ye be there, my sweet Sir Hugh, / I pray you to me speak.'

She's doen her to the Jew's garden, / Thought he had been gathering fruit; / [50] 'Gin ye be there, my sweet Sir Hugh, / I pray you to me speak.'

She neard Our Lady's deep draw-well, / Was fifty fathom deep; / 'Whare'er ye be, my sweet Sir Hugh, / *[55]* I pray you to me speak.'

'Gae hame, gae hame, my mither dear; / Prepare my winding sheet; / And, at the back o merry Lincoln, / The morn I will you meet.'                    *[60*

Now Lady Maisry is gane hame; / Made him a winding sheet; / And, at the back o merry Lincoln, / The dead corpse did her meet.

And a' the bells o merry Lincoln, / *[65]* Without men's hands were rung; / And a' the books o merry Lincoln, / Were read without man's tongue; / And neer was such a burial / Sin Adam's days begun.                    *[70*

## 11.4 THE ASSEMBLY OF JEWISH NOTABLES, PARIS, 1806. THE QUESTIONS OF THE EMPEROR AND TWO OF THE ASSEMBLY'S REPLIES

### 11.4.1 Questions addressed to the Assembly of Jews by His Majesty the Emperor and King, that they might deal with the matters pertaining thereto

1. Is it lawful for Jews to marry more than one wife?                    *[1*

2. Is divorce allowed by the Jewish religion? Is divorce valid, even when it is not pronounced by the Courts of Justice, and by virtue of laws contrary to those of the French Code?                    *[2*

3. Can a Jewess marry a Christian, or a Christian woman a Jew? Or does the Law ordain that Jews shall marry only among themselves?                    *[3*

4. In the eyes of Jews, are Frenchmen their brethren or strangers?                    *[4*

5. In either case what relations does the Law prescribe for them towards Frenchmen who are not of their religion?                    *[5*

6. Do Jews born in France, and treated by the law as French citizens, acknowledge France as their country? Are they bound to defend it? Are they bound to obey its laws and to follow all the provisions of the Civil Code?                    *[6*

7. Who appoints the Rabbis?                    *[7*

8. What police jurisdiction do the Rabbis exercise among the Jews? What judicial power do they exercise among them?                    *[8*

9. Are these forms of election [mentioned in q. 7], this police-jurisdiction [mentioned in q. 8], laid down in their laws, or are they sanctioned only by custom?                    *[9*

10. Are there professions which are forbidden to Jews by their Law?                    *[10*

11. Does the Law of the Jews forbid them to take interest [*usure*] from their brethren?                    *[11*

12. Does it forbid them or permit them to take interest [*usure*] from strangers?                    *[12*

### 11.4.2 Reply of the assembly to question 3

The Law does not say that a Jewess cannot marry a Christian, nor a Christian woman a Jew; nor does it state that Jews can only marry among themselves.                                                                    [13

The only marriages expressly forbidden by the Law are those with the seven Canaanite nations, with Amon and Moab, and with the Egyptians. The prohibition is absolute with regard to the seven Canaanite nations. In the case of Amon and Moab, it is confined, in the view of many Talmudists, to the men of these two nations, but does not extend to the women, though one assumes that it would be necessary for the latter to have embraced the Jewish religion. As for the Egyptians, the prohibition is limited to the third generation. The prohibition applies only to idolatrous peoples. The Talmud formally declares that the modern nations are not to be considered as such, since, like ourselves, they worship the God of heaven and earth. Moreover, there have been, at different periods, marriages between Jews and Christians in France, Spain and Germany. These marriages are sometimes tolerated and sometimes forbidden by the laws of the princes into whose domains the Jews had been received.   [14

A number of these unions are to be found today in France, but we ought not to conceal the fact that the opinion of the Rabbis is against such marriages. According to their teaching, although the religion of Moses has not forbidden the Jews to marry those who are not of their religion, yet, since marriage, in the view of the Talmud, requires for its celebration certain religious ceremonies called *Kiduschim* [Qiddushin], together with the blessing used on such occasions, a marriage is religiously valid only to the extent that these ceremonies have been performed. They could not be performed in the case of two persons who would not equally recognise these ceremonies as sacred; and in this case the married couple could separate without a religious divorce. They would be regarded as married civilly but not religiously.                    [15

Such is the opinion of the Rabbis who are members of the Assembly. In general, they would be no more inclined to bless the marriage of a Christian woman with a Jew, or of a Jewess with a Christian, than Catholic priests would agree to bless unions of this kind. However, the Rabbis acknowledge that the Jew who marries a Christian woman, does not cease on that account to be a Jew in the eyes of his co-religionists, any more than he who marries a Jewess civilly and not religiously.                                                         [16

### 11.4.3 Reply of the assembly to question 6

Men who have adopted a country, who have resided there for many generations; who, even under the rule of certain laws which curtailed their civil rights, were so attached to it that they preferred the misfortune of not enjoying all the advantages of other citizens to that of leaving it, cannot but be regarded in France as Frenchmen; and the obligation of defending it is, in their eyes, a duty at once honourable and precious.                                        [17

Jeremiah, chap. XXIX, strongly advises the Jews to regard Babylon as their country, even though they were to remain there only for seventy years. He exhorts them to till the fields, to build houses, to sow and to plant. His advice was followed to such an extent that Ezra, chap. II, says that when Cyrus allowed them to return to Jerusalem to build the second Temple, only forty-two thousand three hundred and sixty of them left Babylon, that this number was composed only of the poorer people, and that the rich remained in Babylon. *[18*

Love of one's country is, among the Jews, a sentiment so natural, so lively, and so much in harmony with their religious belief, that a French Jew in England regards himself as a stranger, even in the company of fellow Jews, and the same is true of English Jews in France. *[19*

This sentiment reaches such a pitch that French Jews could be seen during the last war fighting against Jews of other countries with which France was at war. *[20*

Many of them are covered with honourable wounds, and others have won on the field of honour resounding testimonies to their bravery. *[21*

## 11.5 HOLOCAUST DOCUMENTS

### 11.5.1 Dieter Wisliceny's account of Himmler's antisemitic 'world-view' (November 1946)

Before I go into developments since the outbreak of the Russian war, I must touch briefly on a subject which in all previous accounts of these events is barely mentioned, but without which it is impossible to obtain a clear view of the situation. I refer to the reasons which led Hitler and Himmler to undertake the destruction of European Jewry. *[1*

Antisemitism constituted one of the basic elements of the Nazi party's programme. Essentially it was the product of two ideas: (1) the pseudo-scientific biological theories of Professor Günther, and (2) a mystical-religious notion that the world is ruled by good and evil powers. According to this view the Jews represented the evil principle, aided and abetted by the Church (the Jesuit Order), Freemasonry and Bolshevism. The literature of this viewpoint is well known; the older writings of the Nazi party teem with such ideas. A straight line leads from the *Protocols of the Elders of Zion* to Rosenberg's *Myth*. These ideas are particularly explicit in the writings of Mathilde Ludendorff, whose excessively sectarian views were later, of course, frowned upon. It is absolutely impossible to make any impression on this outlook by means of logical or rational argument; it is a sort of religiosity which compels men to form themselves into a sect. Under the influence of this literature millions of people believed these things – an event which can only be compared with similar phenomena of the Middle Ages such as witch mania. Against this world of evil the race-mystics set the world of good, of light, embodied in blond, blue-eyed people who alone were supposed to possess the capacity for creating civilisation or building a State. Now these two worlds were allegedly locked together in constant strife, and the war of 1939, which Hitler started, represented only the final battle between these two powers. People are strongly tempted to see Himmler as an ice-cold, cynical politician. This view is certainly incorrect. In his whole attitude Himmler was a mystic, who embraced this 'world view' with religious fanaticism.                                                                            [2

Once possessed of the necessary power, he began to translate into reality his new 'Religion of Race' with the sort of icy fanaticism that is characteristic of someone afflicted with religious mania. So he wanted to turn the SS organisation into a 'Nordic blood brotherhood', to act as 'a bulwark against Jewry, the Church and Bolshevism'. All aspects of life which did not fit in with this concept were either swept aside or destroyed. While he for his part consulted astrologers and dabbled in all the occult sciences, the SS gradually evolved into a new kind of religious sect, with its own forms and customs, in which crude materialism was mixed up with vague deistical notions. Personal achievement was no longer recognised, but advancement depended on the number of one's children, or leaving the Churches, and other such things. Himmler called for the severest measures against the 'World of the Sub-humans'. So the concentration camps came into being. In Himmler's opinion feelings of humanity were only a case of Christian 'spinelessness'. On Himmler's orders Nietzsche's saying, 'Praised be whatever makes for hardness', hung as a text on the wall of almost every SS office. There can be no doubt that Hitler was aware of Himmler's attitude and approved of it, since his own ideas were so similar. The more Himmler's power increased in the sphere of domestic affairs, the more the Jews and their fate fell under his control. In Himmler's opinion to seek for a solution to the Jewish question through emigration or colonial settlement was no solution, but only a shelving of the problem, so strongly did the idea of 'world domination' take possession of him. Certainly, as Eichmann once observed, he had agreed to the Madagascar plan only out of regard to world publicity, and from political motives. That in his own mind he was thinking of the destruction of European Jewry is shown by events after the outbreak of the war with Russia. He, as well as Heydrich and his aides Müller and Eichmann, were determined 'to deliver to Jewry a blow from which it would never recover', as Eichmann put it with cynical candour in 1944.      [3

### 11.5.2 A letter from Hermann Göring to Reinhard Heydrich instructing him to implement the 'Final Solution' of the Jewish question

The Reich Marshal of the Greater German Reich          Berlin, July [31], 1941
Commissioner for the Four Year Plan
Chairman of the Ministerial Council for National Defence
To: The Chief of the Security Police and the Security Service
      SS Gruppenführer Heydrich, Berlin                                            [1

Complementing the task already assigned to you in the decree of 24 January 1939 to undertake, by emigration or evacuation, a solution of the Jewish question as advantageous as possible under the conditions at the time, I hereby charge you with making all necessary organisational, functional and material preparations for a complete solution of the Jewish question [*eine Gesamtlösung der Judenfrage*] in the German sphere of influence in Europe.                          [2

In so far as the jurisdiction of other central agencies may be touched thereby, they are to be involved. [3

I charge you furthermore with submitting to me in the near future an overall plan of the organisational, functional and material measures necessary for the implementation of the aspired final solution of the Jewish question [*der angestrebten Endlösung der Judenfrage*]. [4

Signed: Göring

# APPENDIX A. SCRIPTURAL READINGS FOR SABBATHS (*PARASHIYYOT* FOR THE ANNUAL CYCLE)

*Note.* Parentheses indicate Sefardi custom. A brace indicates two portions sometimes combined.

| | Torah | Haftarah |
|---|---|---|
| *Genesis* | | |
| 1. Bere'shit | 1:1–6:8 | Isa. 42:5–43:11 (42:5–21) |
| 2. Noah | 6:9–11:32 | Isa. 54:1–55:5 (54:1–10) |
| 3. Lekh lekha | 12:1–17:27 | Isa. 40:27–41:16 |
| 4. Vayyera | 18:1–22:24 | 2 Kgs 4:1–37 (4:1–23) |
| 5. Hayyei Sarah | 23:1–25:18 | 1 Kgs 1:1–31 |
| 6. Toledot | 25:19–28:9 | Mal. 1:1–2:7 |
| 7. Vayyeze | 28:10–32:3 | Hos. 12:13–14:10 (11:7–12:12) |
| 8. Vayyishlah | 32:4–36:43 | Hos. 11:7–12:12 (Obad. 1:1–21) |
| 9. Vayyeshev | 37:1–40:23 | Amos 2:6–3:8 |
| 10. Miqqez | 41:1–44:17 | 1 Kgs 3:15–4:1 |
| 11. Vayyiggash | 44:18–47:27 | Ezek. 37:15–28 |
| 12. Vayehi | 47:28–50:26 | 1 Kgs 2:1–12 |
| | | |
| *Exodus* | | |
| 13. Shemot | 1:1–6:1 | Isa. 27:6–28:13; 29:22–3 |
| | | (Jer. 1:1–2:3) |
| 14. Va'era | 6:2–9:35 | Ezek. 28:25–29:21 |
| 15. Bo | 10:1–13:16 | Jer. 46:13–28 |
| 16. Be-shallah | 13:17–17:16 | Judges 4:4–5:31 (5:1–31) |
| 17. Yitro | 18:1–20:23 | Isa. 6:1–7:6; 9:5–6 (6:1–13) |
| 18. Mishpatim | 21:1–24:18 | Jer. 34:8–22; 33:25–6 |
| {19. Terumah | 25:1–27:19 | 1 Kgs 5:26–6:13 |
| {20. Tezavveh | 27:20–30:10 | Ezek. 43:10–27 |
| 21. Ki Tissa | 30:11–34:35 | 1 Kgs 18:1–39 (18:20–39) |
| {22. Vayyaqhel | 35:1–38:20 | 1 Kgs 7:40–50 (7:13–26) |
| {23. Pequdei | 38:21–40:38 | 1 Kgs 7:51–8:21 (7:40–50) |

| | Torah | | Haftarah |
|---|---|---|---|

*Leviticus*

| 24. | Vayyiqra | 1:1–5:26 | Isa. 43:21–44:23 |
|---|---|---|---|
| 25. | Zav | 6:1–8:36 | Jer. 7:21–8:3; 9:22–3 |
| 26. | Shemini | 9:1–11:47 | 2 Sam. 6:1–7:17 (6:1–19) |
| 27. | Tazri'a | 12:1–13:59 | 2 Kgs 4:42–5:19 |
| 28. | Mezora | 14:1–15:33 | 2 Kgs 7:3–20 |
| 29. | Aharei mot | 16:1–18:30 | Ezek. 22:1–19 (22:1–16) |
| 30. | Qedoshim | 19:1–20:27 | Amos 9:7–15 (Ezek. 20:2–20) |
| 31. | Emor | 21:1–24:23 | Ezek. 44:15–31 |
| 32. | Be-har | 25:1–26:2 | Jer. 32:6–27 |
| 33. | Be-huqqotai | 26:3–27:34 | Jer. 16:19–17:14 |

*Numbers*

| 34. | Be-midbar | 1:1–4:20 | Hos. 2:1–22 |
|---|---|---|---|
| 35. | Naso | 4:21–7:89 | Judges 13:2–25 |
| 36. | Be-ha'alotkha | 8:1–12:16 | Zech. 2:14–4:7 |
| 37. | Shelah lekha | 13:1–15:41 | Josh. 2:1–24 |
| 38. | Qorah | 16:1–18:32 | 1 Sam. 11:14–12:22 |
| 39. | Huqqat | 19:1–22:1 | Judges 11:1–33 |
| 40. | Balaq | 22:2–25:9 | Micah 5:6–6:8 |
| 41. | Pinhas | 25:10–30:1 | 1 Kgs 18:46–19:21 |
| 42. | Mattot | 30:2–32:42 | Jer. 1:1–2:3 |
| 43. | Mas'ei | 33:1–36:13 | Jer. 2:4–28; 3:4 (2:4–28; 4:1–2) |

*Deuteronomy*

| 44. | Devarim | 1:1–3:22 | Isa. 1:1–27 |
|---|---|---|---|
| 45. | Va'ethannan | 3:23–7:11 | Isa. 40:1–26 |
| 46. | Eqev | 7:12–11:25 | Isa. 49:14–51:3 |
| 47. | Re'eh | 11:26–16:17 | Isa. 54:11–55:5 |
| 48. | Shofetim | 16:18–21:9 | Isa. 51:12–52:12 |
| 49. | Ki Teze | 21:10–25:19 | Isa. 54:1–10 |
| 50. | Ki Tavo | 26:1–29:8 | Isa. 60:1–22 |
| 51. | Nizzavim | 29:9–30:20 | Isa. 61:10–63:9 |
| 52. | Vayyelekh | 31:1–30 | Isa. 55:6–56:8 |
| 53. | Ha'azinu | 32:1–52 | 2 Sam. 22:1–51 |
| 54. | *Ve-zot ha-berakhah | 33:1–34:12 | Josh. 1:1–18 (1:1–9) |

*Parashah 54 (Ve-zot ha-berakhah) is read not on Sabbath but on Simhat Torah.

# APPENDIX B. THE JEWISH LITURGICAL YEAR 5745 (1984–85)

Jewish dates are commonly reckoned from the Creation of the World (Anno Mundi = A.M.). To convert dates from A.M. to C.E. subtract 3,761/60 from the A.M. date. Thus 5745 A.M. = 1984–85 C.E.

*Note.* *Pilgrim festival. Italicised dates are Sabbaths. Major festivals are in heavy type. Sabbath *Parashiyyot* are italicised (see Appendix A). The Fast of Gedaliah (Tishri 3), the Fast of 17 Tammuz, and the Fast of 9 Av fall on Sabbath in 5745 A.M., and so are postponed till the Sunday.

| *Tishri (27 Sept.)* | | | *Heshvan (27 Oct.)* | | | *Kislev (25 Nov.)* | | |
|---|---|---|---|---|---|---|---|---|
| 1 | **Rosh Ha-Shanah** (I) | | *1* | Rosh Hodesh | | 1 | Rosh Hodesh | |
| 2 | **Rosh Ha-Shanah** (II) | | | *Noah* | | 2 | | |
| *3* | Shabbat Shuvah | | 2 | | | 3 | | |
| | *Ha'azinu* | | 3 | | | 4 | | |
| 4 | Fast of Gedaliah | | 4 | | | 5 | | |
| 5 | | | 5 | | | 6 | | |
| 6 | Ten Days of Penitence | | 6 | | | 7 | *Vayyeze* | |
| | (Yamim Nora'im) | | 7 | | | 8 | | |
| 7 | | | 8 | *Lekh lekha* | | 9 | | |
| 8 | | | 9 | | | 10 | | |
| 9 | | | 10 | | | 11 | | |
| *10* | **Yom Kippur** | | 11 | | | 12 | | |
| 11 | | | 12 | | | 13 | | |
| 12 | | | 13 | | | *14* | *Vayyishlah* | |
| 13 | | | 14 | | | 15 | | |
| 14 | | | *15* | *Vayyera* | | 16 | | |
| 15 | *****Sukkot** (I) | | 16 | | | 17 | | |
| 16 | **Sukkot** (II) | | 17 | | | 18 | | |
| *17* | | | 18 | | | 19 | | |
| 18 | Hol ha-Mo'ed | | 19 | | | 20 | | |
| 19 | | | 20 | | | *21* | *Vayyeshev* | |
| 20 | | | 21 | | | 22 | | |
| 21 | Hosha'na Rabbah | | *22* | *Hayyei Sarah* | | 23 | | |
| 22 | **Shemini Azeret** | | 23 | | | 24 | | |
| | **Simhat Torah** | | | | | | | |
| | (Israel) | | 24 | | | 25 | **Hanukkah** (I) | |
| 23 | **Simhat Torah** | | | | | | | |
| | (Diaspora) | | 25 | | | 26 | **Hanukkah** (II) | |
| | *Ve-zot ha-berakhah* | | 26 | | | 27 | (III) | |
| *24* | *Bere'shit* | | 27 | | | 28 | *Miqqez* (IV) | |
| 25 | | | 28 | | | 29 | (V) | |
| 26 | | | *29* | *Toledot* | | 30 | Rosh Hodesh (VI) | |
| 27 | | | | | | | | |
| 28 | | | | | | | | |
| 29 | | | | | | | | |
| 30 | Rosh Hodesh | | | | | | | |

| *Tevet (25 Dec.)* | | | *Shevat (23 Jan.)* | | | *Adar (22 Feb.)* | | |
|---|---|---|---|---|---|---|---|---|
| 1 | Rosh Hodesh | | 1 | Rosh Hodesh | | 1 | Rosh Hodesh | |
| | **Hanukkah** (VII) | | 2 | | | *2* | *Terumah* | |
| 2 | **Hanukkah** (VIII) | | 3 | | | 3 | | |
| 3 | | | *4* | *Bo* | | 4 | | |
| 4 | | | 5 | | | 5 | | |
| *5* | *Vayyiggash* | | 6 | | | 6 | | |

| Tevet | | Shevat | | Adar | |
|---|---|---|---|---|---|
| 6 | | 7 | | 7 | |
| 7 | | 8 | | 8 | |
| 8 | | 9 | | 9 | Shabbat Zakhor |
| 9 | | 10 | | | *Tezavveh* |
| 10 | Fast of 10 Tevet | 11 | *Be-shallah* | 10 | |
| 11 | | 12 | | 11 | |
| 12 | *Vayehi* | 13 | | 12 | |
| 13 | | 14 | | 13 | Fast of Esther |
| 14 | | 15 | Tu bi-Shevat | 14 | **Purim** |
| 15 | | | (New Year for Trees) | 15 | Shushan Purim |
| 16 | | 16 | | 16 | *Ki Tissa* |
| 17 | | 17 | | 17 | |
| 18 | | 18 | *Yitro* | 18 | |
| 19 | *Shemot* | 19 | | 19 | |
| 20 | | 20 | | 20 | |
| 21 | | 21 | | 21 | |
| 22 | | 22 | | 22 | |
| 23 | | 23 | | 23 | Shabbat Parah |
| 24 | | 24 | | | *Vayyaqhel* |
| 25 | | 25 | Shabbat Sheqalim | | *Pequdei* |
| 26 | *Va'era* | | *Mishpatim* | 24 | |
| 27 | | 26 | | 25 | |
| 28 | | 27 | | 26 | |
| 29 | | 28 | | 27 | |
| | | 29 | | 28 | |
| | | 30 | Rosh Hodesh | 29 | |

| Nisan (23 Mar.) | | Iyyar (22 Apr.) | | | Sivan (21 May) | | |
|---|---|---|---|---|---|---|---|
| 1 | Rosh Hodesh | 1 | Rosh Hodesh | (16) | 1 | Rosh Hodesh | (45) |
| | Shabbat Ha-Hodesh | 2 | | (17) | 2 | | (46) |
| | *Vayyiqra* | 3 | | (18) | 3 | | (47) |
| 2 | | 4 | Yom ha-Azma'ut | (19) | 4 | | (48) |
| 3 | | | (Israel Independence | | 5 | *Be-midbar* | (49) |
| 4 | | | Day) | | 6 | *Shavu'ot* (I) | |
| 5 | | 5 | | (20) | 7 | **Shavu'ot** (II) | |
| 6 | | 6 | *Tazria* | (21) | 8 | | |
| 7 | | | *Mezora* | | 9 | | |
| 8 | Shabbat ha-Gadol | 7 | | (22) | 10 | | |
| | *Zav* | 8 | | (23) | 11 | | |
| 9 | | 9 | | (24) | 12 | *Naso* | |
| 10 | | 10 | | (25) | 13 | | |
| 11 | | 11 | | (26) | 14 | | |
| 12 | | 12 | | (27) | 15 | | |
| 13 | | 13 | *Aharei mot* | (28) | 16 | | |
| 14 | Fast of the Firstborn | | *Qedoshim* | | 17 | | |
| 15 | *Pesah* (I) | 14 | | (29) | 18 | | |
| 16 | **Pesah** (II) | 15 | | (30) | 19 | *Be-ha'alotkha* | |
| | Sefirat ha-Omer (1) | 16 | | (31) | 20 | | |

### Nisan | Iyyar | Sivan

| Nisan | | | Iyyar | | | Sivan | |
|---|---|---|---|---|---|---|---|
| 17 | | (2) | 17 | | (32) | 21 | |
| 18 | Hol ha-Mo'ed | (3) | 18 | Lag ba-Omer | (33) | 22 | |
| 19 | | (4) | 19 | | (34) | 23 | |
| 20 | | (5) | *20* | *Emor* | (35) | 24 | |
| 21 | **Pesah** (VII) | (6) | 21 | | (36) | 25 | |
| *22* | **Pesah** (VIII) | (7) | 22 | | (37) | *26* | *Shelah lekha* |
| 23 | | (8) | 23 | | (38) | 27 | |
| 24 | | (9) | 24 | | (39) | 28 | |
| 25 | | (10) | 25 | | (40) | 29 | |
| 26 | | (11) | 26 | | (41) | 30 | Rosh Hodesh |
| 27 | Yom ha-Sho'ah | (12) | *27* | *Be-har* | (42) | | |
| | (Holocaust Day) | | | *Be-huqqotai* | | | |
| 28 | | (13) | 28 | | (43) | | |
| *29* | *Shemini* | (14) | 29 | | (44) | | |
| 30 | Rosh Hodesh | (15) | | | | | |

### Tammuz (20 June) | Av (19 July) | Elul (18 Aug.)

| Tammuz (20 June) | | Av (19 July) | | Elul (18 Aug.) | |
|---|---|---|---|---|---|
| 1 | Rosh Hodesh | 1 | Rosh Hodesh | 1 | Rosh Hodesh |
| 2 | | *2* | *Mattot* | 2 | |
| *3* | *Qorah* | | *Mas'ei* | 3 | |
| 4 | | 3 | | 4 | |
| 5 | | 4 | | 5 | |
| 6 | | 5 | | 6 | |
| 7 | | 6 | | *7* | *Shofetim* |
| 8 | | 7 | | 8 | |
| 9 | | 8 | | 9 | |
| *10* | *Huqqat* | 9 ⌐ | *Devarim* | 10 | |
| 11 | | 10 ↓ | Tish'ah be-Av | 11 | |
| 12 | | | (Fast of 9 Av) | 12 | |
| 13 | | 11 | | 13 | |
| 14 | | 12 | | *14* | *Ki Teze* |
| 15 | | 13 | | 15 | |
| 16 | | 14 | | 16 | |
| *17* ⌐ | *Balaq* | 15 | | 17 | |
| 18 ↓ | Fast of 17 Tammuz | *16* | *Va'ethannan* | 18 | |
| 19 | | 17 | | 19 | |
| 20 | | 18 | | 20 | |
| 21 | | 19 | | *21* | *Ki Tavo* |
| 22 | | 20 | | 22 | |
| 23 | | 21 | | 23 | |
| *24* | *Pinhas* | 22 | | 24 | |
| 25 | | *23* | *Eqev* | 25 | |
| 26 | | 24 | | 26 | |
| 27 | | 25 | | 27 | |
| 28 | | 26 | | *28* | *Nizzavim* |
| 29 | | 27 | | 29 | |
| | | 28 | | *5746 (1985–86)* | |
| | | 29 | | *Tishri (16 Sept.)* | |
| | | *30* | Rosh Hodesh | 6 | Shabbat Shuvah |

| Av (5745) | | Tishri (5746) | |
|---|---|---|---|
| 30 | Re'eh | 6 | Vayyelekh |
| | | 13 | Ha'azinu |
| | | 23 | **Simhat Torah** |
| | | | Ve-zot ha-berakhah |

# NOTES

## 1. Introduction

1. In the context of Judaism and Christianity 'Bible' is an ambiguous term. To Jews it means the Hebrew Bible – what Christians call the Old Testament. Jews often refer to the Bible as 'Tanakh', an acronym formed from the names of the three divisions of the Hebrew canon: Torah, Nevi'im and Ketuvim.

2. Singer, *Prayer Book*, pp. 91–2, 252.

3. Note, e.g., Kierkegaard's powerful analysis of the Aqedah in 'Fear and Trembling' (1843) (trans. W. Lowrie, *Søren Kierkegaard: Fear and Trembling and Sickness unto Death* [Princeton, 1968]); or Wilfred Owen's poem, 'So Abram rose, and clave the wood, and went . . .', which Benjamin Britten used in *War Requiem*. Perhaps the best known allusion to the Aqedah in contemporary Israeli literature is Amir Gilboa's poem 'Isaac'. On this see T. Carmi (ed.), *The Penguin Book of Hebrew Verse* (Harmondsworth, 1981), pp. 48–50, 560; L. I. Yudkin, *Escape into Siege* (London, 1974), pp. 135–9.

4. This is the position argued by B. Z. Wacholder: see his *Essays on Jewish Chronology and Chronography* (New York, 1976), pp. 212–39.

5. The Vilna edition of the Talmud in fact reads, 'the blessing relating to the Sadducees' (Birkat ha-Zeduqim), but this is an alteration introduced by a Christian censor who detected an anti-Christian reference in the word *minim*. The text of the Amidah quoted in 3.1.2 also does not refer to the minim, but uses the more neutral word *malshinim*, 'slanderers' or 'informers'.

6. Petuchowski, *Contributions to the Scientific Study of Jewish Liturgy*, p. 376.

7. Petuchowski, *Contributions to the Scientific Study of Jewish Liturgy*, p. 376.

8. Singer, *Prayer Book*, p. 317.

9. Singer, *Prayer Book*, p. 7.

10. J. Neusner, *The Academic Study of Judaism* (New York, 1976), p. 39.

11. The wonder-worker Haninah ben Dosa is called repeatedly in rabbinic literature 'a man of deed' (*ish ma'aseh*). See, e.g., Mishnah, Sotah 9:15: 'When Rabbi Haninah ben Dosa died men of deed ceased'. For a discussion of the meaning of the expression *ish ma'aseh* see Vermes, *Post-biblical Jewish Studies*, pp. 187–8.

12. See, further, B. S. Jackson, 'Legalism', *Journal of Jewish Studies*, 30 (1979), pp. 1–22.

13. I follow here Menachem Elon, 'Codification of law', *Encyclopaedia Judaica*, vol. 5, col. 633.

14. For the distinction between 'books of halakhot' and 'books of pesaqim' see Menachem Elon, 'Codification of law', *Encyclopaedia Judaica*, vol. 5, col. 634.

15. Ibn Khaldun, *The Muqaddimah*, ed. Quatremère, III 27 and III 42. Translation: F. Rosenthal, *Ibn Khaldun: The Muqaddimah* (Princeton, 1967), vol. 3, pp. 34 and 53.

16. For text and translation of the

Jerusalem Epistle see A. L. Tibawi, *Al-Ghazali's Tract on Dogmatic Theology* (London, 1956). See also Nabih Amin Faris, *The Foundations of the Articles of Faith* (Lahore, 1963).

**17.** Text: A. Lichtenberg (ed.), *Qovez Teshuvot ha-Rambam ve-Iggerotav* (Leipzig 1859; repr. Farnborough, Hants., 1969), Part II, p. 28d. Translation: F. Kobler (ed.), *Letters of Jews through the Ages*, vol. 1 (London, 1953), pp. 212–13.

**18.** However, he revised it a number of times later. This is evident from autograph manuscripts that survive. Note also the reference to the *Moreh Nevukhim* at 7.3.5.

**19.** Singer, *Prayer Book*, pp. 3–4. The *Yigdal* inspired the Christian hymn 'The God of Abraham praise' by the Weslyan minister Thomas Olivers, first printed in 1770.

**20.** Singer, *Prayer Book*, pp. 89–90.

**21.** The quotations are from one of Adret's letters on philosophy: see B. Halper (ed.), *Post-biblical Hebrew Literature: an Anthology* (Philadelphia, 1921), vol. 1, pp. 137–41 (text); vol. 2, pp. 176–82 (translation). Further, Kobler, *Letters of Jews through the Ages*, vol. 1, pp. 248–59 [n. 17 above]. The ban itself stated: 'We have decreed and agreed for ourselves and our seed and all attached to us, by the power of the ban [*herem*], that for a period of fifty years no member of our congregation shall study the books of the Greeks which have been written on the subject of natural philosophy and metaphysics, whether they be composed in their language, or translated into another, before he reaches the age of twenty-five; and that no member of our community should teach anybody these philosophical studies until he reaches twenty-five; lest they be drawn after those sciences and turn aside from the Torah of Israel which is above all these sciences. . . . We exclude from our decree the study of the science of medicine. Although it

too is based upon the study of Nature, nevertheless the Torah itself accords the physician permission to heal.' See S. B. Freehof, *The Responsa Literature* (Philadelphia, 1955), pp. 105–9.

**22.** Scholem, *Kabbalah*, p. 23.

**23.** G. Vajda, 'Jewish Mysticism', *Encyclopaedia Britannica*, 15th ed,. *Macropaedia*, vol. 10, p. 184.

**24.** Scholem, *Kabbalah*, pp. 27–8.

**25.** See especially the Qedushah de-Yozer, 3.1.1.*2–3*.

**26.** Scholem, *Major Trends in Jewish Mysticism*, pp. 156–204; Scholem, *Kabbalah*, pp. 213–43.

**27.** Though it is a matter of scholarly debate, the 'modern' era of Jewish history may be defined as beginning with the French revolution.

**28.** The Lurianic prayer books contain the Sefardi rite, but have been edited in certain ways to make them conform to the mystical interpretations of the prayers propounded by the great Safed Qabbalist Isaac Luria (1534–72) and his followers. See, further, Blumenthal, *Understanding Jewish Mysticism*, pp. 169–80.

**29.** 'Rabbi Leib son of Sarah, the hidden Zaddik who wandered over the earth, following the course of rivers, in order to redeem the souls of the living and the dead, said this: "I did not go to the maggid [Dov Baer of Mezhirech, d. 1772, one of the most important of the early Hasidic masters] in order to hear Torah from him, but to see how he unlaces his felt shoes and laces them up again" ' (Martin Buber, *Tales of the Hasidim: the Early Masters* [London, 1956], p. 107).

**30.** Philipson, *The Reform Movement*, pp. 491–2.

**31.** Plaut, *Growth of Reform Judaism*, p. 100.

**32.** Plaut, *Growth of Reform Judaism*, p. 242.

**33.** The pamphlet was signed, 'Your most sincere admirer S*** – Vienna, June 12, 1782.' While he was writing *Jerusalem* Mendelssohn was under the impression that the author of the pamphlet was Josef von Sonnenfels – a high-ranking politician and leader of the Viennese Enlightenment, well known as an admirer of Mendelssohn. However, he was the victim of a hoax: the real author was August Friedrich Cranz, a much less eminent figure, once dismissed by a contemporary as 'a scribbler esteemed by nobody here'. See, further, Altmann, *Mendelssohn*, pp. 502–13.

**34.** Hirsch thus defined his concept of *derekh erez*: '*Derekh erez* embraces everything which is conditioned by the fact that man has to cope with his existence upon earth, his destiny and his common life with others, and has to achieve this by the earthly means at his disposal. Hence it signifies especially the means of subsistence and of a respectable conduct of life, as well as everything connected with general human and civil education.' Quoted from Hirsch's *Uebersetzung und Erklaerung zu Israels Gebeten* by E. W. Jalenko, in S. Noveck (ed.), *Great Jewish Personalities in Modern Times* (London, 1964), p. 89. The phrase *Torah im derekh erez* was lifted by Hirsch from Mishnah, Pirqei Avot 2:2. It is translated 'Torah with a secular occupation' in 6.1.*1*.

**35.** The principal Allied Powers constituting the Supreme Council of the Paris peace conference assigned the mandate for Palestine to Great Britain during the San Remo conference in April 1920. This decision was then ratified by the Council of the League of Nations on 24 July 1922. Article 2 of the mandate for Palestine stated: 'The Mandatory shall be responsible for placing the country under such political, administrative and economic conditions as will secure the establishment of the Jewish national home, as laid down in the preamble, and the development of self-governing institutions, and also for safeguarding the civil and religious rights of all the inhabitants of Palestine, irrespective of race and religion.' For the text of the mandate see J. N. Moore, (ed.), *The Arab–Israeli Conflict*, vol. 3, *Documents* (Princeton, 1974), pp. 75–84.

**36.** The basic account of the York massacre is William of Newburgh, *Historia Rerum Anglicarum* IV 10. Latin text: *William of Newburgh: Historia Rerum Anglicarum I–IV*, ed. R. Howlett (London, 1884), pp. 317–22. English trans.: J. Stevenson, *The Church Historians of England*, vol. 4, pt. 2 (London, 1856), pp. 568–71. See also J. Jacobs, *The Jews of Angevin England* (London, 1893), pp. 123–30. Jacobs rightly raises the question of whether William of Newburgh knew Josephus's account of the fall of Masada (*Jewish War* 7:320–406) and modelled his treatment of the York massacre on it.

**37.** See *Annals of Waverly*, ed. H. R. Luard (London, 1865), pp. 346–8 (= *Annales Monastici*, vol. 2); *Matthew Paris: Chronica Majora*, ed. H. R. Luard, vol. 5 (London, 1880), pp. 516–19. For an English version of the latter see *Matthew Paris's English History*, trans. J. A. Giles, vol. 5 (London, 1854), pp. 138–41.

**38.** Hugh's feast day is 27 July: see *Acta Sanctorum* (Antwerp, 1729), *July*, vol. 6, pp. 494–5. William was supposed to have been done to death by the Jews of Norwich in 1144. His feast is 25 March: see *Acta Sanctorum: March*, vol. 3, pp. 588–91.

## 2. Scripture and tradition

**1.** For a form-critical analysis of the Chain of Tradition see J. Neusner, *Rabbinic Traditions about the Pharisees before 70* (Leiden, 1971), vol. 1, pp. 15–23.

**2.** The examples do not form an integral part of the Baraita. I have introduced them in an attempt to clarify the often cryptic rules.

3. The example illustrates only the technique of constructing a general principle on the basis of *two* verses. Construction on the basis of *one* is much more complicated.

4. Rules 5–11 explore further the relationship between the general and the specific. They have been omitted for the sake of brevity and simplicity.

5. The example illustrates determination from the immediate context; determination 'from its end' will obviously follow similar lines.

6. It is possible to offer here only an anthology of the Mekhilta's very extensive comments on these two chapters.

7. The usual rendering of this verse is: 'God has spoken once, twice have I heard this'.

### 3. Liturgy

1. The bracketed words are said in a whisper.

2. The two extracts come respectively from the beginning and towards the end of the Maggid section of the Passover Seder.

### 4. Tales of the saints and scholars

1. See above, 3.1.1.*8*.

### 5. Religious law

1. That is, forgot to say grace.

2. = Mishnah, Shabbat 7:2.

3. More literally, 'fathers of works' (*avot mela'khot*): see n. 7 below.

4. English versions usually translate *mela'khah* here as 'stuff' or 'material'.

5. A name for Abaye. He was so called because his distinguished uncle Rabbah bar Nahmani was one of his teachers.

6. 'Eleazar' is the reading of the Munich manuscript.

7. More literally, '. . . who imposed liability on an offspring [*toladah*] along with a father [*av*]'. See further n. 3 above.

8. 'Gentile judges': literally, 'judges of star-worshippers' (or 'idolators') (*ovedei khokhavim*).

### 6. Ethical literature

1. For further maxims from Pirqei Avot, see 2.1.1 above.

2. 'A good eye', i.e. goodwill, or liberality. Conversely, 'an evil eye' means ill-will or selfishness; see 6.1.*18*.

3. More literally, 'his eye is evil towards what belongs to others'. See n. 2 above.

4. Bahya uses the Arabic term *al-hawa* as equivalent to the Hebrew *yezer ha-ra*, 'the evil inclination'.

5. The inclination is personified throughout this passage.

6. Luzzato's quotations from classic rabbinic texts are often rather inexact, and from time to time he simply alludes to his sources, leaving it to the learned reader to fill in the details from memory. The texts needed for understanding this passage will be found in 6.3, 'Luzzato's sources'.

7. Genesis Rabbah 94:9 has another version of the story. For an attractive analysis see D. Daube, *Collaboration with Tyranny in Rabbinic Law* (London, 1965), pp. 5–27.

### 7. Philosophy and theology

1. In *Kuzari* 4:25 (ed. Baneth, p. 183; trans. Hirschfeld, p. 238) Judah Ha-Levi gives a fuller account of the doctrine of emanation to which he alludes here. The curious explanation of the revolution of the celestial sphere is found also in al-Ghazali, *Tahafut al-Falasifah* 15 (ed. Bouyges, pp. 250 f). See Al-Ghazali's *Tahafut al-Falasifah* (*Incoherence of the Philosophers*), trans. S. A. Kamali (Lahore, 1963), p. 169.

2. Sometimes translated 'The eternal God'.

3. Maimonides explains in *Guide of the Perplexed*, Introduction (ed. Munk, 5b) that he finally gave up the attempt to write these two works. For the relevant passage see *Moses Maimonides: The Guide of the Perplexed*, trans. S. Pines

(Chicago and London, 1963), vol. 1, pp. 9–10.

**4.** *Mehoqeq* here is usually translated 'ruler', 'leader' or 'lawgiver', but an early Jewish tradition, found e.g. in the Targumim, took it as meaning 'scribe' and saw in it a reference to Moses.

**5.** The *parashah* is usually called 'Balaq'. Maimonides is probably thinking of Num. 24:17.

**6.** Maimonides is probably thinking of Deut. 30:1–10.

**7.** The passage in brackets is found a little earlier in Maimonides' *Commentary on the Mishnah*, Sanhedrin 10. It appears to be the explanation of the doctrine of the resurrection to which he refers here.

## 8. Mystical literature

**1.** The manuscripts and editions of the *Sefer Yezirah* differ greatly from each other. The translation is based upon an eclectic text. Only extracts from the work have been given: they have been chosen with a view to making clear its basic structure and leading ideas.

**2.** Reading *kidodiyyot esh* for *kykywt esh*, on the basis of Job 41:11, 'From his mouth torches [*lappidim*] proceed, sparks of fire [*kidodei esh*] escape'.

**3.** Hebrew: *mashhitim mi-yoredei merkavah ve-lo be-yoredei merkavah she-lo bi-reshut*. The sense of this is much disputed.

**4.** It has long been suspected that some of the magical names and formulae in the Heikhalot texts are Greek transliterated into Hebrew. J. H. Levy suggested that ABYRGHYDRYHM is a corrupt transliteration of the Greek names of the four primal elements: *aēr, gē, hudōr, pur* – air, earth, water and fire. See J. H. Levy, 'Remnants of Greek sentences and names in "Heikhalot Rabbati" ', in Levy, *Studies in Jewish Hellenism* (Jerusalem, 1969), pp. 259–65 [in Hebrew].

**5.** Levy suggests that if we ignore the divine name YHVH, we may have here

a garbled transliteration of the Greek: *Theos ouranōn zē(i)s pur gēs sigē esti*. Unfortunately this does not make much sense. The first two and the last three words make a kind of sentence which reads: 'The God of heaven [and] of earth is silence'. This would fit in with the name DVMY'EL which in Hebrew could mean 'The Silence of God'. See n. 4 above.

**6.** Again Levy detects Greek behind the gibberish: *Aristēn hēmeran, aristēn tuchēn, phēnon sēmeion, eirēnē*, 'Excellent day, the best of luck, show the sign, peace!' This would be a greeting from DVMY'EL to the adept. However, at some point the greeting was misunderstood and turned into a magical name by the addition of 'YHVH the God of Israel'. See n. 4 above.

**7.** Levy suggests the underlying Greek words: *Theos, ouranos, gē, ho despotēs*, 'God, heaven, earth, the Lord'. See n. 4 above.

**8.** Kol (All) and Zaddiq (Righteous One) are alternative names of the Sefirah Yesod (Foundation).

**9.** Though the general drift of this passage is clear enough, it is very difficult to put into good English. The reading of the original text is also doubtful at a number of points. I have leaned heavily in my version on Tishby, *Mishnat ha-Zohar*, vol. 2, pp. 55–7.

## 9. Modern movements, modern thinkers

**1.** A hymn for Sabbath composed by the great Qabbalist Isaac ben Solomon Luria (1534–72): see *Sefer Yefeh Nof* (Venice, 1564–76), p. 40b.

**2.** 'The Ari' is a name for the Qabbalist Isaac Luria: see n. 1 above.

**3.** The reference here is to David Ernst Moerschel, an army chaplin in Berlin who wrote a postscript to *The Search for Light and Right*: see Mendes-Flohr and Reinharz, *The Jew in the Modern World*, p. 85; further, *Moses Mendelssohn: Jerusalem*, trans. M.

Samuels (London, 1838), vol. 1, pp. 144–5. Samuels gives a full English version of *The Search for Light and Right.*

**4.** Gen. 12:8 is usually rendered 'Abraham called on the name of the Lord'. Hirsch, however, takes it to mean 'Abraham called [men together] in the name of the Lord'. Abraham ibn Ezra (1089–1164), following earlier authorities, thus glosses the verse: '*Vayyiqra be-shem Adonai* means either that Abraham prayed to the Lord, or that he called on mankind to worship the Lord'.

## 11. Society and the Jews

**1.** I have followed here the printed text of King John's charter: 'Vel coram illis qui turres nostras custodierint, in quorum bailiis Judei manserint. Et ubicunque Judei fuerint, liceat eis ire, etc.' This makes rather better sense than the printed text of Richard's charter: 'Vel coram eis qui terras illas custodierint, in quorum bailiis manserint et ubicunque fuerint. Liceat eis ire, etc.' Either the editors of the charter mistranscribed it, or, perhaps, a medieval secretary miscopied.

**2.** Again I follow King John's text: 'Neque hoc eis prohibere'. Richard's charter as printed has 'Neque illas eis prohibere'.

# BIBLIOGRAPHY

## A. Primary sources

Ahad Ha-Am (Asher Ginsberg). 10.1.2 is from an essay which appeared in the periodical *Ha-Shiloah* in 1897. It is reprinted in Ahad Ha-Am's collected essays, *Al Parashat Derakhim*, vol. 2 (Berlin, 1921), pp. 22–35, under the title 'The Jewish State and the Jewish problem'. English translation: H. Kohn (ed.), *Nationalism and the Jewish Ethic: Basic Writings of Ahad Ha'am* (New York, 1962), pp. 66–89. See also Hertzberg, *Zionist Idea*, pp. 262–9.

Amidah. See under Liturgy.

Assembly of Jewish Notables. Text: D. Tama, *Organisation civile et religieuse des Israelites de France et du royaume d'Italie* (Paris, 1808), Part 1, pp. 132 f., 151 f., 173 f. English translation: D. Tama, *Transactions of the Parisian Sanhedrin*, trans. F. D. Kirwan (London, 1807; repr. Farnborough, Hants., 1971). See also Mendes-Flohr and Reinharz, *The Jew in the Modern World*, pp. 112–24.

Avot de-Rabbi Natan. Text: S. Schechter, *Aboth deRabbi Nathan* (Vienna, 1887).

Translations: J. Goldin, *The Fathers according to Rabbi Nathan* (New Haven, 1955) – Recension A; A. J. Saldarini, *The Fathers according to Rabbi Nathan* (Leiden, 1975) – Recension B.

Babylonian Talmud. Text: *Talmud Bavli* (Vilna, 1886). Translation: I. Epstein (ed.), *The Babylonian Talmud* (London, 1935–48).

Bahya ibn Paquda. *The Duties of the Heart.* Text: J. Qafih, *Sefer Torat Hovot ha-Levavot* (Jerusalem, 1973). Translation: M. Mansoor, *The Book of Direction to the Duties of the Heart* (London, 1973).

Ballad of Hugh of Lincoln. F. J. Child (ed.), *English and Scottish Ballads* (New York, 1882–98), No. 155 (= vol. 3, pp. 233–54).

Baraita of Rabbi Ishmael. Text: M. Friedmann, *Sifra, der älteste Midrasch zu Levitikus* (Breslau, 1915; repr. Jerusalem, 1967), pp. 9–28. See also Singer, *Prayer Book*, pp. 14 f. Commentary: Mielziner, *Introduction to the Talmud*, pp. 117–87.

Columbus platform. Reprinted from *Central Conference of American Rabbis Yearbook* vol. 47 (1937).

Declaration of the State of Israel. See under Laws of the State of Israel.

Fourth Lateran Council. Text: M. Stern, *Urkundliche Beiträge über die Stellung der Päpste zu den Juden*, zweite Lieferung, II Band, I Heft (Kiel, 1895: repr. Farnborough, Hants., 1970), pp. 4–11. For the full text of the canons of the Council see J. D. Mansi, *Sacrorum Conciliorum ... Collectio*, vol. 22 (Venice, 1778), and, with commentary, C. J. Hefele and H. Leclercq, *Histoire des Conciles d'après les documents originaux*, V. 2 (Paris, 1913), pp. 1316–1398.

Freehof, S. B. The Responsum cited in 9.2.3 was first published in the *Central Conference of American Rabbis Yearbook*, vol. 76 (1966); repr. in Freehof, *Current Reform Responsa* (Cincinnati, 1969), pp. 103–6.

Göring, Herman. See under Holocaust documents.

Havdalah service. See under Liturgy.

Heikhalot Rabbati. The translation is based on ms. Ebr. 228 of the Vatican Library, Rome. The standard printed editions are very corrupt: see S. A. Wertheimer, *Batei Midrashot*, vol. 1 (2nd ed., Jerusalem, 1954), pp. 67–136; A. Jellinek, *Bet ha-Midrasch*, vol. 3 (Leipzig, 1885), pp. 83–108. For an important new edition of the major Heikhalot manuscripts see P. Schäfer, *Synopse zur Hekhalot-Literatur* (Tübingen, 1981). Chapter and verse divisions in 8.2.1 follow Wertheimer. There is a partial, and very inaccurate, translation of *Heikhalot Rabbati* in Blumenthal, *Understanding Jewish Mysticism*.

Herzl, T. 10.1.1 is from Herzl's *The Jewish State*. Text: *Der Judenstaat* (Leipzig and Vienna, 1896; repr. Osnabrück, 1968). The passage quoted is on pp. 24–9. Translation: S. d'Avigdor, *Theodor Herzl: The Jewish State* (6th ed., London, 1972). See also

Hertzberg, *Zionist Idea*, pp. 204–26.

Hirsch, S. R. 9.3.2 is from an essay which was published in the first issue of Hirsch's periodical *Jeschurun* (October 1854) and repr. in Hirsch's *Gesammelte Schriften*, ed. N. Hirsch, vol. 1 (Frankfurt a.M., 1902), pp. 149–59, under the title 'Der Jude und seine Zeit'. Translation: I. Grunfeld, *Judaism Eternal*, vol. 2 (London, 1956), pp. 213–23.

Holocaust documents. 11.5.1. Text: L. Poliakov and J. Wulf, *Das Dritte Reich und die Juden* (Berlin, 1961), pp. 50–2. 11.5.2. Text: Poliakov and Wulf, *Das Dritte Reich*, pp. 70 f.

Jerusalem Talmud. Text: *Talmud Yerushalmi* (Krotoschin, 1866).

Judah Ha-Levi. *The Kuzari*. Text: D. Baneth, *Kitab al-Radd wa-'l-Dalil fi'l-Din al-Dhalil (Al-Kitab al-Khazari) by Judah Ha-Levi* (Jerusalem, 1977). Translation: H. Hirschfeld, *Judah Hallevi's Kitab al-Khazari* (London, 1905; repr. New York, 1964). This translation is very poor. Scarcely better are the selections in I. Heinemann, *Jehuda Halevi: Kuzari* (Oxford, 1946; repr. in *Three Jewish Philosophers*, New York, 1960). The modern Hebrew translation by Yehuda Even Shmuel, *The Kosari of R. Yehuda Halevi* (Tel Aviv, 1972), is useful.

Law of Return. See under Laws of the State of Israel.

Laws of the State of Israel. With the exception of 10.2.4 the translations are taken from *Laws of the State of Israel: Authorised Translation from the Hebrew prepared at the Ministry of Justice*. 10.2.1 is from *Laws of the State of Israel* vol. 1 (5708/1948), pp. 3–5. 10.2.2 is from vol. 4 (5710/1950), p. 114. For later amendments to this law see vol. 8 (5714/1954), p. 144, and vol. 24 (5730/1970), p. 28. 10.2.3 is from vol. 7 (5713/1953), pp. 139–40. 10.2.4 is taken from A. F. Landau (ed.), *Selected Judgements of the Supreme Court of Israel*, Special Volume (Jerusalem, 1971), pp. 1–34.

Leviticus Rabbah. Text: M. A. Mirkin, *Midrash Rabbah* (Tel Aviv, 1956–64). Translation: H. Freedman and M. Simon, *Midrash Rabbah* (London, 1939).

Liturgy. *Weekday and Sabbath*. Text and translation: S. Singer, *The Authorized Daily Prayer Book* (new ed., London, 1962). 3.1.1 is on pp. 38–46, 116–21. 3.1.2 is on pp. 46–55. 3.2.1 is on pp. 169 f. 3.2.2 is on pp. 292 f. *Passover Haggadah*. Text: E. D. Goldschmidt, *The Passover Haggadah: its History and Sources* (Jerusalem, 1960). Translations and commentaries: N.N. Glatzer, *The Passover Haggadah* (rev. ed., New York, 1969); C. Roth, *The Haggadah* (London, 1975).

Luzzato, M. H. *The Path of the Upright*. The text used is that printed in the bilingual edition by M. M. Kaplan, *Mesillat Yesharim: The Path of the Upright, by M. H. Luzzato* (Philadelphia, 1948).

Maimonides. *Commentary on the Mishnah*. Text: J. Qafih, *Mishnah im Persuh Rabbenu Mosheh ben Maimon* (Jerusalem, 1963–8). The Thirteen Principles are in the vol. on *Seder Neziqin*, pp. 210–7. English translation and commentary in Jacobs, *Principles of the Jewish Faith*.

Mekhilta of Rabbi Ishmael. Text and translation: J. Z. Lauterbach, *Mekilta deRabbi Ishmael* (Philadelphia, 1933–35).

Mendelssohn. 9.3.1 is from *Jerusalem, Part 2*. Text: G. B. Mendelssohn (ed.), *M. Mendelssohn: Gesammelte Schriften*, vol. 3 (Leipzig, 1843), pp. 255–362. Translation: A. Jospe, *Jerusalem and other Jewish Writings by Moses Mendelssohn* (New York, 1969), pp. 11–110.

Mishnah. Text: H. Albeck and H. Yalon, *Shishah Sidrei Mishnah* (Jerusalem and Tel Aviv, 1952–56). Translation: H. Danby, *The Mishnah* (Oxford, 1933).

Passover Haggadah. See under Liturgy.

Pesiqta de-Rav Kahana. Text: B. Mandelbaum, *Pesikta deRav Kahana* (New York, 1962). Translation: W. G. Braude and I. J. Kapstein, *Pesikta de-Rab Kahana: R. Kahana's Compilation of Discourses for Sabbaths and Festal Days* (London, 1975).

Pittsburgh platform. Text first published in 'Authentic Report of the Proceedings of the Rabbinical Conference held in Pittsburgh, Nov. 16, 17, 18, 1885', *Jewish Reformer*, 15 January 1886, p. 4.

Qiddush. See under Liturgy.

*Qizzur Shulhan Arukh*. Text: S. Ganzfried, *Qizzur Shulhan Arukh* (new. ed., Jerusalem, 1974). Translation: J. Goldin, *Code of Jewish Law: Kitzur Shulhan Aruch* (rev. ed., New York, 1963).

Rabbinical Courts Jurisdiction (Marriage and Divorce) Law. See under Laws of the State of Israel.

Richard I's charter. Text: T. Rymer, *Foedera, Conventiones, Litterae et cujuscunque generis Acta Publica inter Reges Angliae et alios*, ed. Clarke and Holbrooke, vol. 1, part 1 (London, 1816), p. 51. Translation: J. Jacobs, *The Jews of Angevin England* (London, 1893), pp. 134–6. King John's charter of 10 April 1201 may be found in T. D. Hardy (ed.), *Rotuli Chartarum in Turri Londinensi asservati*, vol. 1, part 1 (London, 1837), p. 93, and for a translation see Jacobs, *Jews of Angevin England*, pp. 212–14.

Sa'adiah Gaon. *The Book of Beliefs and Opinions*. Text: J. Qafih, *Sefer ha-Nivhar be-Emunot uve-De'ot* (Jerusalem, 1970). Translation: S. Rosenblatt, *Saadia Gaon: The Book of Beliefs and Opinions* (New Haven, 1948).

Schechter, S. 9.3.3 is taken from the introduction to Schechter's *Studies in Judaism*, First Series (London, 1896), pp. xi–xxx.

*Sefer Yezirah*. Text: I. Gruenwald, 'A preliminary critical edition of *Sefer Yezira*', *Israel Oriental Studies*, 1

(1971), pp. 132–77. Translation: K. Stenring, *The Book of Formation (Sepher Yetzirah) by Rabbi Akiba ben Joseph* (London, 1923; repr. New York, 1970). There is also a translation with brief commentary in Blumenthal, *Understanding Jewish Mysticism.*

Shema. See under Liturgy.

*Shivhei Ha-Besht.* Text: S. A. Horodezky, *Shivhei Ha-Besht* Tel Aviv, 1947). Translation: D. Ben-Amos and J. R. Mintz, *In Praise of the Baal Shem Tov* (Bloomington, Indiana, 1970).

*Shulhan Arukh.* Text: *Shulhan Arukh im Rabbenu Aqiva Eger ha-Shalem,* 8 vols (Tel Aviv, 1977). This contains the major commentaries. See also the bilingual edition by C. N. Denburg, *Code of Hebrew Law; Shulhan 'aruk,* vol. 1, *Yoreh De'ah,* 335–403; vol. 2, *Hoshen Ha-Mishpat,* 1–27 (Montreal, 1954–55).

Silberg, Judge. For Judge Silberg's verdict in the 'Brother Daniel' case see under Laws of the State of Israel.

Targum Pseudo-Jonathan. Text: D. Rieder, *Pseudo-Jonathan: Targum Jonathan ben Uzziel on the Pentateuch* (Jerusalem, 1974). Translation: J. W. Etheridge, *The Targums of Onkelos and Jonathan ben Uzziel on the Pentateuch with Fragments of the Jerusalem Targumim* (London, 1862–65; repr. New York, 1968). For selections with commentary see J. Bowker, *The Targums and Rabbinic Literature.*

Wisliceny, Dieter. See under Holocaust documents.

Zechariah Mendel of Jaroslav. The text of the letter quoted in 9.1.2 may be found in *Sefer No'am Elimelekh* (Lemberg, 1874), towards the end. Translation: L. Jacobs, *Jewish Mystical Testimonies* (New York, 1977), pp. 208–16.

*Zohar.* Text: R. M. Margaliot, *Sefer ha-Zohar al Hamishah Humshei Torah* (Jerusalem, 1956). Translation: H. Sperling and M. Simon, *The Zohar* (London, 1949). This is not complete.

Useful are the Hebrew selections with notes by I. Tishby, *Mishnat Ha-Zohar* (Jerusalem, 1961–71).

## B. Secondary sources

Abrahams, I., *A Companion to the Authorized Daily Praybook* (London, 1922; repr. New York, 1966).

Altmann, A., *Moses Mendelssohn: a Biographical Study* (London, 1973).

Baron, S. W., *A Social and Religious History of the Jews,* 3 vols (New York, 1937).

— *A Social and Religious History of the Jews,* 2nd ed. revised and enlarged. 17 vols to date (New York and Philadelphia, 1952–80).

Bavier, R., *et al., The Study of Judaism. Bibliographical Essays* (New York, 1973). A useful bibliographical guide. See also under Yerushalmi below.

Ben-Sasson, H. H. (ed.), *A History of the Jewish People* (London, 1976).

Ben-Sasson, H. H., and Ettinger, S. (eds.), *Jewish Society through the Ages* (London, 1971).

Blau, J. L., *Modern Varieties of Judaism* (New York, 1966).

— *Judaism in America: from Curiosity to Third Faith* (Chicago, 1976).

Blumenthal, D. R. (ed.), *Understanding Jewish Mysticism: a Source Reader* (New York, 1978).

Bowker, J., *The Targums and Rabbinic Literature* (Cambridge, 1969).

Chazan, R., *Church, State and Jew in the Middle Ages,* ed. N. Kozodoy (New York, 1979).

Clement, L. S., *The Rift in Israel: Religious Authority and Secular Democracy* (New York, 1971).

Cohn, N., *Warrant for Genocide: the Myth of the Jewish World-Conspiracy and the Protocols of the Elders of Zion* (New York, 1969).

Corre, A. (ed.), *Understanding the Talmud* (New York, 1975).

Dawidowicz, Lucy, *The War against the Jews* (Penguin: Harmondsworth, 1977).

Elon, M. (ed.), *The Principles of Jewish*

*Law* (Jerusalem, 1975). A collection of articles from the *Encyclopaedia Judaica*.

*Enclyclopaedia Judaica*, 16 vols and *Year Books* (Jerusalem, 1972). This is the standard reference work on all matters relating to the Jews and Judaism.

Finkelstein, L. (ed.), *The Jews: their History, Culture and Religion*, 4th ed., 3 vols (New York, 1970).

Fox, M. (ed.), *Modern Jewish Ethics: Theory and Practice* (Columbus, Ohio, 1975).

Guttmann, J., *Philosophies of Judaism* (New York, 1964).

Heinemann, J., and Petuchowski, J. J., *Literature of the Synagogue, edited with introduction and notes* (New York, 1975).

Hertzberg, A. (ed.), *The Zionist Idea: a Historical Analysis and Reader* (New York, 1959).

Idelsohn, A. Z., *Jewish Liturgy and its Development* (New York, 1960).

Jacobs, L., *Principles of the Jewish Faith: an Analytical Study* (London, 1964).

— *A Jewish Theology* (London, 1973).

— *Hasidic Prayer* (London, 1972).

Katz, J., *Tradition and Crisis: Jewish Society at the End of the Middle Ages* (New York, 1961).

— *Exclusiveness and Tolerance: Studies in Jewish–Gentile Relations in Medieval and Modern Times* (Oxford, 1961).

Katz, S. (ed.), *Jewish Philosophers* (Jerusalem, 1975). Articles from the *Encyclopaedia Judaica*, with a new section on the modern period.

Laqueur, W., *A History of Zionism* (London, 1972).

Mendes-Flohr, P. R., and Reinharz, J. (eds.), *The Jew in the Modern World: a Documentary History* (Oxford, 1980).

Mielziner, M., *Introduction to the Talmud*, 4th ed. by A. Guttmann (New York, 1968).

Montefiore, C. G., and Loewe, H. (eds.), *A Rabbinic Anthology: Selected and arranged with Comments and*

*Introductions* (London, 1938).

Moore, G. F., *Judaism in the First Three Centuries of the Christian Era* (Cambridge, Mass., 1927–30).

Neusner, J., *Invitation to Talmud* (New York, 1973).

— *Form-Analysis and Exegesis: a Fresh Approach to the Interpretation of the Mishnah* (Minneapolis, 1981).

— *Judaism: the Evidence of the Mishnah* (Chicago, 1981).

Neusner, J. (ed.), *The Modern Study of the Mishnah* (Leiden, 1973).

— *The Formation of the Babylonian Talmud* (Leiden, 1970).

Petuchowski, J. J. (ed.), *Contributions to the Scientific Study of Jewish Liturgy* (New York, 1972).

Philipson, D., *The Reform Movement in Judaism*, revised ed. (New York, 1931.

Plaut, W. G., *The Rise of Reform Judaism* (New York, 1963–65).

— *The Growth of Reform Judaism* (New York, 1965).

Poliakov, L., *A History of Anti-Semitism*, 3 vols (London, 1974–75).

Rabinowicz, H., *The World of Hasidism* (London, 1970).

Sachar, H., *The Course of Modern Jewish History* (New York, 1958).

Schauss, H., *Guide to Jewish Holy Days* (New York, 1970).

Schechter, S., *Aspects of Rabbinic Theology* (London, 1909).

Scholem, G. G., *Major Trends in Jewish Mysticism*, 3rd ed. (New York, 1954).

— *Jewish Gnosticism, Merkabah Mysticism and Talmudic Tradition*, 2nd ed. (New York, 1965).

— *On the Kabbalah and its Symbolism* (New York, 1965).

— *Kabbalah* (Jerusalem, 1974). Articles from the *Encyclopaedia Judaica*.

Steinsaltz, A., *The Essential Talmud* (London, 1976).

Urbach, E. E., *The Sages: their Concepts and Beliefs* (Jerusalem, 1975).

Vermes, G., *Scripture and Tradition in Judaism. Haggadic Studies*, 2nd ed. (Leiden, 1973).

— *Post-biblical Jewish Studies* (Leiden,

1975).

Vital, D., *Zionism: the Formative Years* (Oxford, 1982).

Waxman, M., *A History of Jewish Literature*, 5 vols. (New York, 1960).

Werblowsky, R. J. Z., *Joseph Karo: Lawyer and Mystic* (Oxford, 1962).

Yerushalmi, Y. H., *et al.*, *The Study of Judaism: Bibliographical Essays in Medieval Jewish Studies* (New York, 1976). Useful annotated bibliographies. For the companion volume see under Bavier above.

# GLOSSARY

*Aliyyah.* Immigration to the Land of Israel.

*Amidah.* One of the major prayers of the Jewish liturgy. Plur.: *Amidot.* Also known as the Eighteen Benedictions.

*Aqedah.* The story of the 'binding' of Isaac (Gen. 22).

*Ashkenazi.* A Jew of German, Central or Eastern European origin, wherever resident in the world. Cf. 'Sefardi'.

*Bavli.* The Babylonian Talmud. Cf. 'Yerushalmi' and 'Talmud'.

*Berakhah.* A 'blessing': a liturgical formula of praise and thanksgiving. Plur. *berakhot.*

*Ein Sof.* 'The Unlimited': a Qabbalistic designation for God.

*Erez Israel.* The Land of Israel; Palestine.

*Gemara.* The part of the Palestinian and Babylonian Talmuds which comments on and supplements the Mishnah. Cf. 'Talmud'.

*Haftarah.* A section from the Prophets read in synagogue on Sabbaths and festivals immediately following the section from the Pentateuch. Cf. 'parashah', and see Appendix A.

*Haggadah.* The text containing the story of the Exodus from Egypt, recited at the Passover *Seder.* Plur. *Haggadot.*

*Halakhah.* Traditional religious law dealing with matters of ritual and behaviour: the Jewish legal tradition.

*Halizah.* The ceremony of 'drawing off' the shoe, performed when a man refuses to marry his brother's childless widow (see Deut. 25: 9–10).

*Hasidism.* East European religious movement, initially revivalist in character, founded by Israel Ba'al

Shem Tov in the first half of the eighteenth century.

*Haskalah.* 'Enlightenment': a movement, flourishing *c.* 1750–1880, whose main aim was to spread European culture among Jews.

*Havdalah.* Ceremony to mark the end of Sabbath.

*Hibbat Ziyyon.* 'Lion of Zion': see 'Hovevei Ziyyon'.

*Hovevei Ziyyon.* 'Lovers of Zion': an early (pre-Herzl) Zionist movement in Russia.

*Kalam.* Islamic theology.

*Kasher/kosher.* Adjective meaning 'ritually permissible', most commonly applied to foot.

*Lulav.* 'Palm branch': one of the 'four species' (palm branch, citron, myrtle, willow) used to celebrate the festival of Sukkot.

*Midrash.* A rabbinic method of interpreting Scripture; also a rabbinic Bible commentary which employs this method.

*Minhag.* Religious custom; the distinctive religious practices of a particular Jewish community. Plur. *minhagim.*

*Mishnah.* A code of Jewish compiled (*c.* 210 C.E.) by Judah Ha-Nasi.

*Mitnaggedim.* The opponents of the Hasidim in Eastern Europe.

*Miqveh.* A ritual bath.

*Mizvah.* 'Commandment': a biblical or rabbinic injunction. Plur. *mizvot.*

*Musaf.* Additional service for Sabbaths and festivals.

*Musar.* Traditional religious ethics.

*Nefesh.* 'Soul': in the Qabbalah the lowest level of man's spiritual nature. Cf.

'Neshamah' and 'Ruah'.

*Neshamah.* 'Super-soul': in the Qabbalah the highest level of man's spiritual nature. Cf. 'Nefesh' and 'Ruah'.

*Parashah.* A section of the Pentateuch read on Sabbath in synagogue. Plur. *parashiyyot.* Cf. 'Haftarah', and see Appendix A.

*Pesaq.* A legal decision; a 'cut-and-dried' statement of religious law. Plur. *pesaqim.*

*Qabbalah.* The Jewish mystical tradition, especially the mystical system associated with the *Zohar.*

*Qaraism.* A Jewish religious movement, originating in the eighth century C.E., which rejected rabbinic Judaism, and accepted only Scripture as authoritative.

*Qedushah.* A prayer dwelling on God's holiness and majesty. Plur. *qedushot.*

*Qiddush.* A prayer recited over wine or bread to mark the beginning of Sabbaths and festivals. Cf. 'Havdalah'.

*Rosh Ha-Shanah.* The Jewish New Year, falling on 1 Tishri. See Appendix B.

*Ruah.* 'Spirit': in the Qabbalah the intermediate level of man's spiritual nature. Cf. 'Nefesh' and 'Neshamah'.

*Seder.* The ceremonies observed in the home to celebrate Passover.

*Sefardi.* A Jew of Spanish or Portuguese origin, wherever resident in the world. Cf. 'Ashkenazi'.

*Sefirah.* A mystical term denoting one of the ten spheres or emanations through which the Divine manifests itself. Plur. *sefirot.*

*Shavu'ot.* The festival of Pentecost or Weeks, falling on 6 Sivan. See Appendix B.

*Shekhinah.* Th Divine Presence, in the Qabbalah identified with the tenth of the *Sefirot.*

*Shema.* One of the main prayers of the Jewish liturgy, deriving its name from its central affirmation, 'Hear (*Shema*), O Israel, the Lord our God, the Lord is one' (Deut. 6:4).

*Shulhan Arukh.* An important Jewish law code, compiled by Joseph Caro, and

first published in 1565.

*Siddur.* The name given among Ashkenazi Jews to the weekday and Sabbath prayer book.

*Sukkot.* The festival of Tabernacles, falling on 15 Tishri. See Appendix B.

*Talmud.* 'Talmud' *par excellence* means the Babylonian Talmud, a fundamental work of halakhah, embodying a commentary on the Mishnah edited in Babylonia *c.* 499 C.E. There is also a Palestinian Talmud, edited in Palestine *c.* 390 C.E. Cf. 'Balvi', 'Yerushalmi' and 'Gemara'.

*Tanna.* A rabbinic scholar of the period of the Mishnah (first and second centuries C.E.). Plur. *Tanna'im.*

*Targum.* An Aramaic translation of the Bible.

*Tiqqun.* 'Restitution': a mystical term denoting the act of restoring the divine and natural worlds to their original unity and harmony.

*Torah.* The key term in Judaism, basically meaning 'teaching' or 'instruction'. Can denote: (a) the idea of divine revelation, (b) the whole body of traditional law and doctrine, or (c) the first five books of the Hebrew Bible.

*Tosafot.* Additions to Rashi's commentary on the Talmud, composed mainly by French Jewish scholars of the twelfth to fourteenth centuries.

*Yerushalmi.* The Palestinian Talmud. See 'Bavli' and 'Talmud'.

*Yeshivah.* A traditional Jewish academy devoted primarily to the study of the Talmud and other classic rabbinic texts. Plur. *Yeshivot.*

*Yom Kippur.* The Day of Atonement, falling on 10 Tishri. See Appendix B.

*Yoredei Merkavah.* 'Those who descend to the Merkavah': mystics who had visions of God's heavenly Chariot (*Merkavah*).

*Zaddiq.* The spiritual leader of a Hasidic community.

*Zohar.* 'The Book of Splendour': the central work of the Qabbalah, probably composed in Spain in the thirteenth century by Moses de Leon.

# INDEX